TITLES IN THE CYBERSECURITY SERIES

The Comprehensive Guide to Cybersecurity Careers:
A Professional's Roadmap for the Digital Security Age
Jason Edwards
ISBN 13: 978-1-60427-202-4, 262 pages

The Comprehensive Guide to Cybersecurity Hiring:
Strategies, Trends, and Best Practices
Jason Edwards
ISBN 13: 978-1-60427-203-1, 278 pages

The Comprehensive Guide to Cybersecurity's Most Infamous
Hacks: 70 Case Studies of Cyberattacks
Jason Edwards
ISBN 13: 978-1-60427-208-6, 340 pages

T0414080

THE COMPREHENSIVE GUIDE TO CYBERSECURITY'S MOST INFAMOUS HACKS

70 Case Studies of Cyberattacks

By Dr. Jason Edwards

CONTENTS

INTRODUCTION TO CYBERSECURITY AND DIGITAL THREATS

The journey of cybersecurity, a reflection of the rapid advancement and growing complexity of digital technology over the past several decades, is a fascinating historical evolution. The early Internet, a network primarily used by academics and researchers, was relatively benign compared to today's complex cyber landscape. The advent of the Morris Worm in 1988, created by a Cornell University student ostensibly to gauge the size of the Internet, marked a significant milestone in cybersecurity history. This incident underscored the potential for substantial damage from even unintended attacks and highlighted the necessity for security measures.

As the Internet expanded during the 1990s, cyber threats evolved. The early 90s saw the rise of viruses, often spread via floppy disks and later through email attachments as internet connectivity became more ubiquitous. Notable examples from this period include the Michelangelo virus, designed to activate on the sixth of March and potentially erase data on infected systems, and the Melissa virus, which spread rapidly by exploiting vulnerabilities in Microsoft Word's macro feature. These incidents were primarily motivated by a desire for notoriety or curiosity but laid the groundwork for more malicious forms of cybercrime.

The late 1990s and early 2000s marked the beginning of organized cybercrime. With the growth of e-commerce and online banking, cybercriminals began targeting financial institutions and personal data for profit. The 1994 Citibank hack, orchestrated by Russian hacker Vladimir Levin, involved illegally transferring millions of dollars from customer accounts. This period also saw the emergence of sophisticated social engineering techniques, such as phishing and pretexting, as seen in the Rome Laboratory hack, where attackers used social engineering to access sensitive military information.

The twenty-first century brought a proliferation of Internet-connected devices, expanding the attack surface available to cybercriminals. The adoption of the Internet continued unabated with access increasing exponentially each year (see Figure I.1). The rise of social media, cloud computing, and mobile technology further complicated the cybersecurity landscape. Malware became more sophisticated with the development of polymorphic viruses that could change their code to evade detection by antivirus software. Additionally, the commercialization of cybercrime, exemplified by the emergence of ransomware as a service, enabled even nontechnical individuals to launch attacks.

Cybersecurity is a critical concern for governments, businesses, and individuals today. The rise of nation-state-sponsored cyberattacks, such as the 2010 Stuxnet worm that targeted Iran's nuclear facilities, highlights the geopolitical dimensions of cybersecurity. These attacks, often backed by the resources and expertise of a nation-state, can have far-reaching implications, from disrupting critical infrastructure to influencing political processes. Similarly, the increasing frequency of data breaches, affecting millions of users' personal information, underscores the importance of robust cybersecurity

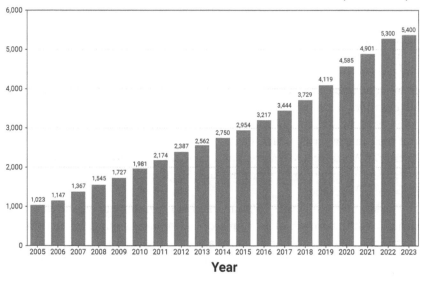

Figure I.1   The explosion of internet users worldwide (*source*: Statista Search Department)

measures in an era of digital interconnectedness. As digital technologies evolve, so does the landscape of threats, making cybersecurity an ever-present concern in modern society.

THE CRITICAL NEED FOR UNDERSTANDING CYBERSECURITY ATTACKS

The necessity of understanding cybersecurity attacks extends beyond IT professionals and into the broader public and private sectors. Each cyberattack serves as a case study in vulnerability and defense, offering lessons that can help prevent future incidents. For example, understanding the anatomy of a phishing attack, where attackers impersonate trusted entities to steal sensitive information, is crucial for training employees and individuals to recognize and avoid such scams. Phishing remains one of the most common and effective cyberattack methods due to its reliance on human psychology rather than technical vulnerabilities.

Analyzing past cyber incidents also helps organizations develop more effective security policies and incident response plans. The 2017 WannaCry ransomware attack, which exploited a vulnerability in the Windows operating system, demonstrated the importance of timely software updates and the need for robust backup systems. This attack affected over 200,000 computers in 150 countries, including critical infrastructure like the UK's National Health Service, which faced significant disruptions. By studying the spread and impact of WannaCry, cybersecurity professionals have developed better detection and response strategies for similar ransomware threats.

Furthermore, understanding cybersecurity attacks involves examining the broader economic, political, and social factors contributing to the threat landscape. Cybercrime is a global issue, with many attacks originating from regions with limited law enforcement capabilities or regulatory frameworks. This includes the rise of underground markets on the dark web, where stolen data, malware, and hacking tools are bought and sold. These markets have facilitated the commodification of cybercrime, making sophisticated attacks accessible to a broader range of actors.

The political dimensions of cybersecurity are also significant. Nation-states increasingly engage in cyber espionage and cyber warfare to achieve strategic objectives, such as the theft of intellectual property, disruption of critical infrastructure, and influencing political processes. The 2016 DNC email leak, widely attributed to Russian state actors, is a prominent example of how cyber operations can impact the political landscape. Understanding the motivations

and methods behind such attacks is essential for developing effective deterrence and defense strategies at the national level.

In addition to technical defenses, the human element plays a crucial role in
cybersecurity. Social engineering attacks exploit human psychology to bypass
technical defenses, often with devastating effectiveness. Training and awareness programs are vital for educating users about common attack vectors and
best practices for securing information. For example, regular phishing simu-
lations can help employees recognize and report suspicious emails, reducing
the likelihood of a successful attack. Similarly, promoting an organization's
security culture encourages individuals to follow security protocols and report potential threats.

EMERGING TECHNOLOGIES AND THEIR IMPACT ON CYBERSECURITY

The ongoing development of emerging technologies presents both opportunities and challenges for cybersecurity. Artificial intelligence (AI) and machine
learning (ML) are particularly transformative among these technologies.
These technologies are increasingly integrated into cyber defense and offense,
offering new capabilities and raising concerns.

Artificial Intelligence and Machine Learning in Cyber Defense and Offense

AI and ML are powerful cybersecurity tools, providing advanced threat
detection and response capabilities. On the defensive side, ML algorithms can
analyze vast amounts of data to identify patterns indicative of malicious activity. These algorithms can detect anomalies in network traffic, user behavior,
and system performance that may signal an ongoing attack. For instance, ML
can help identify unusual login patterns or access requests, flagging potential
insider threats or compromised accounts.

AI-driven security systems can also automate responses to detected threats,
such as isolating affected systems, blocking malicious IP addresses, and alerting security teams. This automation is particularly valuable in reducing the time
between detecting and mitigating an attack and limiting potential damage.
Additionally, AI can enhance the accuracy of threat intelligence by correlating
data from multiple sources and providing insights into emerging threats and
attack trends.

However, the use of AI and ML in cybersecurity also poses challenges. These
technologies are not infallible and can be exploited by attackers in various

ways. Adversarial ML, where attackers manipulate data to deceive ML models, is a growing concern. For example, attackers can craft inputs that cause an AI-powered security system to misclassify malicious activity as benign, allowing the attack to proceed undetected. Moreover, as defenders use AI to enhance security, attackers are increasingly employing AI to improve the effectiveness of their attacks. AI can be used to automate phishing campaigns, craft more convincing social engineering attacks, and even identify vulnerabilities more efficiently.

The dual-use nature of AI in cybersecurity creates an ongoing arms race between attackers and defenders. As both sides continue to innovate, cybersecurity professionals must stay abreast of the latest developments in AI and ML and the associated risks. This includes investing in AI research, developing new defensive strategies, and fostering collaboration between industry, academia, and government to address AI's ethical and security implications in cybersecurity.

Quantum Computing: Opportunities and Challenges

Still in its developmental stages, quantum computing represents a potential paradigm shift in computing power and capability. Quantum computers operate on fundamentally different principles compared to classical computers, using qubits that can represent multiple states simultaneously due to the phenomenon known as superposition. This capability enables quantum computers to perform calculations much more efficiently than classical computers.

The implications of quantum computing for cybersecurity are profound, particularly concerning cryptography. Many cryptographic algorithms currently used to secure communications and data, such as the Rivest-Shamir-Adleman algorithm and elliptic-curve cryptography, rely on the difficulty of specific mathematical problems, like factoring large numbers or computing discrete logarithms. Quantum computers could solve these problems exponentially faster than classical computers, rendering current cryptographic techniques obsolete.

The prospect of a quantum computer breaking widely used encryption methods has led to concerns about a *quantum apocalypse*, where sensitive data could be decrypted en masse. This has spurred efforts to develop quantum-resistant cryptographic algorithms, also known as post-quantum cryptography. These new algorithms aim to provide security against classical and quantum attacks, ensuring the confidentiality and integrity of data in a post-quantum world.

In addition to threats, quantum computing also offers potential benefits for cybersecurity. Quantum key distribution (QKD), a method for securely exchanging cryptographic keys using quantum mechanics principles, provides a way to detect eavesdropping. In QKD, any attempt to intercept the key exchange alters the system's quantum state, alerting the communicating parties to the presence of an intruder. While QKD has yet to be widely adopted, it represents a promising avenue for enhancing the security of communication channels.

The development and deployment of quantum computing technologies will likely take years if not decades. However, the potential impact on cybersecurity is significant, and organizations must begin preparing for a future where quantum computing is a reality. This preparation includes investing in quantum-safe cryptography, understanding the capabilities and limitations of quantum computing, and considering the broader implications for cybersecurity strategy and policy.

Geopolitical Cybersecurity Dynamics

The geopolitical landscape is increasingly intertwined with cybersecurity, as nation-states use cyber operations to achieve strategic objectives. Cyber espionage, sabotage, and influence operations are becoming more common, targeting critical infrastructure, intellectual property, and political processes. The SolarWinds hack, attributed to Russian state actors, demonstrated the potential for wide-reaching impacts on public and private sector organizations.

The rise of nation-state cyber activities has led to a growing emphasis on cybersecurity as a component of national security. Governments invest in cyber defense capabilities, develop strategies to protect critical infrastructure, and establish norms and agreements to govern state behavior in cyberspace. International cooperation is essential in this area since cyber threats often transcend national borders and require coordinated responses.

At the same time, greater resilience against cyberattacks is needed. This includes improving critical infrastructure security such as power grids, transportation systems, and healthcare facilities, which are often targeted in cyber operations. It also enhances the ability to detect, respond to, and recover from cyber incidents. Public-private partnerships are crucial in this effort, as private entities operate many critical systems.

Privacy and Data Protection

As digital technologies continue to permeate all aspects of life, privacy and data protection concerns are becoming more prominent. The practice of collection and processing of personal data by companies and governments has raised concerns about surveillance, data breaches, and the misuse of information. High-profile incidents, such as the Facebook-Cambridge Analytica scandal, have highlighted the potential for data misuse and the need for stronger data protection measures.

Regulations such as the General Data Protection Regulation in the European Union and the California Consumer Privacy Act in the United States are steps toward addressing these concerns. These regulations impose stricter requirements on collecting, using, and protecting personal data, giving individuals more control over their information. However, the implementation and enforcement of these regulations vary, and there are ongoing debates about the balance between security, privacy, and innovation.

The trend toward greater data protection will likely continue, with more jurisdictions enacting regulations to safeguard personal information. Organizations must navigate these regulations, ensuring compliance while protecting their users' data. This includes implementing robust security measures, such as encryption and access controls, and adopting the best data governance and privacy practices by design.

THE STRUCTURE AND APPROACH OF THIS BOOK

This book comprehensively explores significant developments in cybersecurity through detailed case studies of noteworthy cyber incidents. It is structured to guide readers through the historical evolution of cyber threats, from the Internet's early days to the present-day challenges and prospects.

Each chapter focuses on a specific theme or type of attack, such as early malware, nation-state cyber operations, ransomware, and emerging technologies. These case studies illustrate key events within these chapters, dissecting the methods, responses, and lessons learned. This approach provides a chronological overview of cybersecurity developments and allows for in-depth analysis of critical incidents that have shaped the field.

This book bridges the gap between technical and nontechnical readers by explaining complex concepts in an accessible manner. Each chapter will include case studies that provide detailed accounts of significant cyber incidents, including the methods used, the impact of the attacks, and the lessons learned. The book seeks to equip readers with the knowledge and insights to navigate cybersecurity's complex and ever-changing landscape by examining past and present cyber incidents. Whether you are a cybersecurity professional, a policymaker, or simply interested in understanding the world of digital threats, this book offers valuable insights and practical guidance for staying secure in the digital age.

ABOUT THE AUTHOR

Dr. Jason Edwards is a seasoned cyberse-curity expert with extensive experience across many industries, including technology, finance, insurance, and energy. His professional journey is enriched by a Doctorate in Management, Information Systems, and Information Technology, along with profound roles that have contributed to cybersecurity resilience and regulatory compliance for diverse organizations. Each role reflects Jason's depth of expertise and strategic approach, demonstrating his capability to enhance organizational cybersecurity frameworks and navigate complex risk and compliance landscapes.

A Bronze Star punctuates his remark-able 22-year career as an Army officer, a testament to his extraordinary service and dedication. Beyond organizational contributions, Jason is a stalwart in the cybersecurity community. He engages a broad audience through insightful publications on LinkedIn and steers a comprehensive cybersecurity newsletter, reaching tens of thousands of readers weekly. Jason is the author of several books and lives with his family in San Antonio, Texas.

At J. Ross Publishing we are committed to providing today's professional with practical, hands-on tools that enhance the learning experience and give readers an opportunity to apply what they have learned. That is why we offer free ancillary materials available for download on this book and all participating Web Added Value™ publications. These online resources may include interactive versions of material that appears in the book or supplemental templates, worksheets, models, plans, case studies, proposals, spreadsheets and assessment tools, among other things. Whenever you see the WAV™ symbol in any of our publications, it means bonus materials accompany the book and are available from the Web Added Value Download Resource Center at www.jrosspub.com.

Downloads for *The Comprehensive Guide to Cybersecurity's Most Infamous Hacks* include additional stories and case studies.

1

THE DAWN OF CYBERSECURITY

Ah, the early days of the Internet—when dial-up modems serenaded us with their digital screeches and the most sophisticated *hack* that most people knew about involved remembering your AOL password. Back then, *cybersecurity* was as foreign as carrying a computer in your pocket. It was an era when floppy disks were the cutting-edge technology, and the biggest digital threat for many was accidentally overwriting your thesis with a game of Oregon Trail. As quaint as it all sounds now, the late 1980s and early 1990s were formative years for what would become a battleground in the digital age.

But behind the nostalgia of dial-up tones and pixelated screens, a different, darker story was unfolding—a story that would shape the future of cybersecurity. As networks began to connect more computers across the globe, they also opened doors to a new breed of criminals, activists, and digital mischiefmakers. These early hackers weren't just interested in causing chaos for fun; they were exploring the very limits of this new technology, often outpacing the defensive measures that organizations had in place. From the first ransomware attack to bold exploits against financial institutions and military networks, these early breaches laid bare the vulnerabilities of a world still learning to grapple with its newfound connectivity.

This chapter explores several pivotal moments in the early history of cybersecurity, focusing on key case studies that illustrate the evolving nature of cyber threats during the digital age's infancy. Each incident showcases a mixture of innovative attacks and organizational blind spots, revealing both the hackers' boldness and their targets' vulnerabilities. By revisiting these cases, we gain insight into the strategies and tools used by early cybercriminals and uncover the valuable lessons learned—many of which remain highly relevant for today's cybersecurity professionals. These events are not merely historical curiosities; they laid the groundwork for the principles that now guide modern cybersecurity practices.

In this chapter, we dive deeply into these foundational cybersecurity breaches, analyzing how they unfolded, the methods behind them, and their impacts on the organizations involved. It is important to acknowledge that, over time, detailed records of these attacks may be sparse or fragmented. Where necessary, informed analysis based on the author's professional expertise fills these gaps to offer a fuller picture of what likely transpired. By reflecting on these early incidents, we better understand the crucial need for constant vigilance, proactive defenses, and the ability to adapt to a rapidly shifting threat landscape. So, let's journey back to when the Internet was still uncharted territory and see how these early clashes shaped the cybersecurity practices we rely on today.

WHAT IS A CYBERATTACK?

Cybersecurity attacks refer to a wide range of malicious activities to compromise digital assets and systems' confidentiality, integrity, or availability. These attacks can target individuals, businesses, governments, and critical infrastructure, causing disruptions, financial loss, data theft, or national security risks. Cyberattacks have evolved significantly over the past four decades, becoming more sophisticated and harder to detect as attackers employ advanced tools and techniques. Cybersecurity attacks have become a persistent threat in the digital age, from early computer viruses to modern ransomware, distributed denial-of-service attacks, and state-sponsored espionage (see Figure 1.1).

These attacks can happen in various ways, often beginning with exploiting vulnerabilities in software, networks, or human behavior. One common entry point is phishing, where attackers trick individuals into revealing sensitive information or installing malware by posing as legitimate entities in emails or messages. Other attacks may exploit unpatched software vulnerabilities, as seen in zero-day exploits, where attackers leverage undiscovered flaws to gain access. Once inside a network, attackers may use malware, ransomware, or advanced persistent threats to carry out their objectives, whether stealing data, disrupting operations, or demanding a ransom for encrypted files. Attackers also employ social engineering by manipulating human trust to gain access to systems.

Defending against cybersecurity attacks requires a multi-layered approach. At the technical level, organizations should implement firewalls, intrusion

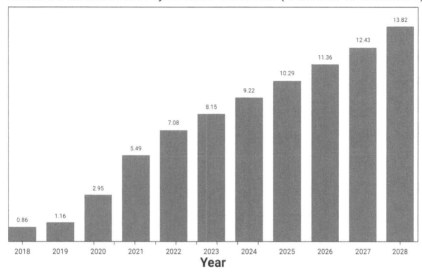

Cybercrime expected to skyrocket
Estimated annual cost of cybercrime worldwide (in trillions of U.S. Dollars)

Figure 1.1   Cybercrime is exploding worldwide (*source*: Statista Search Department)

detection systems, and endpoint protection to monitor and block unautho-rized access. Regular patch management and software updates are crucial to prevent attackers from exploiting known vulnerabilities. Additionally, encryption of sensitive data both in transit and at rest can protect against data breaches. Network segmentation also helps isolate critical systems from less sensitive ones, reducing the attack surface. Beyond technology, security awareness training is vital to educate users about phishing schemes, social en-gineering tactics, and best practices for maintaining secure behavior online.

A robust incident response plan ensures organizations can quickly detect, respond to, and recover from cybersecurity incidents. Threat intelligence can help organizations avoid emerging threats, while penetration testing and red teaming exercises simulate attacks to identify vulnerabilities. In addition to these proactive measures, organizations must remain vigilant, as the cyber-security landscape is constantly evolving, with attackers developing new tac-tics and techniques (see Figure 1.2). By staying updated on the latest threats and employing a combination of technical, procedural, and human defenses, organizations can significantly reduce their risk of falling victim to cyberse-curity attacks.

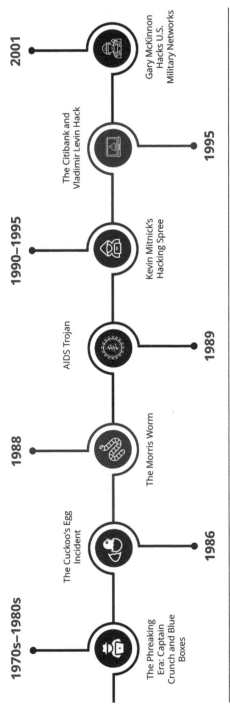

Figure 1.2   The timeline of cyberattacks discussed in this chapter

THE PHREAKING ERA: CAPTAIN CRUNCH AND BLUE BOXES (1970s–1980s)

The era of phreaking marked a unique chapter in the history of cybersecurity, characterized by a blend of curiosity, rebellion, and the developing understanding of telecommunications networks. *Phreaking*, a term derived from *phone freak*, involved manipulating the telephone system to make free calls, exploiting its vulnerabilities long before the Internet became a mainstream platform for cyber activities. This phenomenon primarily took root in the 1970s and 1980s, when analog phone networks were the backbone of global communications.

John Draper, also known as Captain Crunch, was the most infamous phreaker of this era. Draper's moniker was derived from the toy whistles in Cap'n Crunch cereal boxes, which emitted a perfect 2600 Hz tone—the exact frequency needed to exploit the phone system's switches and make free calls. Draper's exploits with the *blue box*, a device he developed that mimicked the various tones used by phone systems to route calls, gained significant notoriety. This device allowed users to bypass telephone company billing systems, causing a considerable stir among telecommunications providers and law enforcement agencies.

The technological landscape of the time was one of transition and vulnerability. Analog systems, while revolutionary, lacked the security features necessary to protect against such exploits. The key stakeholders in this narrative included major telecommunications companies like AT&T, who were both pioneers in their field and, ironically, the entities most vulnerable to phreaking activities. As the 1970s progressed into the 1980s, these companies, law enforcement, and the growing hacker subculture played critical roles in the unfolding drama of phreaking.

Unfolding the Attack

The phreaking era began in earnest with Draper's discovery of the 2600 Hz tone in the late 1960s. Using the toy whistle from Cap'n Crunch cereal, Draper and his fellow phreakers realized they could manipulate the phone system to their advantage. This simple yet effective exploit allowed them to seize control of telephone lines, making long-distance calls without incurring charges. Draper soon moved from using the whistle to designing more sophisticated devices (blue boxes), which could replicate the various tones used by telephone switches to control call routing.

The blue box was a game changer in the world of phreaking. These devices, often handmade by phreakers, enabled them to generate a sequence of tones that manipulated the phone systems just like a legitimate operator would. This technology allowed phreakers to make free calls and explore the inner workings of the global phone network, sometimes accessing restricted lines used by government agencies. The attacks were not centralized events but a series of individual exploits carried out by numerous phreakers worldwide, driven by curiosity, rebellion, and the thrill of bypassing the system.

The vulnerabilities exploited during this era were intrinsic to the analog nature of the telephone system itself. The system's reliance on in-band signaling, where control signals were sent over the same channel as voice communication, meant that anyone who could mimic those signals could potentially manipulate the network. This lack of separation between data and control channels represented a significant security flaw that phreakers like Draper quickly exploited. The timeline of phreaking exploits spans from the late 1960s into the 1980s, with each phreaker's discovery further highlighting the telephone system's weaknesses.

Detection and Response Efforts

The response to the phreaking phenomenon was initially slow, largely because telecommunications companies like AT&T were unaware of the scale and nature of the exploits occurring. Detecting phreaking activities was particularly challenging since phreakers often made legitimate calls that bypassed the billing system, leaving no immediate signs of foul play. The complexity of the attacks made it difficult to differentiate between legitimate network traffic and fraudulent activity. However, as the use of blue boxes became more widespread and the financial losses mounted, telecommunications companies began to realize the seriousness of the threat.

AT&T, recognizing the potential for abuse of their network, initiated efforts to detect and counteract phreaking by monitoring unusual patterns in long-distance call routing. They focused on identifying calls that bypassed billing mechanisms and began implementing targeted surveillance techniques. Law enforcement became involved, and through sting operations and investigations, key figures like John Draper were arrested for toll fraud. This marked a shift in the response to phreaking, as law enforcement and judicial systems began taking a more structured and serious approach to combating these activities.

In many ways, the phreakers of the 1970s share similarities with modern hackers who use *living-off-the-land* tactics, where attackers exploit legitimate tools and processes to evade detection. Whereas phreakers used normal call routing mechanisms in their exploits, today's hackers manipulate built-in system tools and trusted software to stay under the radar. These modern attacks are similarly hard to detect because they blend in with regular, sanctioned activity, making it difficult for defenders to distinguish between normal operations and malicious intent. As with phreaking, where new security measures led to evolving tactics, the cybersecurity community now faces a similar challenge of constantly adapting defenses to keep pace with attackers' increasingly stealthy methods.

Despite efforts to stamp out phreaking, the decentralized and intellectually driven nature of the phreaking community made it difficult to eradicate. The response timeline saw incremental improvements, but the phreakers met each new countermeasure with new tactics. This cat-and-mouse game between attackers and defenders echoes the ongoing battle between modern cybersecurity professionals and sophisticated adversaries continually evolving their methods to exploit even the most advanced systems.

Assessing the Impact

The immediate impact of phreaking on telecommunications companies was primarily financial, with significant revenue losses reported due to the unbilled long-distance calls facilitated by blue boxes. For companies like AT&T, these losses underscored the vulnerabilities in their network and the need for more robust security measures. Beyond financial implications, the reputations of these companies also took a hit as public awareness of phreaking exploits grew, and media coverage often portrayed these organizations as being outwitted by a group of tech-savvy rebels.

In the long term, the phreaking era had far-reaching consequences beyond direct financial and reputational damage to telecommunications companies. It catalyzed the development of more secure telecommunications technologies, most notably the transition from in-band signaling to out-of-band signaling, where control and data signals are sent over separate channels, significantly reducing the risk of such exploits. The impact also extended to the legal and regulatory landscapes, prompting stricter laws and penalties around toll fraud and unauthorized network access.

For the phreakers themselves, the consequences varied. While some, like Draper, faced legal repercussions, others used their skills to transition into legitimate careers in technology. The lessons learned from the phreaking era, particularly around network security and the importance of safeguarding critical infrastructure, have had lasting implications. The techniques and ethos of the phreakers laid the groundwork for what would later become the cybersecurity profession, highlighting both the potential for innovation and the risks associated with technological advancements.

Lessons Learned and Takeaways

The phreaking era provides several critical lessons for modern cybersecurity practices. One of the primary takeaways is the importance of understanding and securing the fundamental infrastructure of communication networks. The exploits carried out by phreakers like Captain Crunch were possible due to inherent weaknesses in the design of the telephone system, underscoring the need for security considerations to be integrated into the design and development stages of technology rather than being an afterthought.

The response to phreaking also highlights the value of proactive monitoring and detection mechanisms. Telecommunications companies were initially reactive in their approach, only recognizing the scale of the problem after significant losses had been incurred. This underscores the importance of establishing robust monitoring systems that detect anomalies and potential exploits in real time, allowing organizations to respond quickly to emerging threats. Additionally, the collaborative efforts between telecommunications companies and law enforcement illustrate the benefits of a coordinated response to cybersecurity threats.

Another key lesson from the phreaking era is the role of the hacker ethos in advancing technological understanding. While many phreakers were motivated by the thrill of bypassing the system, their actions also highlighted significant flaws in the telecommunications infrastructure that needed to be addressed. This dual role of hackers as both threats and catalysts for improvement is a recurring theme in cybersecurity history, emphasizing the importance of engaging with the hacker community to gain insights into potential vulnerabilities and foster a culture of security awareness and innovation.

Case Study Summary

The phreaking era, epitomized by figures like Captain Crunch and the widespread use of blue boxes, represents a foundational chapter in the history of cybersecurity. The exploits of these early hackers demonstrated both the vulnerabilities in existing telecommunications infrastructure and the potential for unauthorized access and control over critical systems. The response by telecommunications companies and law enforcement marked the beginning of more structured cybersecurity practices and the recognition of the need for robust network security measures.

continued

From this case study, we see the importance of understanding the underlying technologies within our communication systems and the potential risks associated with their exploitation. The lessons learned from the phreaking era resonate today, highlighting the need for proactive monitoring, collaboration, and an appreciation for the hacker ethos as a driver of technological advancement and security improvement. As we continue to navigate the evolving landscape of cyber threats, these early examples remind us of the dynamic nature of cybersecurity and the importance of remaining vigilant and adaptable in the face of emerging challenges.

THE CUCKOO'S EGG INCIDENT (1986)

The Cuckoo's Egg Incident of 1986 is one of the earliest and most significant examples of cybersecurity breaches, highlighting the budding awareness of network security in the early days of the Internet. The incident is named after the book *The Cuckoo's Egg* by Clifford Stoll, an astronomer-turned-system administrator who played a pivotal role in uncovering an international cyber-espionage ring. This case is noteworthy for its technical details and narrative of one man's relentless pursuit of a hacker that would lead to finding vulnerabilities in numerous U.S. military and research networks.

The event unfolded at the Lawrence Berkeley National Laboratory (LBNL), California's U.S. Department of Energy laboratory. While investigating a minor accounting discrepancy of 75 cents in the laboratory's computer usage records, Stoll discovered unauthorized activity on the network. This small anomaly would ultimately reveal a massive, coordinated effort to penetrate military, academic, and corporate computer systems across the United States and beyond. The unauthorized access pointed to vulnerabilities in these networks, which were relatively unprotected due to the nascent stage of cybersecurity practices at the time.

During the mid-1980s, the technological landscape rapidly evolved with the advent of early computer networks like ARPANET, the precursor to the modern Internet. However, security was not a primary concern for many organizations, as *hacking* was poorly understood outside of niche circles. Key stakeholders involved in the Cuckoo's Egg incident included government agencies like the Department of Defense, academic institutions, private companies, and international intelligence services. These stakeholders, largely unaware of the vulnerabilities within their systems, would soon find themselves in the crosshairs of a determined adversary exploiting these weaknesses.

Unfolding the Attack

The Cuckoo's Egg incident began in 1986 when Clifford Stoll, a system administrator at LBNL, was tasked with investigating a minor accounting error in the lab's computer network. His investigation revealed an unauthorized user logging in and exploiting the system to access other networks. This intruder used stolen passwords and manipulated known vulnerabilities in the Berkeley Software Distribution (BSD) UNIX operating system, which is widely used in academic and research environments. The intruder's technique involved exploiting a bug in the GNU Emacs program, which allowed them to elevate privileges and gain root access to compromised systems.

The timeline of events spanned several months, with Stoll meticulously tracking the hacker's activities. The initial entry point was traced to a compromised account on the LBNL network, which the hacker used as a launching pad to access other systems. The intruder utilized simple yet effective techniques, such as brute-force password attacks and exploiting weak password policies. These methods allowed the hacker to gain unauthorized access to various systems, including those belonging to the U.S. military and defense contractors.

As Stoll continued his investigation, he discovered that the intruder was part of a larger, coordinated espionage effort. The hacker, later identified as Markus Hess, was a German computer programmer working for the KGB, the Soviet Union's primary security agency. Hess and his associates systematically targeted networks in search of sensitive military and research data. The vulnerabilities exploited were primarily due to weak password policies, unpatched software, and a general lack of awareness regarding network security. This situation underscored the urgent need for improved security measures in computer networks that were becoming increasingly interconnected and accessible.

Detection and Response Efforts

The detection of the unauthorized access was purely accidental, prompted by an anomaly that might have otherwise gone unnoticed. Clifford Stoll's curiosity and persistence were crucial in uncovering the hacker's activities. Using various tools and techniques, including custom scripts and log analysis, Stoll could track intruders' movements across the network. He employed honeypots—decoy systems designed to lure attackers—to gather more information about the hacker's methods and objectives. This approach allowed Stoll to observe the intruder in real time, documenting his every move.

Once it became apparent that the breach was not an isolated incident, Stoll contacted several organizations, including the Federal Bureau of Investigation (FBI), the Central Intelligence Agency, and the National Security Agency.

However, the response from these agencies was initially slow, since cybersecurity was not yet a primary focus for many government institutions. Over time, as the scale of the espionage effort became clear, these agencies coordinated their efforts to monitor the hacker's activities and prevent further damage.

The timeline of the response efforts extended over a year, during which Stoll collaborated with law enforcement and intelligence agencies to build a case against the hacker. This collaboration eventually led to Hess's arrest in 1988 in Germany, marking one of the earliest cases of international cyber espionage. The involvement of external parties, such as law enforcement and intelligence agencies, was crucial in bringing the hacker to justice and highlighting the importance of cybersecurity collaboration across borders.

Assessing the Impact

The Cuckoo's Egg incident had profound and immediate impacts on the organizations involved and broader implications for cybersecurity. The immediate effects included exposing sensitive military and research data to a foreign adversary, potentially compromising national security. The breach also revealed the widespread vulnerability of computer networks that were becoming increasingly interconnected but lacked robust security measures to protect sensitive information.

In the long term, the incident significantly affected the cybersecurity community and the general public's awareness of cyber threats. It underscored the need for stronger cybersecurity practices, including better password management, regular software updates, and increased network activity monitoring. Organizations began to realize cybersecurity was not just an IT issue but a critical aspect of national security and business operations. This realization led to the development of more comprehensive security policies and practices that are now standard in the industry.

The impact on stakeholders extended beyond the organizations directly affected by the breach. The incident highlighted the vulnerabilities of global networks and the potential for malicious actors to exploit them for espionage and other nefarious purposes. It also demonstrated the need for international cooperation in combating cyber threats since the hacker operated across multiple countries and targeted systems worldwide. The Cuckoo's Egg incident thus served as a wake-up call for organizations to take cybersecurity seriously and invest in protecting their digital assets.

Lessons Learned and Takeaways

The Cuckoo's Egg incident provides several critical lessons for modern cybersecurity practices. One of the primary lessons is the importance of vigilance and attention to detail. Clifford Stoll's discovery of the breach directly resulted from his meticulous approach to investigating a seemingly insignificant anomaly. This highlights the value of thorough monitoring and analysis of network activity to detect potential security breaches before they escalate into more significant threats.

Another key lesson from the incident is the importance of implementing robust security measures to protect sensitive information. The hacker exploited weak passwords, unpatched software, and other vulnerabilities that could have been mitigated with more stringent security policies. This underscores the need for organizations to prioritize cybersecurity and adopt a proactive approach to protecting their networks. Regular security audits, employee training, and the implementation of best practices are essential to safeguard against potential threats.

The Cuckoo's Egg incident also emphasizes the importance of collaboration and communication in responding to cyber threats. Stoll's efforts to involve law enforcement and intelligence agencies were crucial in bringing the hacker to justice and preventing further damage. This collaboration highlights the value of effectively sharing information and resources to combat cyber threats. It also underscores the need for organizations to work together to develop a more secure and resilient digital environment.

Case Study Summary

The Cuckoo's Egg incident is a seminal case in the history of cybersecurity, illustrating the vulnerabilities of early computer networks and the potential for malicious actors to exploit them for espionage and other purposes. The incident underscores the importance of vigilance, robust security measures, and collaboration in protecting sensitive information and responding to cyber threats. It also serves as a reminder of the need for organizations to take cybersecurity seriously and invest in protecting their digital assets.

This case study teaches the value of thorough monitoring and analysis of network activity, the importance of implementing robust security measures, and the need for collaboration and communication in responding to cyber threats. The lessons learned from the Cuckoo's Egg incident continue to resonate today, highlighting the dynamic nature of cybersecurity and the importance of remaining vigilant and proactive in the face of emerging challenges. As we continue to navigate the evolving landscape of cyber threats, these early examples remind us of the critical need to prioritize cybersecurity and invest in protecting our digital assets.

THE MORRIS WORM (1988)

The Morris Worm of 1988 is widely regarded as one of the first significant computer worms to spread extensively via the Internet, marking a pivotal moment in the history of cybersecurity. Released by Robert Tappan Morris, a graduate student at Cornell University, the worm inadvertently exposed critical vulnerabilities in networked systems across the United States. Initially intended as an experiment to gauge the size of the Internet, the worm quickly spiraled out of control, affecting thousands of computers and causing widespread disruption.

At the time of the incident, the Internet was still in its infancy, primarily used by academic institutions, government agencies, and a few corporations. The ARPANET, the precursor to the modern Internet, had only recently transitioned to the TCP/IP protocol suite, which became the standard for network communications. Most systems connected to the Internet ran on UNIX, a relatively new operating system with several vulnerabilities that the Morris Worm would ultimately exploit. These systems were largely unprotected by today's cybersecurity standards since the concept of a global network worm was not yet fully understood or anticipated.

Key stakeholders involved in the Morris Worm incident included major universities, government agencies such as the Defense Advanced Research Projects Agency (DARPA), and private companies connected to the network. The worm's spread highlighted the interconnected nature of these entities and underscored the need for improved security measures to protect networked systems. As the worm wreaked havoc, these organizations grappled with an unprecedented cybersecurity threat, laying the groundwork for future developments.

Unfolding the Attack

The Morris Worm was released on November 2, 1988, from a computer at the Massachusetts Institute of Technology to obfuscate its origins from Cornell University. The worm was designed to exploit known vulnerabilities in UNIX-based systems, including weaknesses in the BSD Unix sendmail program, rsh/rexec services, and weak password protection in finger daemon. Once a system was infected, the worm would replicate itself and attempt to spread to other systems within the network, effectively acting as a self-propagating virus.

The worm's propagation followed a rapid timeline, infecting approximately 6,000 computers within hours. Although Morris did not intend for the worm to be malicious, a bug in its code caused it to repeatedly reinfect machines, significantly increasing the load on infected systems. This flaw led to widespread network congestion and system crashes, as the worm overwhelmed servers and rendered them inoperable. The entry point for the worm was typically through exploiting the vulnerabilities mentioned earlier, allowing it to gain unauthorized access to systems and execute its code.

The methods used by the worm were relatively simple but highly effective. The worm could access systems without sophisticated hacking techniques using weak passwords, unpatched software, and inadequate security measures. Once inside a system, it utilized a combination of brute-force attacks and buffer overflow exploits to propagate itself further. These methods indicated the state of cybersecurity at the time, where basic security practices such as strong password management and regular software updates were not yet widely implemented.

Detection and Response Efforts

The detection of the Morris Worm was a chaotic process because organizations were initially unsure of what was happening or how to respond. Many systems administrators noticed their systems slowing down or crashing but did not immediately understand the cause. As the worm spread, the scale of the attack became apparent, prompting a rapid and somewhat frantic response from the affected organizations. The first step in detecting the worm involved identifying unusual network traffic and high CPU usage on infected machines.

Organizations responded by attempting to isolate and remove the worm from infected systems—a task made difficult by the worm's self-replicating nature and the lack of precedent for such an attack. The response efforts involved turning off vulnerable services, disconnecting affected machines from the network, and sharing information about the worm's behavior with other administrators. This collaborative approach was critical in slowing the worm's spread and mitigating its impact, highlighting the importance of communication and coordination in cybersecurity response efforts.

The involvement of external parties, including DARPA, cybersecurity experts, and law enforcement, was crucial in developing a comprehensive response to the worm. DARPA, which funded the development of ARPANET, played a significant role in coordinating the response efforts, bringing together experts from various fields to analyze the worm and develop countermeasures. This collaborative effort ultimately created the Computer Emergency Response Team (CERT) at Carnegie Mellon University, the first organization dedicated to responding to cybersecurity incidents and sharing information about emerging threats.

Assessing the Impact

The Morris Worm profoundly impacted the organizations and the broader cybersecurity community. In the immediate aftermath, the worm caused significant operational disruptions, with many systems rendered inoperable due to the heavy load caused by the worm's replication process. The financial impact was also considerable, with estimates of the damage ranging from $100,000 to $10 million, depending on the cost of system downtime, labor, and lost productivity.

In the long term, the incident had several important consequences for cybersecurity. It highlighted the need for improved security measures to protect networked systems, which lead to increased awareness of the importance of patch management, password security, and regular system monitoring. The incident also underscored the need for a more coordinated approach to cybersecurity, prompting the establishment of CERT and more robust response frameworks for dealing with cybersecurity incidents.

The impact of the Morris Worm extended beyond the immediate effects on the organizations involved by influencing the broader perception of cybersecurity risks and the importance of proactive measures to protect networked systems. The incident demonstrated that even well-intentioned experiments could have unintended and far-reaching consequences, underscoring the need for responsible behavior and ethical considerations in cybersecurity research and development. It also highlighted the vulnerabilities inherent in interconnected networks, emphasizing the importance of robust security practices in mitigating the risk of similar incidents.

Lessons Learned and Takeaways

The Morris Worm incident provides several critical lessons for modern cybersecurity practices. One of the primary lessons is the importance of proactive security measures and the need to stay ahead of potential threats. The worm exploited known vulnerabilities that could have been mitigated through regular software updates, strong password policies, and turning off unnecessary services. This underscores the need for organizations to adopt a proactive approach to cybersecurity, regularly reviewing and updating their security measures to protect against emerging threats.

Another key takeaway from the incident is the importance of collaboration and information sharing in responding to cybersecurity threats. The response to the Morris Worm was marked by a collaborative effort among various organizations and experts, highlighting the value of sharing information and resources to combat cyber threats effectively. This approach laid the foundation for establishing CERT and developing a more coordinated response framework for cybersecurity incidents, emphasizing the need for ongoing collaboration in the face of an ever-evolving threat landscape.

The Morris Worm also serves as a reminder of the ethical considerations inherent in cybersecurity research and development. While the worm was not intended to cause harm, its release had significant unintended consequences, underscoring the need for responsible behavior and consideration of potential risks when conducting cybersecurity experiments. This lesson is particularly relevant today as the cybersecurity community grapples with the ethical implications of new technologies and their potential impact on society.

Case Study Summary

The Morris Worm incident represents a significant milestone in the history of cybersecurity, highlighting the vulnerabilities of early networked systems and the potential for even well-intentioned experiments to cause widespread disruption. The incident underscores the importance of proactive security measures, collaboration, and ethical considerations in protecting networked systems and responding to cyber threats. It also serves as a reminder of the need for ongoing vigilance and adaptability in the face of an ever-evolving cybersecurity landscape.

This case study teaches the value of proactive security measures, the importance of collaboration and information sharing, and the need for ethical considerations in cybersecurity research and development. The lessons learned from the Morris Worm continue to resonate today, emphasizing the dynamic nature of cybersecurity and the importance of remaining vigilant and proactive in protecting our digital assets. As we continue to navigate the evolving landscape of cyber threats, these early examples remind us of the critical need to prioritize cybersecurity and invest in protecting our networks.

AIDS TROJAN (1989)

The AIDS Trojan, also known as the P.C. Cyborg Trojan, represents one of the earliest examples of ransomware, highlighting the evolving nature of cyber threats in the late 1980s. Released in 1989, the AIDS Trojan was created by Dr. Joseph Popp, a Harvard-educated biologist. Popp claimed his motivation was to raise awareness and funds for AIDS research, but his method—coercing victims into paying for a decryption key—was unprecedented. The incident marked a significant shift in the tactics employed by cybercriminals, introducing the concept of digital extortion.

The attack primarily targeted users within the medical and scientific communities, leveraging their trust to gain access to their computer systems. The AIDS Trojan was distributed via physical floppy disks, which were sent to individuals and organizations across the globe. At the time, many users were not accustomed to digital threats, and the concept of a Trojan horse program—malware disguised as a legitimate application—was relatively new. The AIDS Trojan exploited this lack of awareness, demonstrating the importance of cybersecurity education and the need for vigilance against emerging threats.

The technological landscape of the late 1980s was characterized by a rapidly growing personal computer market and the increasing use of computers in professional environments. Despite this growth, cybersecurity measures were rudimentary, and many systems lacked basic protections against malware. Key stakeholders involved in the AIDS Trojan incident included medical researchers, scientific institutions, and the broader technology community. The attack underscored the vulnerabilities of early computing systems and the importance of developing more robust security measures to protect against similar threats.

Unfolding the Attack

The AIDS Trojan was distributed in December 1989 via 20,000 floppy disks mailed to individuals and organizations worldwide. The disks were labeled as containing a program called "AIDS Information—Introductory Diskette," purportedly an educational tool for learning about the AIDS virus. Recipients were unaware that the diskette contained malicious software that would, after being installed, encrypt the file names on the infected system, rendering them inaccessible. The Trojan was designed to activate after several reboots, effectively lying dormant and allowing it to spread further before detection.

The entry point of the attack was straightforward—users inserted the floppy disk into their computers and followed the instructions to install what they believed was a legitimate program. Once the AIDS Trojan was activated, it would display a message demanding payment of $189 to a post office box in Panama to receive a decryption key. This ransom demand marked the first recorded instance of ransomware in history, setting a precedent for future attacks that would use similar tactics of coercion and extortion.

The methods employed by the AIDS Trojan were simple but effective, exploiting both the technological limitations of the time and the trust users placed in seemingly legitimate sources. By leveraging social engineering, the attacker could bypass minimal security measures and gain access to many systems. The Trojan exploited a critical vulnerability—the lack of user awareness and education regarding cybersecurity threats. This vulnerability, combined with little robust antivirus software or other protective measures, allowed the Trojan to spread quickly and cause significant disruption.

Detection and Response Efforts

Detection of the AIDS Trojan was relatively slow, primarily because ransomware was new and unfamiliar to most users and organizations. Many victims did not immediately understand what had happened when their files became inaccessible, attributing the issue to a technical malfunction rather than a deliberate attack. As reports of the incident began to surface, it became apparent that a malicious program was at play, prompting a broader investigation into its origins and methods.

Organizations responded by attempting to remove the Trojan and recover their data, often resorting to reformatting their hard drives or restoring from backups, if available. This process was time-consuming and often resulted in the loss of valuable data. Some victims paid the ransom in hopes of recovering their files, but there was no guarantee doing so would result in the return of their data. The incident highlighted the need for better detection and response mechanisms to mitigate the impact of such attacks.

The involvement of external parties, including cybersecurity experts and law enforcement agencies, was crucial in developing a comprehensive response to the AIDS Trojan. These efforts included analyzing the malware, understanding its behavior, and developing tools to remove it from infected systems. Law enforcement agencies also launched investigations to track down the perpetrator, eventually leading to the arrest of Dr. Joseph Popp in January 1990. The incident underscored the importance of a coordinated response to cybersecurity threats involving technical expertise and legal action.

Assessing the Impact

The immediate impact of the AIDS Trojan was significant, causing widespread disruption to the individuals and organizations affected. Many victims lost access to critical files, resulting in financial losses, operational disruptions, and damaged reputations. The attack also exposed the vulnerabilities of early computer systems and the lack of preparedness among users and organizations to deal with such threats. The incident served as a wake-up call, highlighting the need for improved cybersecurity measures and greater awareness of digital threats.

In the long term, the AIDS Trojan had several important consequences for cybersecurity. It was one of the first instances to highlight the potential for malware to be used for financial gain, introducing the concept of digital extortion and setting a precedent for future ransomware attacks. The incident also underscored the importance of user education and awareness, as many victims were unaware of the risks associated with installing unknown software from untrusted sources. This realization prompted a greater emphasis on cybersecurity training and developing more robust security measures to protect against similar threats.

The impact of the AIDS Trojan extended beyond the immediate effects on the victims, influencing the broader perception of cybersecurity risks and the importance of proactive measures to protect computer systems. The incident demonstrated that even seemingly innocuous software could be used for malicious purposes, emphasizing the need for vigilance and caution when dealing with unknown programs. It also highlighted the importance of developing a more comprehensive approach to cybersecurity, involving technical measures, user education, and legal action to address the growing threat of digital extortion.

Lessons Learned and Takeaways

The AIDS Trojan incident provides several critical lessons for modern cybersecurity practices. One of the primary lessons is the importance of user education and awareness in preventing cybersecurity threats. The attack exploited users' trust in seemingly legitimate sources, highlighting the need for greater caution and skepticism when dealing with unknown software. This underscores the importance of cybersecurity training and awareness programs to educate users about potential risks and best practices for protecting their systems.

Another key lesson from the incident is the importance of proactive security measures to protect against emerging threats. The AIDS Trojan spread widely due to the lack of robust security measures at the time, including antivirus software, firewalls, and other protective technologies. This highlights the need for organizations to adopt a proactive approach to cybersecurity, regularly reviewing and updating their security measures to protect against new and evolving threats.

The AIDS Trojan also serves as a reminder of the importance of a coordinated response to cybersecurity incidents. The response to the attack involved a combination of technical expertise, user education, and legal action, high-lighting the need for a comprehensive approach to addressing cyber threats. This approach underscores the importance of collaboration and information sharing when responding to cybersecurity incidents, emphasizing the need for ongoing cooperation between stakeholders to protect against digital ex-tortion and other malicious activities.

Case Study Summary

The AIDS Trojan incident represents a significant milestone in the history of cybersecurity, introducing the concept of ransomware and highlighting the vulnerabilities of early computer systems. The incident underscores the importance of user education, proactive security measures, and a coordinated response in protecting against cybersecurity threats.

The lessons learned from the AIDS Trojan continue to resonate today, emphasizing the dynamic nature of cybersecurity and the importance of remaining vigilant and proactive in protecting our digital assets. As we continue to navigate the evolving landscape of cyber threats, these early examples remind us of the critical need to prioritize cybersecurity and invest in protecting our networks.

KEVIN MITNICK'S HACKING SPREE (1990–1995)

Kevin Mitnick's hacking spree from 1990 to 1995 represents one of the most notorious episodes in the early years of cybersecurity. Mitnick, a highly skilled hacker, became infamous for unauthorized access to numerous computer systems, including those of major corporations and government organizations. His activities highlighted the vulnerabilities in computer networks and the dangers posed by individuals who could exploit them. Mitnick's hacking spree captured the public's imagination and elevated concerns about cybersecurity to a national level, prompting significant changes in how digital security was perceived and managed.

During his hacking spree, Mitnick targeted several high-profile companies, including Digital Equipment Corporation (DEC), Motorola, Nokia, NEC, and Sun Microsystems. His attacks were not motivated by financial gain but rather by the challenge of breaking into secure systems and gaining access to sensitive information. Mitnick's ability to infiltrate these organizations exposed significant weaknesses in their cybersecurity defenses, leading to substantial financial losses and reputational damage. His activities also demonstrated the growing importance of digital security in an increasingly interconnected world.

The technological landscape at the time was evolving rapidly, with the rise of personal computers, the proliferation of the Internet, and the increasing reliance on digital communication and information storage. However, many organizations were still unprepared for the security challenges posed by this new environment. Key stakeholders involved in Mitnick's hacking spree included the companies he targeted, law enforcement agencies such as the FBI, and the cybersecurity community, which was beginning to take shape as a field of expertise and professional practice.

Unfolding the Attack

Kevin Mitnick's hacking spree began in earnest in 1990 after he violated the terms of his probation for a previous hacking conviction by accessing Pacific Bell's voicemail computers. This marked the start of a five-year period during which Mitnick conducted a series of high-profile cyber intrusions. He utilized various techniques to gain unauthorized access to computer systems, including social engineering, phishing, and exploiting software vulnerabilities. Mitnick's attacks often began with social engineering, where he would manipulate individuals into revealing sensitive information, such as usernames and passwords, which he then used to infiltrate networks.

One of Mitnick's most significant attacks occurred in 1992 when he targeted DEC's computer network. Mitnick could access DEC's source code for its VMS operating system by exploiting vulnerabilities in the company's systems. The stolen source code represented a considerable intellectual property loss for DEC, and the breach was a significant embarrassment for the company, showcasing the need for stronger cybersecurity measures.

Mitnick continued his hacking activities, targeting several other major corporations over the next few years. He employed various methods to compromise these systems, including password guessing, brute-force attacks, and exploiting flaws in network security protocols. In many cases, Mitnick used compromised systems as a base to launch further attacks, expanding his reach and making it more challenging for authorities to track his activities. By 1994, Mitnick had become the most-wanted computer criminal in the United States, leading to an extensive manhunt by law enforcement.

Detection and Response Efforts

Detecting Kevin Mitnick's activities was a challenging and lengthy process, complicated by his extensive use of social engineering and his ability to cover his tracks. Mitnick's hacking was detected through a combination of suspicious network activity, internal audits, and reports from employees targeted by his social engineering tactics. Once organizations realized they had been breached, they worked quickly to identify the scope of the damage and secure their systems. However, Mitnick's ability to move swiftly from one target to another made it difficult to contain the damage.

In response to Mitnick's attacks, many organizations strengthened their cybersecurity defenses, implemented stricter access controls, and began to prioritize cybersecurity as a critical component of their operations. Law enforcement agencies, led by the FBI, launched an extensive investigation to locate and apprehend Mitnick. The investigation involved collaboration between multiple agencies and private sector cybersecurity experts, highlighting the importance of cooperation in responding to cyber threats. Mitnick was eventually tracked down by Tsutomu Shimomura, a computer security expert whose own systems had been compromised by Mitnick.

The response efforts culminated in Mitnick's arrest on February 15, 1995, in Raleigh, North Carolina. The arrest marked the end of a two-year pursuit and underscored the growing importance of cybersecurity expertise in law enforcement efforts. The case attracted significant media attention, emphasizing the importance of cybersecurity in the public consciousness and the need for robust defenses against increasingly sophisticated cyber threats. Mitnick's capture also illustrated the value of cross-sector collaboration in combating cybercrime, as law enforcement agencies and cybersecurity experts worked together to bring him to justice.

Assessing the Impact

The immediate impact of Kevin Mitnick's hacking spree was significant, causing substantial financial losses and reputational damage to the organizations he targeted. Companies such as DEC, Motorola, and Nokia were forced to invest heavily in cybersecurity improvements and legal fees to address the breaches and mitigate the damage caused by the theft of intellectual property and sensitive information. The incident also exposed the vulnerabilities in their cybersecurity defenses, highlighting the need for more robust security measures and greater awareness of the risks posed by cyber threats.

In the long term, Mitnick's hacking spree had far-reaching consequences for cybersecurity. It brought widespread attention to the issue of cybersecurity and underscored the importance of protecting digital assets against unauthorized access and exploitation. The case also highlighted the need for improved cybersecurity policies and practices, including stronger access controls, better network monitoring, and more effective incident response plans. Additionally, the incident increased awareness of the importance of ethical behavior and responsible conduct within the cybersecurity community.

The impact of Mitnick's activities extended beyond the organizations directly affected, influencing the broader perception of cybersecurity risks and the importance of proactive measures to protect against emerging threats. The case demonstrated the potential for individuals to cause significant harm through unauthorized access to computer systems, emphasizing the need for organizations to prioritize cybersecurity as a critical component of their operations. It also underscored the importance of collaboration between stakeholders in responding to cyber threats, highlighting the value of information sharing and cooperation in combating cybercrime.

Lessons Learned and Takeaways

Kevin Mitnick's hacking spree provides several critical lessons for modern cybersecurity practices. One of the primary lessons is the importance of robust access controls and authentication mechanisms to protect against unauthorized access. Mitnick's ability to gain access to sensitive systems through social engineering and other tactics underscores the need for organizations to implement strong authentication measures, such as multifactor authentication, to safeguard their networks and prevent unauthorized access.

Another key lesson from the incident is the importance of cybersecurity awareness and employee training. Many of Mitnick's attacks relied on social engineering tactics to manipulate individuals into revealing sensitive information, highlighting the need for organizations to educate their employees about cybersecurity risks and best practices. This includes training employees to recognize and respond to phishing attempts, suspicious communications, and other social engineering tactics that could compromise their security.

The case also emphasizes the importance of collaboration and information sharing in responding to cyber threats. The response to Mitnick's hacking spree involved a combination of technical expertise, coordination among affected organizations, and the involvement of external parties, such as law enforcement and cybersecurity experts. This collaborative approach underscores the need for ongoing stakeholder cooperation to protect against cyber threats and develop more resilient cybersecurity defenses.

Case Study Summary

Kevin Mitnick's hacking spree represents a significant chapter in the history of cybersecurity, highlighting the vulnerabilities of early networked systems and the potential for individuals to exploit them for personal gain. The incident underscores the importance of robust access controls, cybersecurity awareness and training, and collaboration in responding to cyber threats. It also serves as a reminder of the need for ongoing vigilance and adaptability.

This case study teaches the value of robust access controls, the importance of cybersecurity awareness and training, and the need for a collaborative approach to responding to cybersecurity incidents. The lessons learned from Mitnick's hacking spree continue to resonate today, emphasizing the dynamic nature of cybersecurity and the importance of remaining vigilant and proactive in protecting our digital assets. As we continue to navigate the evolving landscape of cyber threats, these early examples remind us of the critical need to prioritize cybersecurity and invest in protecting our networks.

THE CITIBANK AND VLADIMIR LEVIN HACK (1995)

The Citibank and Vladimir Levin hack of 1995 is one of the most notable early incidents of cybercrime involving financial institutions, highlighting the vulnerabilities of banking systems in the emerging digital age. Vladimir Levin, a Russian hacker and mathematician, orchestrated a sophisticated cyber heist that targeted Citibank's computer network, successfully siphoning millions of dollars from accounts worldwide. This attack underscored the potential financial risks associated with cyber threats and marked a turning point in how banks and other financial institutions viewed cybersecurity.

Citibank, one of the world's largest financial institutions, was the primary target of Levin's cyberattack. At the time, Citibank pioneered online banking and global funds transfers, making it a prime target for cybercriminals seeking to exploit the burgeoning digital banking landscape. The attack revealed significant weaknesses in the bank's security infrastructure and highlighted the need for more robust defenses to protect against increasingly sophisticated cyber threats.

The technological landscape of the mid-1990s was characterized by rapid advancements in computer technology and the growth of the Internet, which facilitated greater connectivity but also introduced new security challenges. Key stakeholders involved in the Citibank and Vladimir Levin hack included Citibank, its customers, law enforcement agencies like the FBI, and the broader financial industry; all were forced to reevaluate their cybersecurity strategies in light of the attack.

Unfolding the Attack

The Citibank hack began in the summer of 1994 when Vladimir Levin, operating from St. Petersburg, Russia, managed to gain unauthorized access to Citibank's cash management system. Levin exploited vulnerabilities in Citibank's network, using dial-up modems to access the bank's computers remotely. Once inside, he manipulated the system to transfer funds from various accounts to accounts under his control in different countries, including the United States, Finland, Israel, and Germany.

The timeline of the attack extended over several months, with Levin initiating multiple unauthorized transactions between June and October 1994. He transferred approximately $10 million to accounts he controlled, using stolen credentials and unauthorized access to the bank's cash management system. Levin's methods primarily involved password guessing and exploiting weak authentication mechanisms, allowing him to bypass security controls and execute fraudulent transactions.

The vulnerabilities exploited by Levin included weak security protocols, inadequate monitoring of network activity, and insufficient authentication measures. By exploiting these weaknesses, Levin could access Citibank's system without triggering any alarms or alerts. The attack demonstrated the risks associated with remote access technologies and underscored the importance of robust authentication and monitoring systems to protect against unauthorized access.

Detection and Response Efforts

The detection of the Citibank hack was not immediate because Levin's activities were initially concealed by the limitations of the bank's monitoring systems. Citibank's internal security team eventually discovered the unauthorized transfers when they noticed unusual bank fund transfer patterns. Once the breach was identified, Citibank immediately moved to contain the damage by freezing affected accounts, reversing unauthorized transactions where possible, and implementing stricter security controls to prevent further unauthorized access.

Citibank's response to the attack involved a combination of internal investigations and collaboration with law enforcement agencies, including the FBI. The bank worked closely with these agencies to track down Levin and his accomplices, gathering evidence and monitoring the flow of funds to identify the perpetrators. The investigation revealed that Levin was not acting alone; he was part of a larger group that included several accomplices who helped facilitate the transfers and withdraw funds from different locations worldwide.

The response efforts culminated in Levin's arrest in March 1995 at London's Heathrow Airport, following a coordinated operation by the FBI and British law enforcement. His arrest began a lengthy legal process that underscored the complexities of prosecuting cybercriminals operating across international borders. Levin was eventually extradited to the United States, where he pled guilty to conspiracy to commit bank fraud in 1997. The case highlighted the importance of international cooperation in combating cybercrime and demonstrated the challenges of bringing cybercriminals to justice.

Assessing the Impact

The immediate impact of the Citibank hack was significant, causing financial losses and reputational damage to the bank. Although Citibank managed to recover most of the stolen funds, the attack exposed significant weaknesses in its cybersecurity defenses and raised concerns about the security of online banking services. The incident also underscored the potential risks to customers, who were left vulnerable to fraud and unauthorized access due to the bank's inadequate security measures.

In the long term, the Citibank hack had several important consequences for the financial industry and the broader field of cybersecurity. The incident prompted a reevaluation of security practices and led to the adoption of more robust cybersecurity measures across the banking sector. This included the implementation of stronger authentication protocols, enhanced monitoring and detection systems, and more rigorous security policies to protect against unauthorized access and cyber threats.

The impact of the Citibank hack extended beyond the immediate effects on the bank and its customers, influencing the broader perception of cybersecurity risks and the importance of proactive measures to protect against emerging threats. The incident demonstrated the vulnerabilities inherent in financial systems and the potential for cybercriminals to exploit these weaknesses for financial gain.

Lessons Learned and Takeaways

The Citibank and Vladimir Levin hack provides critical lessons for modern cybersecurity practices. One of the primary lessons is the importance of robust authentication and access controls to protect against unauthorized access. Levin's ability to gain access to Citibank's systems using stolen credentials and weak authentication mechanisms underscores the need for organizations to implement strong authentication measures, such as multifactor authentication, to safeguard their networks and prevent unauthorized access.

Another key lesson from the incident is the importance of effective monitoring and detection systems to identify and respond to suspicious activity. The delay in detecting Levin's unauthorized transfers highlights the need for organizations to invest in advanced monitoring tools and systems that can detect anomalies and potential security breaches in real time. This includes implementing automated alerts and response protocols to quickly identify and mitigate potential threats before they can cause significant damage.

The case also emphasizes the importance of international cooperation and collaboration in responding to cybercrime. Levin and his accomplices' successful investigation and prosecution were made possible through close cooperation between Citibank, law enforcement agencies, and international partners. This underscores the need for ongoing cooperation and information sharing between stakeholders to protect against cyber threats and develop more resilient cybersecurity defenses. Ultimately, Levin was convicted and served three years in jail in the United States.

Case Study Summary

The Citibank and Vladimir Levin hack represents a significant chapter in the history of cybersecurity, highlighting the vulnerabilities of early banking systems and the potential for cybercriminals to exploit them for financial gain. The incident underscores the importance of robust authentication and access controls, effective monitoring and detection systems, and international cooperation in responding to cyber threats.

The lessons learned from the Citibank hack continue to resonate today, emphasizing the dynamic nature of cybersecurity and the importance of remaining vigilant and proactive in protecting our digital assets. As we continue to navigate the evolving landscape of cyber threats, these early examples remind us of the critical need to prioritize cybersecurity and invest in protecting our networks.

GARY MCKINNON (SOLO) HACKS U.S. MILITARY NETWORKS (2001)

The case of Gary McKinnon's 2001 hacking of U.S. military and NASA systems stands as one of the most audacious individual cyberattacks in history. McKinnon, a British hacker, gained unauthorized access to these highly sensitive systems over a 13-month period—an unprecedented breach when cybersecurity was still evolving. McKinnon aimed to uncover information related to UFOs and free energy technology, claiming U.S. authorities were concealing these. Despite the seemingly innocuous motive, his actions severely disrupted operations within critical U.S. defense and research institutions.

At the time of the attack, the U.S. military and NASA were among the world's largest and most technologically advanced organizations. They were key players in national defense and space exploration, and their systems contained information critical to national security and scientific research. In the early 2000s, cybersecurity practices were advancing, but vulnerabilities in many systems still existed, particularly in legacy systems that were slow to adopt new security protocols. McKinnon exploited these weaknesses in ways that shook the confidence in the defense community and public trust in the security of government systems.

The attack also brought international attention to cybercrime laws and the treatment of non-U.S. citizens in cases involving U.S. national security. McKinnon's extradition case generated widespread debate about his guilt and the rights of individuals charged with cybercrimes across international borders. This added a significant legal and diplomatic dimension to an already high-profile case.

Unfolding the Attack

The attack began in February 2001 and spanned until March 2002. During that time, McKinnon successfully breached dozens of U.S. military networks, including those of the Army, Navy, Air Force, Department of Defense, and NASA. McKinnon operated alone from his home in the United Kingdom, using a dial-up internet connection and a simple program to search for systems with open administrative access. He took advantage of weak passwords and unsecured networks, bypassing outdated security measures to access sensitive data.

Once inside these systems, McKinnon left messages mocking U.S. authorities for their inadequate security. He also deleted critical files, rendering some systems inoperable. At one point, he caused the shutdown of 300 computers at a U.S. Navy weapons station, temporarily disrupting operations. The simplicity of McKinnon's methods stood in stark contrast to the damage he inflicted, highlighting the critical importance of strong passwords and robust system defenses.

U.S. cybersecurity teams eventually detected McKinnon's activities, but not before he had caused considerable disruption. His methods—largely centered around exploiting weak security configurations—underscored the growing gap between technological capabilities and cybersecurity preparedness.

While McKinnon's motives were not driven by traditional criminal intent like financial gain, his actions exposed serious vulnerabilities within critical U.S. infrastructure.

Detection and Response Efforts

McKinnon's activities were detected after months of suspicious activity on the compromised networks. U.S. cybersecurity personnel began noticing unauthorized access to systems, missing files, and messages left by the hacker. Initially, McKinnon's intrusions were believed to be the work of a larger, organized group, given the attack's scale and the targets' high-profile nature. However, once forensic teams began analyzing the digital footprints left behind, it became clear that a single individual was behind the attack.

Upon discovery, the U.S. launched a full-scale investigation involving multiple government agencies, including the FBI and the Department of Defense. International cooperation with British authorities was crucial in tracking McKinnon, given that the attacks originated overseas. Despite the severity of the breaches, the response was complicated by the international legal complexities of extraditing a non-U.S. citizen for cybercrimes against the U.S. government.

Immediate response actions included isolating affected systems, conducting internal audits to assess the extent of the damage, and implementing stronger security protocols across the affected networks. However, the incident also exposed significant gaps in the U.S. government's ability to quickly detect and respond to cyberattacks on its critical infrastructure, leading to more robust cybersecurity frameworks in the years following the attack.

Assessing the Impact

Gary McKinnon's cyberattack was felt on multiple levels. Operationally, the breach caused significant disruption within the U.S. military and NASA, with some systems rendered temporarily inoperable. Financially, the estimated cost of the damage caused by McKinnon's actions was around $700,000. However, the cost of lost productivity and resource allocation to address the breach was likely much higher.

Beyond the immediate operational effects, the long-term consequences included a loss of trust in the security of U.S. government networks, both domestically and internationally. The incident also highlighted the vulnerabilities within military and research systems, prompting a reassessment of cybersecurity policies and practices. The breach raised concerns about how easily a lone hacker with limited resources could compromise systems critical to national security, leading to a renewed focus on strengthening cybersecurity defenses across government agencies.

McKinnon's case also had significant legal and diplomatic ramifications. His extradition case became a highly publicized legal battle, sparking widespread debate over the treatment of non-U.S. citizens in cybercrime cases. The drawn-out extradition process strained relations between the U.S. and the UK, with many in the UK opposing McKinnon's extradition due to concerns over his health and the severity of potential U.S. penalties. After a 10-year legal battle, the UK finally blocked McKinnon's extradition to the U.S. on health grounds.

Lessons Learned and Takeaways

One of the key lessons from the Gary McKinnon case is the importance of basic cybersecurity hygiene, particularly the use of strong passwords and secure system configurations. McKinnon gained access to highly sensitive systems using relatively simple methods, exploiting weak security measures that could have been easily addressed with more stringent controls. This underscores the critical need for organizations to implement basic security protocols and ensure that legacy systems are properly secured.

The case also highlights the evolving nature of cyber threats, particularly the ability of individual actors to cause significant disruption to large organizations. McKinnon's actions demonstrated that cyberattacks do not always require sophisticated tools or techniques—even simple vulnerabilities can be exploited to devastating effect. This has implications for how organizations prioritize their cybersecurity efforts, emphasizing the need for continuous monitoring and regular security assessments.

Additionally, the international dimension of the case raises important questions about the legal frameworks for addressing cybercrime. McKinnon's extradition case brought to the forefront the challenges of prosecuting individuals across borders for cyber offenses, an issue that has become increasingly relevant as cybercrime continues to grow. The case underscores the need for greater international cooperation and clearer legal processes for handling cross-border cyber incidents.

Case Study Summary

The Gary McKinnon cyberattack on U.S. military and NASA networks serves as a critical case study in the evolution of cybersecurity. McKinnon's relatively unsophisticated methods exposed significant vulnerabilities in some of the most secure systems in the world. The incident had far-reaching

continued

consequences for the U.S. government and the global conversation around cybersecurity, international law, and the treatment of cyber criminals.

Key takeaways from this case include the importance of basic cybersecurity practices, the potential for lone actors to cause significant disruption, and the legal complexities of prosecuting cybercrimes across borders. The case also serves as a reminder of the need for vigilance and proactive cybersecurity strategies, particularly in an era where the cyber-threat landscape continues to evolve rapidly.

This case illustrates the broader impact of seemingly small vulnerabilities on large organizations, particularly those involved in national defense and critical infrastructure. As such, it provides valuable lessons for organizations of all sizes on securing their systems against even the most unexpected threats.

CHAPTER CONCLUSION

The early years of cybersecurity, as highlighted through these case studies, reveal a rapidly evolving landscape that can be deeply vulnerable. From the first ransomware attacks and politically motivated hacks to the pioneering days of digital espionage and financial cybercrime, each incident exposed fundamental weaknesses in the burgeoning digital infrastructure. The common themes that emerge from these cases are the importance of vigilance and robust security measures, along with the ever-present human element, that is, the attackers exploiting trust and weak protocols and the defenders scrambling to respond. These early attacks taught the world that cybersecurity is not just a technical challenge but a dynamic, multidisciplinary field that requires continuous adaptation and learning.

For today's cybersecurity professionals, these historical incidents serve as both a warning and a guide. They underscore the importance of understanding the full spectrum of potential threats—from technically sophisticated exploits to simple social engineering tactics. The attackers in these cases were often successful because they identified and exploited systemic vulnerabilities, whether through software flaws, poor authentication practices, or inadequate monitoring. Therefore, cybersecurity professionals must prioritize a comprehensive approach to security, including regular vulnerability assessments, patch management, and advanced authentication mechanisms. It is also crucial to foster a culture of security awareness among all users, as human error remains a significant risk factor.

Additionally, the case studies demonstrate the critical role of collaboration and information sharing in combating cyber threats. From early efforts to coordinate between different organizations and law enforcement agencies to creating specialized cybersecurity response teams, the value of collective defense is clear. Today, cybersecurity professionals should continue to build on this legacy by engaging in active collaboration with peers, participating in threat intelligence networks, and maintaining open lines of communication with both public and private sector partners. The ability to rapidly share information and coordinate responses can mean the difference between a contained incident and a widespread breach.

Looking forward, cybersecurity professionals should also remain mindful of the evolving nature of threats. The attacks of the past were often unexpected because they represented new kinds of challenges. Similarly, the future will undoubtedly bring new technologies and attack vectors to test our defenses. Therefore, professionals must invest in ongoing education, stay informed about emerging trends, and adopt a proactive mindset. By learning from the past, staying vigilant in the present, and preparing for the future, today's cybersecurity professionals can build stronger defenses against the ever-changing landscape of digital threats.

2

THE RISE OF MALWARE
AND VIRUSES

Ah, the early 2000s—when people were still getting used to the idea of having email on their phones, social media was just a glimmer in a coder's eye, and everyone thought opening that email from a mysterious *Nigerian prince* was their ticket to riches. It was also a time when cybersecurity threats started to get . . . let's say, *creative*. From worms named after tennis stars to viruses that claimed to profess love but instead trashed your inbox, this period in cyber history was like a digital Wild West, where anything could—and did—happen. If you remember the days when the words "You've got mail" filled you with excitement instead of dread, you probably lived through some of these iconic attacks.

But behind the humor of catchy virus names and curious attachments was a serious wake-up call for organizations and individuals alike. The rise of malware and viruses exposed the vulnerabilities in the rapidly expanding digital world. Many threats that emerged during this time were not just technological nuisances; they were harbingers of a new age where digital security would be as crucial as physical security. This chapter closely examines the major malware and virus outbreaks of the early 2000s, breaking down how they spread, what vulnerabilities they exploited, and how organizations responded—when they did respond, that is.

This chapter aims to analyze these infamous attacks and draw lessons that remain highly relevant for today's cybersecurity professionals. In many cases, I've had to extrapolate details about response efforts and detection from media reports and other available sources because direct accounts from affected organizations were often incomplete or unavailable. This indicates how chaotic those early days of cybersecurity were; many organizations were so overwhelmed by these attacks that detailed postmortems were not always possible. However, by piecing together the available information, we can still glean valuable insights into how these attacks unfolded and how they were managed.

As we dive into the case studies, it is clear that while the technology has evolved, many fundamental challenges remain. Whether it is poor patch management, user susceptibility to phishing, or the failure to adopt proactive security measures, these attacks offer a roadmap for what not to do. But more important, they provide lessons on staying vigilant and proactive in a landscape where cyber threats are constantly evolving. So, while we can laugh a little about the absurdity of some of these early threats, the lessons they provide are anything but a joke.

WHAT ARE MALWARE AND VIRUSES?

Malware and viruses have been fundamental to cybersecurity attacks for decades, each representing a significant threat to individual users, organizations, and critical infrastructure. Malware, short for malicious software, refers to any software designed to cause harm, disrupt operations, or steal data. Viruses are a specific type of malware that replicates by attaching itself to legitimate programs or files. Once the infected file is executed, the virus spreads to other programs, continuing its damage. While viruses represent an early form of malware, modern threats include various malicious software types such as ransomware, worms, spyware, and Trojans (see Figure 2.1).

The attack begins when a user inadvertently executes malware, often through phishing emails, downloading compromised software, or visiting malicious websites. For viruses, the attack relies on the host file being opened or run, allowing the virus to propagate to other files or systems. Malware, in general, may exploit vulnerabilities in software or networks, allowing attackers to gain unauthorized access, steal data, or disrupt services. For example, ransomware encrypts data and demands a ransom payment for decryption, while spyware quietly monitors a system's activity, sending sensitive information back to the attacker.

Protection against malware and viruses requires a multilayered approach. Antivirus software is critical in scanning for known malicious signatures and behaviors. Keeping systems and software updated with the latest security

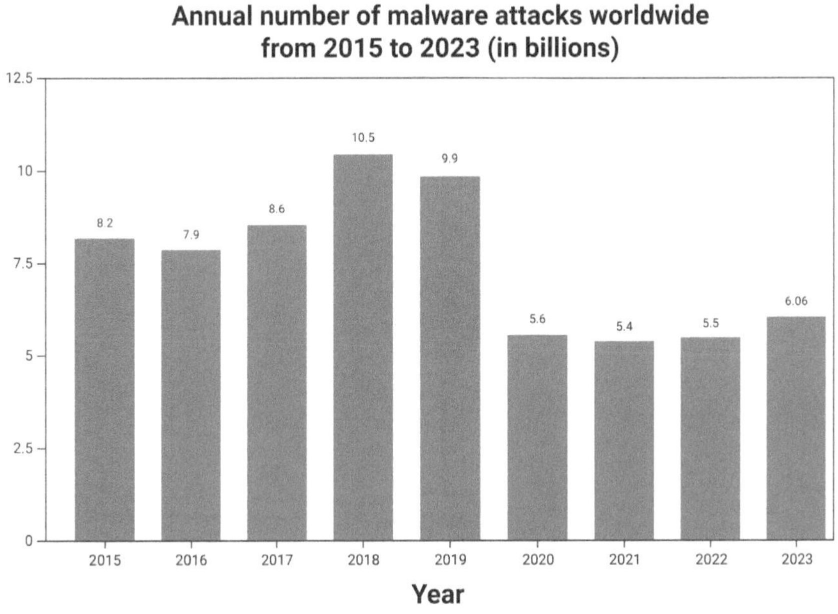

**Annual number of malware attacks worldwide
from 2015 to 2023 (in billions)**

Figure 2.1 Malware attacks worldwide (*source*: Statista Search Department)

patches helps prevent the exploitation of vulnerabilities often used to spread malware. Additionally, practicing cyber hygiene, such as avoiding suspicious emails, using strong and unique passwords, and implementing network defenses like firewalls and intrusion detection systems, can significantly reduce the risk of infection. Organizations also benefit from regular backups, security awareness training for employees, and implementing least-privilege access controls, ensuring that the damage from any successful attack is minimized.

As malware continues to evolve, so too must defense strategies. The rise of polymorphic malware that can alter its code to avoid detection, and fileless attacks that operate solely in memory without leaving a file footprint, demonstrate that malware is becoming increasingly sophisticated. Proactive cybersecurity measures, including behavioral analytics, endpoint detection, and response systems, are crucial for identifying and neutralizing threats in real time, reducing the attack surface, and mitigating the impact of these pervasive threats.

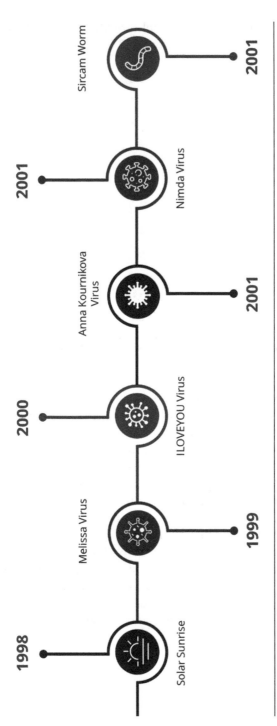

Figure 2.2   The timeline of attacks discussed in this chapter

SOLAR SUNRISE (1998)

The Solar Sunrise attack of 1998 stands out as one of the earliest and most alarming instances of a cyber threat targeting military systems. Set against the backdrop of the burgeoning Internet era, the attack exposed vulnerabilities in U.S. Department of Defense (DoD) systems, which were believed to be secure. The attack occurred when the Internet was rapidly evolving, but cybersecurity practices had yet to mature, leaving many critical systems at risk. The term *Solar Sunrise* was coined after the intruders used solar energy-themed names for their accounts, adding an enigmatic layer to the case.

At the time, the DoD relied heavily on its computer networks to manage critical functions, including communications and operations. This made it an attractive target for cybercriminals or state-sponsored attackers. The key stakeholders included the U.S. military, cybersecurity experts, and law enforcement agencies. Notably, the attack coincided with a period of heightened geopolitical tension in the Middle East, leading to initial speculation that the intrusion was the work of state-sponsored actors, potentially from Iraq.

Technologically, the late 1990s were a time of rapid growth in computer networks, but security often took a backseat to convenience and functionality. Firewalls, intrusion detection systems, and other forms of defense were in their infancy, leaving many systems vulnerable to exploitation. In this context, Solar Sunrise exposed weaknesses not only in the systems themselves but also in the ability of organizations to detect and respond to cyber intrusions.

Unfolding the Attack

The Solar Sunrise attack began with the compromise of U.S. military computer networks, specifically targeting unclassified systems still critical to operations. From the information available, it is assumed that the attackers exploited weak points in the network's security configuration, possibly through poorly secured accounts and outdated software. The entry point appears to have been through relatively simple but effective hacking techniques, likely involving the exploitation of known vulnerabilities in the operating systems of the time.

The attackers infiltrated the networks using a method known as *sniffing*, which allowed them to capture sensitive data, including passwords, as they were transmitted across the network. From there, they could move laterally within the system, gaining access to additional computers and servers. Over several days, the attackers maintained their access, conducting reconnaissance and potentially gathering sensitive information about military operations.

One of the most concerning aspects of the Solar Sunrise attack was the attackers' ability to remain undetected for a significant period. The timeline of the events suggests that the intrusion was ongoing for several weeks before it was detected. While no classified data was reportedly compromised, the attackers' ability to penetrate military networks caused alarm among U.S. defense officials and cybersecurity professionals.

Detection and Response Efforts

The detection of the Solar Sunrise attack was not immediate, reflecting the limitations of intrusion detection systems in the late 1990s. Eventually, the attack was detected through routine monitoring, which revealed unusual activity on the network. Once identified, the response efforts involved coordination between several entities, including the DoD, the Federal Bureau of Investigation (FBI), and private cybersecurity firms. The early response efforts were hampered by the novelty of the attack, with many involved parties struggling to comprehend the full scope of the breach.

The initial response included isolating affected systems to prevent further damage while attempting to trace the source of the attack. It was soon clear that the intrusion was not the work of a state-sponsored actor, as initially feared, but rather a group of young, unsophisticated hackers. Investigators traced the attack to two teenagers in California and another individual based in Israel. The FBI and DoD worked in tandem to apprehend the suspects, eventually bringing the perpetrators to justice.

Despite the attack's seemingly low sophistication, the response required a concerted effort from law enforcement, military personnel, and cybersecurity experts. The response efforts also exposed gaps in communication between military and civilian organizations tasked with defending critical infrastructure. This incident underscored the need for stronger cybersecurity protocols and real-time threat detection capabilities.

Assessing the Impact

The immediate impact of the Solar Sunrise attack was a heightened awareness of vulnerabilities within U.S. military networks. Though no classified information was compromised, the attack had serious implications for national security. The realization that even unclassified systems could be targeted and compromised sent shockwaves through the DoD and other governmental agencies. Financial losses were minimal, but the attack highlighted the potential operational disruptions that cyber incidents could cause, especially in critical sectors like defense.

In the long term, Solar Sunrise significantly impacted the evolution of U.S. cybersecurity policy. The attack exposed the need for improved cybersecurity measures across all levels of government and military operations. One of the most notable consequences was the acceleration of initiatives to strengthen the cybersecurity defenses of critical infrastructure. In addition, the incident pushed the DoD and other agencies to develop stronger relationships with private-sector cybersecurity firms, recognizing the importance of collaboration in defending against future threats.

The attack also had lasting consequences for the individuals involved. For the teenagers who carried out the attack, Solar Sunrise became a cautionary tale about the legal and ethical implications of hacking. The public exposure of their involvement led to legal penalties and a stark reminder that even seemingly harmless hacking activities can have far-reaching consequences.

Lessons Learned and Takeaways

The Solar Sunrise attack provided several critical lessons for the cybersecurity community. First and foremost, it highlighted the importance of securing all systems, not just those handling classified information. Unclassified systems, though seemingly less critical, can still be exploited to cause significant disruption. The attack also underscored the need for constant vigilance and advanced intrusion detection tools capable of detecting sophisticated threats in real time.

One of the main weaknesses identified was the reliance on outdated software and weak password protocols, which allowed the attackers easy access to the system. This case demonstrated the necessity of regular system updates and the enforcement of strong password policies as basic security measures. Additionally, the incident highlighted the importance of collaboration between government agencies and private cybersecurity experts and the need for international cooperation when dealing with cross-border cyber threats.

In response to Solar Sunrise, the DoD and other organizations implemented several changes to improve their cybersecurity posture. These changes included adopting more robust intrusion detection systems, enhancing the training and awareness of staff, and establishing clearer protocols for responding to cyber incidents. The broader implications for the industry were clear: cybersecurity was no longer just a technical issue but a matter of national security.

Case Study Summary

The Solar Sunrise attack of 1998 serves as a crucial chapter in the history of cybersecurity, offering key lessons that remain relevant today. The attack, though carried out by relatively unsophisticated hackers, demonstrated the vulnerabilities within critical U.S. military systems and served as a wake-up call for both the public and private sectors. Key takeaways from this case include the importance of securing all systems, constant vigilance, and the need for robust, real-time threat detection capabilities.

Reflecting on the broader impact of the attack, it is clear that Solar Sunrise played a pivotal role in shaping modern cybersecurity policies and practices. By exposing weaknesses in the early cybersecurity defenses of critical infrastructure, the attack catalyzed a series of improvements that would eventually form the foundation of the robust cybersecurity frameworks in place today.

THE MELISSA VIRUS (1999)

The Melissa virus surfaced in March 1999, becoming one of the earliest and most notorious email-based malware attacks. Created by David L. Smith, the virus was named after a Florida stripper mentioned in the virus code, and it rapidly spread across the globe. At the time, email was becoming a primary communication tool, and the virus exploited this growing dependency. Melissa primarily targeted Microsoft Word and Outlook, leveraging their popularity to achieve mass infection. Its impact was felt by businesses, educational institutions, and government agencies that relied on these systems for daily operations.

The Melissa virus exploited the interconnected nature of email systems, creating widespread disruption. Once a user opened the infected Word document, the virus activated and sent itself to the first 50 contacts in the user's Outlook address book. This caused exponential growth in the number of infections as the virus spread rapidly across networks. In an era when cybersecurity was still maturing, the virus exposed significant vulnerabilities in how email systems were secured and how little awareness users had about the risks of malware.

Key stakeholders impacted by this attack included IT departments, email service providers, and organizations across various sectors. These groups struggled to manage the onslaught of infected emails, which overwhelmed systems and forced temporary shutdowns. Antivirus companies played a critical role in developing patches and fixes, while law enforcement agencies such as the FBI were involved in tracking down the virus's creator. The Melissa attack illustrated the global nature of cyber threats and the need for coordinated response efforts.

Unfolding the Attack

The Melissa virus was initially distributed through an infected Word document, often titled "List.doc," containing adult website passwords. From the information available, I assume this document was circulated through online forums and file-sharing networks, drawing users in with promises of secret content. Once the user opened the document, the virus embedded itself in the system, and Outlook was used to send the infected file to 50 contacts, continuing the chain of infection. This form of self-replication was highly effective in exploiting human curiosity and the ease of sharing email attachments.

The virus's rapid spread was unprecedented, affecting thousands of systems within hours. It overwhelmed email servers with the sheer volume of outgoing messages, often causing servers to crash. Large organizations in particular, saw their communication systems come to a standstill, forcing many to take their servers temporarily offline. Despite the virus's relatively simple nature, its success occurred because of its ability to exploit common user behaviors and weak points in email security protocols.

The attack unfolded over several days, but its impact was felt globally. The virus did not directly damage files or steal sensitive data, but the disruption it caused was significant. Email servers, especially those belonging to major corporations and government institutions, were crippled under the load of Melissa's email bombardment. The reliance on email for business communications meant many organizations suffered operational downtime, resulting in considerable financial losses.

Detection and Response Efforts

The detection of the Melissa virus was rapid due to the high volume of infected emails. IT administrators and cybersecurity firms quickly noticed the spike in email traffic and began investigating. From the information, I assume many organizations were caught off guard by the sheer scale of the infection, with some taking drastic measures like shutting down email servers to prevent further spread. Antivirus companies, such as Symantec and McAfee, worked to develop detection signatures for the virus, and many organizations rushed to implement these updates.

Initial response efforts were largely focused on containment. Organizations worked to isolate infected systems, while antivirus companies provided updates that could identify and remove the virus. Law enforcement agencies, including the FBI, became involved, eventually leading to the arrest of David L. Smith in April 1999. Smith was charged with creating and distributing the virus, and his arrest marked one of the first high-profile cases of legal action against a malware creator.

Despite these response efforts, the damage had already been done. The virus spread so quickly that many organizations were forced to shut down email systems temporarily, resulting in widespread operational disruption. The collaborative response between law enforcement, private companies, and government institutions underscored the importance of swift action in the face of a major cybersecurity incident. This event highlighted the need for better incident response plans and tools to deal with such large-scale infections in the future.

Assessing the Impact

The Melissa virus had a substantial financial and operational impact on organizations across the globe. Though the virus did not directly corrupt data or compromise sensitive information, the indirect costs were significant. Companies experienced email server crashes, productivity loss, and expensive recovery efforts. Estimates of the total damage caused by the virus range from 80 to 100 million dollars, reflecting the widespread disruption across various sectors.

The operational disruption was perhaps the most immediate effect of the Melissa virus. Email systems, which were increasingly critical for business communications, became unusable. Organizations were forced to take servers offline, halting communications for hours or even days. This downtime caused significant productivity losses and led to reputational damage for companies that failed to respond quickly or effectively to the outbreak.

The long-term consequences of the Melissa virus extended beyond financial losses. It served as a wake-up call for organizations to reassess their email security protocols and macro settings in Microsoft Office applications. Many companies implemented stricter policies regarding email attachments and enhanced their incident response strategies. The virus also spurred advancements in antivirus software, leading to more widespread adoption of cybersecurity best practices, including user education about malware and phishing threats.

Lessons Learned and Takeaways

The Melissa virus provided several critical lessons for the cybersecurity industry. First and foremost, it highlighted the importance of securing email systems and educating users about the dangers of opening suspicious attachments. The virus's success relied on exploiting human curiosity, emphasizing the need for stronger user awareness programs and training in recognizing phishing and social engineering tactics. Organizations began to implement stricter controls around email and attachments, particularly restricting the automatic execution of macros in documents.

Another key takeaway was the necessity of rapid detection and response mechanisms. The virus spread so quickly that many organizations were overwhelmed, underscoring the importance of an effective incident response plan. The Melissa virus demonstrated that even seemingly simple malware could have far-reaching consequences if left unchecked. This attack prompted the development of more advanced antivirus solutions and automated detection tools to mitigate future outbreaks.

Finally, the Melissa virus emphasized the value of collaboration in addressing large-scale cyber threats. The response involved cooperation between private companies, law enforcement, and government agencies, illustrating the need for a coordinated approach to cybersecurity. The lessons from Melissa continue to shape modern incident response frameworks and underscore the importance of proactive measures in protecting critical communication systems.

Case Study Summary

The Melissa virus was a landmark event in the evolution of malware, showcasing how quickly a virus could disrupt global email systems. Its rapid spread and reliance on human curiosity made it a cautionary tale about the importance of user education and strong email security policies. Key takeaways include the need for better detection and response mechanisms and the importance of restricting potentially harmful macros and attachments.

Reflecting on the broader impact of the Melissa virus, it played a crucial role in shaping the cybersecurity landscape. After the attack, organizations began to adopt stricter email security measures and improve their incident response plans. The lessons learned from this case continue to inform best practices in cybersecurity, particularly in defending against email-based malware and social engineering attacks.

THE ILOVEYOU VIRUS (2000)

The ILOVEYOU virus, which emerged in May 2000, became one of the most infamous malware attacks in the early days of widespread internet usage. A computer worm spread rapidly via email with the subject line *ILOVEYOU* and an attached file called *LOVE-LETTER-FOR-YOU.txt.vbs*. The virus played on human curiosity and social engineering by luring recipients into opening the attachment, believing it to be a love letter. The virus originated in the Philippines, and within hours of its release, it had infected millions of computers globally.

At the time, the Internet was becoming a more integrated part of daily life, and email had become a crucial tool for personal and business communication. The ILOVEYOU virus capitalized on people's growing trust in electronic communications, taking advantage of the relatively weak security measures that were common at the time. The virus spread through Microsoft Outlook, targeting users on the Windows operating system, particularly those using older email software versions lacking robust security features.

Key stakeholders in the ILOVEYOU virus attack included businesses, government agencies, and individual users impacted by the virus. The malware infected millions of computers worldwide, affecting corporate networks and personal systems. The widespread impact and the speed with which the virus spread forced the cybersecurity community to rethink strategies for email security and highlighted the importance of educating users about social engineering tactics.

Unfolding the Attack

The ILOVEYOU virus began as an email with a seemingly innocent subject line—*ILOVEYOU*. The email contained an attachment that appeared to be a harmless text file but instead was a Visual Basic Script (VBScript) file. From the information available, I assume the virus was initially disseminated through mass emailing techniques, targeting unsuspecting users who opened the attachment without realizing its true nature. Once the attachment was opened, the script would execute, overwriting essential system files and spreading the virus by sending copies of itself to all contacts in the user's Outlook address book.

The timeline of the virus's spread is striking. Within hours of its release, it had infected millions of computers across the globe. The virus spread rapidly and caused significant damage to infected systems by overwriting files, including media files like images and audio. It spread primarily through email, and shared file systems were used to increase its reach. Major corporations, government agencies, and even military systems were affected, highlighting the extensive reach of the attack.

The entry point for the virus was almost always the infected email attachment, which relied on users opening it and unknowingly executing the malicious code. The virus exploited vulnerabilities in email clients and the Windows operating system, particularly in how email attachments were handled. The simplicity of the attack—disguising malicious code in a file that looked like a text document—underscored how effective social engineering could be in compromising systems.

Detection and Response Efforts

The ILOVEYOU virus was detected relatively quickly due to its rapid spread and the immediate effects on infected systems. IT departments and cybersecurity firms soon noticed the high volume of infected emails from compromised accounts. From the information I was able to gather, I assume that initial response efforts focused on containing the spread by shutting down email servers and disconnecting affected systems from networks. The virus's ability to propagate through email made containment challenging because it spread faster than many organizations could respond.

Once the virus was identified, antivirus companies quickly developed and released patches to detect and remove the ILOVEYOU virus. Law enforcement agencies in various countries also became involved, with the investigation eventually leading back to a student in the Philippines. However, the Philippines did not have specific laws against cybercrime then, complicating efforts to prosecute the individual responsible. Despite these legal challenges, the response to the virus marked an important turning point in how cybersecurity incidents were handled internationally.

Assessing the Impact

The immediate impact of the ILOVEYOU virus was massive, affecting millions of computers worldwide. The financial losses from the attack were estimated to be around 10 billion dollars due to the cost of repairing infected systems, lost productivity, and data recovery efforts. Many businesses and government agencies were forced to shut down email servers temporarily, leading to significant operational disruptions. The virus's ability to overwrite system and media files also caused irreversible damage to many users' data, contributing to the overall financial and operational impact.

The long-term consequences of the ILOVEYOU virus extended beyond financial losses. The attack exposed critical weaknesses in email security and user awareness. Many organizations implemented stricter policies around email attachments and began educating users about the risks of opening unsolicited emails. Additionally, the attack underscored the need for stronger antivirus and email filtering systems, prompting advancements in cybersecurity solutions.

For individual users, losing personal files, such as images and documents, caused frustration and highlighted the risks of using outdated or unsecured systems. The ILOVEYOU virus also impacted the developing cybercrime laws, particularly in the Philippines, where the attacker originated. This incident catalyzed legal reforms aimed at addressing cybercrime on a global scale.

Lessons Learned and Takeaways

The ILOVEYOU virus provided several critical lessons for the cybersecurity community. One of the most important takeaways was the need for stronger email security practices, particularly in how attachments are handled. Most organizations began implementing more restrictive policies on email attachments and invested in better email filtering technologies to prevent similar attacks in the future. The virus also emphasized the importance of user education, as many infections could have been prevented if users had been more cautious about opening unsolicited attachments.

Another key lesson was the importance of rapid response in mitigating the spread of malware. The ILOVEYOU virus spread so quickly that many organizations were caught off guard, underscoring the need for robust incident response plans. In the aftermath of the attack, many businesses and government agencies revamped their cybersecurity protocols, emphasizing real-time monitoring and rapid detection of threats.

Finally, the attack highlighted the need for international cooperation in combating cybercrime. The global nature of the ILOVEYOU virus meant that law enforcement agencies and cybersecurity experts from multiple countries had to work together to trace the source of the attack. The incident increased awareness of the importance of international legal frameworks for prosecuting cybercriminals and coordinating responses to global cyber threats.

Case Study Summary

The ILOVEYOU virus of 2000 was a landmark event in cybersecurity, showcasing the devastating potential of email-based malware. The virus spread rapidly, causing widespread financial and operational damage across the globe. Key takeaways include stronger email security policies, better user education, and the importance of international collaboration in responding to cyber threats.

continued

Reflecting on the broader impact of the ILOVEYOU virus, it played a crucial role in shaping modern cybersecurity practices. Organizations began adopting more robust email security measures, and the incident led to significant advancements in antivirus technology. The lessons from this case continue to influence best practices in preventing and responding to email-based malware and other social engineering attacks.

THE ANNA KOURNIKOVA VIRUS (2001)

The Anna Kournikova virus surfaced in February 2001 and was a computer worm that spread rapidly by exploiting human curiosity and social engineering techniques. Named after the famous Russian tennis player Anna Kournikova, the virus used her celebrity status to trick users into opening an infected email attachment. The email subject line read "Here you have," and the attachment appeared to be an image of Kournikova. However, upon opening the attachment, the virus spread to the victim's email contacts via Microsoft Outlook, creating a new wave of infections.

The internet landscape in 2001 was still relatively immature regarding security measures. While some major organizations had implemented robust security protocols, many users and businesses were still vulnerable to simple yet effective social engineering attacks. At the time, Microsoft Outlook was one of the dominant email platforms, and many users were unaware of the dangers posed by seemingly harmless email attachments. This vulnerability, combined with the celebrity appeal of Anna Kournikova, made the virus highly effective in spreading across networks.

Key stakeholders affected by the Anna Kournikova virus included businesses, individual users, and IT departments dealing with the fallout of infected email systems. Although the virus did not directly damage files or systems, the mass distribution of emails caused significant operational disruptions for many organizations. The virus highlighted the continued vulnerability of email systems and the importance of user awareness in preventing malware infections.

Unfolding the Attack

The Anna Kournikova virus spread rapidly through email, exploiting users' trust in receiving attachments from known contacts. From the data I collected, I assume the attacker, a Dutch programmer known as *OnTheFly*, created the virus using a VBScript worm template readily available online. The simplicity of the attack method made it accessible even to individuals with limited programming knowledge, demonstrating how dangerous readily available malware creation tools could be. The email, with the subject line "Here you have" and the attached file "AnnaKournikova.jpg.vbs," played on recipients' curiosity to open what appeared to be an image file.

Once the attachment was opened, the virus activated and immediately sent to all contacts in the victim's Microsoft Outlook address book. This propagation method was identical to previous email worms, such as the ILOVEYOU virus.

The Anna Kournikova virus's timeline unfolded quickly. Within hours of its release, it had spread to thousands of computers worldwide. The attack exploited vulnerabilities in email clients like Outlook, which allowed executable code in attachments to run automatically without significant user intervention. The speed and scale of the virus highlighted how vulnerable even well-established systems could be to relatively unsophisticated attacks when social engineering was involved.

Detection and Response Efforts

The Anna Kournikova virus was detected fairly quickly due to its rapid spread and the immediate disruption it caused in email systems. Many organizations and users reported seeing large volumes of emails sent out without their knowledge, quickly raising red flags. From what information I could gather, I assume cybersecurity firms initially detected the virus by monitoring unusual email activity, and they responded by releasing patches to detect and block it.

Initial response efforts focused on containing the spread of the virus by turning off email servers and advising users not to open suspicious attachments. Many IT departments had to implement manual fixes to remove the virus from infected systems, though the virus was relatively easy to eliminate compared to more destructive malware. Antivirus companies like Symantec and McAfee released updates to their software that could detect the virus and prevent further infections. However, as with many email worms, much of the damage was done within the first few hours of its release.

Law enforcement quickly became involved in investigating the source of the virus, and within days, the Dutch programmer responsible was identified and arrested. *OnTheFly*, who was later revealed to be a 20-year-old student, admitted to creating the virus but claimed it was a prank rather than an attempt to cause significant harm. The legal consequences for OnTheFly were relatively minor since laws against cybercrime were still evolving, but the case became a notable example of the legal challenges involved in prosecuting cybercriminals.

Assessing the Impact

The immediate impact of the Anna Kournikova virus was primarily operational, with businesses and organizations experiencing email system slowdowns and temporary shutdowns. The virus did not cause direct damage to files or data, but the sheer volume of emails it generated created significant disruptions. Many businesses had to halt email services while they worked to clean infected systems, leading to lost productivity and, in some cases, financial losses due to downtime. Estimates of the economic impact were relatively low compared to other major malware incidents, but the attack still highlighted the vulnerability of email systems.

For individual users, the virus served as a reminder of the dangers of opening unsolicited email attachments, even if they appeared to come from a trusted source. While the virus was not malicious regarding data theft or destruction, it exploited a fundamental weakness in human behavior—curiosity and trust in known contacts. This incident underscored the importance of educating users about cybersecurity risks and fostering a healthy skepticism toward email attachments.

In the long term, the Anna Kournikova virus had significant implications for email security. The attack prompted many organizations to rethink their email security policies, leading to stricter controls on attachments and more robust antivirus protection. Additionally, the incident contributed to the growing recognition that social engineering was a powerful tool for cybercriminals, even when combined with relatively simple malware.

Lessons Learned and Takeaways

The Anna Kournikova virus provided several important lessons for the cybersecurity community. First, it reinforced the critical role of user awareness in preventing malware infections. The virus spread not through sophisticated hacking techniques but by exploiting human curiosity and user trust in email attachments. This incident demonstrated that even the most secure systems could be vulnerable if users were not educated about the dangers of opening unsolicited attachments.

Another key takeaway was the importance of implementing stronger email security measures. The virus highlighted the need for email clients to have more robust safeguards to prevent executable code from running automatically. In response, many organizations implemented stricter controls on email attachments and began filtering potentially dangerous file types to reduce the risk of infection.

Finally, the Anna Kournikova virus emphasized the ongoing threat posed by readily available malware creation tools. The attacker used a widely available VBScript worm template, showing how easy it had become for amateur programmers to create and distribute malware. This realization pushed cybersecurity firms and law enforcement agencies to take a more proactive stance in monitoring and preventing the distribution of such tools.

Case Study Summary

The Anna Kournikova virus of 2001 is a key example of how social engineering and simple malware can create significant disruptions. While the virus did not cause direct harm to data or systems, its widespread impact highlighted vulnerabilities in email systems and the importance of user education in preventing cyberattacks. Key takeaways include the need for stronger email security measures, better user awareness, and the dangers posed by the availability of malware creation tools.

Reflecting on the broader impact of the attack, the Anna Kournikova virus played a role in shaping modern email security practices. Organizations began adopting stricter policies on email attachments and investing in better antivirus solutions. The lessons from this case continue to influence how businesses and individuals protect themselves from similar social engineering-based cyber threats.

NIMDA VIRUS (2001)

The Nimda virus emerged in September 2001 and was one of the most complex and rapidly spreading malware attacks. Its name, *Nimda*, is *admin* spelled backward, which hinted at its goal of targeting network administrators and taking over systems. The virus spread through multiple vectors, including email, websites, and file sharing, making it difficult to contain. Nimda arrived just a week after the September 11 attacks in the United States, adding to the chaos of an already tumultuous time.

In 2001, the Internet was increasingly becoming a backbone for business operations, communications, and e-commerce. As organizations became more connected, their systems were exposed to various vulnerabilities. The Nimda virus exploited these vulnerabilities across multiple platforms, affecting personal and enterprise-level systems. The virus targeted Microsoft Windows machines and attacked internet servers, web browsers, and email systems, leaving businesses scrambling to recover from the widespread disruptions it caused.

Key stakeholders in the Nimda virus attack included businesses, government agencies, and individual users, all of whom experienced operational disruptions and data loss. For IT administrators, Nimda represented a critical failure of cybersecurity defenses, as it spread quickly and leveraged multiple attack vectors. Antivirus companies, cybersecurity firms, and law enforcement agencies were called upon to assist in mitigating the damage, but the speed and scope of the attack made response efforts particularly challenging.

Unfolding the Attack

The Nimda virus was notable for its versatility, spreading simultaneously through several channels. From available information, I assume the virus was initially distributed via infected email attachments, compromised websites, and network file shares. Once it gained a foothold in a system, Nimda quickly replicated itself and spread to other machines by exploiting vulnerabilities in Microsoft's Internet Information Services (IIS) web server software. This allowed the virus to propagate at an alarming rate across the Internet, infecting individual computers and network servers.

One of Nimda's most dangerous features was its ability to infect systems without requiring any user interaction. For example, users could become infected simply by visiting a compromised website or opening an infected email attachment. The virus would then use these entry points to spread through network shares, infecting any machine connected. The virus also took advantage of vulnerabilities in Microsoft Outlook, sending itself to all contacts in the user's address book, similar to earlier email worms.

The timeline of the attack unfolded quickly. Nimda was released on September 18, 2001, and within hours, it had infected hundreds of thousands of machines across the globe. Its ability to spread through multiple vectors made it difficult to contain, as standard mitigation methods, such as blocking email attachments, were insufficient to stop the infection. The virus also targeted home users and large organizations, adding to its widespread impact.

Detection and Response Efforts

Nimda's rapid spread and multivector attack strategy made detection difficult in the early stages of the outbreak. IT departments and cybersecurity firms noticed unusual network traffic and a sudden surge in infected emails and website defacements. From the material I obtained, I assume initial response efforts focused on identifying the vulnerabilities Nimda was exploiting, such as the IIS web server flaw, and patching those systems to prevent further infection. However, containment proved to be a major challenge due to the virus's ability to spread through various channels.

Once the nature of the virus was understood, antivirus companies quickly developed and distributed patches to detect and remove the Nimda virus. This was a race against time because many systems had already been compromised when the patches were released. Organizations were advised to update their antivirus software, implement firewalls, and disable vulnerable services to slow the spread of the infection. Many companies also temporarily took their email servers offline to prevent further infections via email attachments.

Law enforcement agencies along with private cybersecurity firms conducted investigations to trace the virus's origin, but the attack's complexity made it difficult to identify the perpetrator. Despite the coordinated response efforts, the Nimda virus continued to cause widespread disruption for several weeks. The incident highlighted the need for faster detection methods and more robust cybersecurity practices, especially in the face of multivector attacks like Nimda.

Assessing the Impact

The Nimda virus had a profound impact on organizations around the world. Financial losses from the attack were estimated to be in the billions as companies dealt with downtime, lost productivity, and the costs of recovering compromised systems. Infected systems often had to be completely wiped and reinstalled, which added to the operational strain on businesses. Many organizations also faced reputational damage, particularly those that were slow to respond to the virus and failed to prevent further spread.

For businesses relying on e-commerce and internet services, the disruptions caused by Nimda were particularly severe. Websites were taken offline, and email systems were crippled, leading to a loss of revenue and customer trust. Government agencies and critical infrastructure systems were also affected, raising concerns about the security of essential services in the face of widespread cyberattacks. The Nimda virus became a wake-up call for industries previously underinvested in cybersecurity measures.

In the long term, Nimda had a lasting impact on cybersecurity policies and practices. The attack prompted many organizations to rethink their network security strategies, leading to greater investment in intrusion detection systems, antivirus software, and regular system patching. The incident also underscored the importance of user awareness in preventing the spread of malware, as many infections could have been avoided if users had been more cautious about opening suspicious emails and visiting untrusted websites.

Lessons Learned and Takeaways

The Nimda virus provided several key lessons for the cybersecurity community. One of the most important takeaways was the need for a multilayered defense strategy to protect against malware that uses multiple attack vectors. The virus's ability to spread through email, websites, and network shares demonstrated that relying on a single security solution, such as antivirus software, was insufficient. Organizations began adopting more comprehensive cybersecurity frameworks, including firewalls, intrusion detection systems, and regular system updates.

Another critical lesson was the importance of patch management. Nimda exploited known vulnerabilities in Microsoft's IIS web server software, which could have been mitigated had organizations applied patches promptly. The incident highlighted the need for businesses to apply security updates and ensure that all systems were protected against the latest threats. Many companies also implemented stricter security policies around email attachments and web browsing to reduce the risk of infection.

Finally, the Nimda virus emphasized the importance of cybersecurity awareness and user education. Many infections occurred because users unknowingly opened infected attachments or visited compromised websites. The attack demonstrated the need for regular cybersecurity training, teaching users how to recognize potential threats and avoid risky behaviors. This focus on user education became a cornerstone of modern cybersecurity strategies to reduce human errors that can lead to infections.

Case Study Summary

The Nimda virus of 2001 was a pivotal moment in the history of cybersecurity, showcasing the destructive potential of multivector malware attacks. The virus's ability to spread through email, websites, and network shares made it particularly challenging to contain, leading to widespread financial losses and operational disruptions. Key takeaways from this case include the importance of multilayered defense strategies, timely patch management, and user education in preventing the spread of malware.

Reflecting on the broader impact of the Nimda virus, it became a catalyst for change in how organizations approached cybersecurity. The lessons learned from Nimda continue to influence modern security practices, particularly in intrusion detection, patch management, and user awareness. The attack underscored the need for businesses and governments to stay vigilant in the face of evolving cyber threats and to adopt more proactive cybersecurity measures.

SIRCAM WORM/VIRUS (2001)

The Sircam worm surfaced in July 2001 and was a particularly insidious piece of malware that combined elements of a worm and a virus, spreading through email and network shares. Sircam's ability to send sensitive personal or business-related documents to random email contacts made it stand out, raising significant concerns about privacy and data leaks. The worm arrived when email worms became a common vector for cyberattacks, but its unique features elevated it as one of the most dangerous threats of the early 2000s.

By mid-2001, email had solidified its role as the primary communication tool for businesses, and organizations were still adapting to the growing risk of email-based malware. The technological landscape was evolving, with many companies becoming more reliant on networked systems, creating a fertile environment for worms like Sircam to spread. Microsoft Windows operating systems, particularly Windows 95, 98, and Millennium Edition, were vulnerable to Sircam, and the worm quickly exploited these weaknesses.

Key stakeholders involved in this attack included businesses and individuals who unwittingly shared private documents via infected email systems. The potential for sensitive data leaks, whether personal or corporate, made Sircam a particularly concerning threat. Additionally, IT departments and cybersecurity firms were on high alert as they raced to contain the spread of the worm.

Unfolding the Attack

The Sircam worm spread primarily through email attachments and network shares, using social engineering to trick users into opening infected attachments. From the information I could put together, I assume that the infected emails often contained subject lines pulled from the titles of documents stored on the victim's computer, making them seem legitimate and increasing the likelihood that recipients would open them. Once the recipient opened the attachment, Sircam activated, spreading itself to all the contacts in the victim's address book.

One of Sircam's most dangerous features was its ability to attach random files from the infected computer to outgoing emails. Personal or sensitive documents could be sent to random people, leading to potentially severe privacy breaches. Additionally, the worm would install itself on shared network drives, spreading its reach across corporate networks. Sircam also included a payload that could potentially delete all files on the infected machine or cause the system to crash after October 16, 2001, though this feature was not always activated.

The timeline of Sircam's spread was swift. Within days of its discovery, it had infected hundreds of thousands of computers globally. The worm's ability to send documents without user knowledge and self-replication across email and networks made it particularly challenging to contain. The worm exploited weaknesses in user behavior—namely, the tendency to open attachments from seemingly trusted sources—making it a textbook example of how social engineering can amplify the impact of a malware attack.

Detection and Response Efforts

Sircam's ability to spread through email and network shares made it difficult to detect initially since many users were unaware that their systems had been compromised until it was too late. IT departments began noticing unusual email activity, with large emails containing attachments being sent from infected accounts. From the available information, I assume the worm was detected through the increased network traffic and reports of users receiving unsolicited emails with sensitive documents attached.

Cybersecurity firms responded quickly, releasing updates to antivirus software that could detect and remove the worm. However, as with many email-based worms, the damage had already been done by the time these updates were widely distributed. Organizations scrambled to contain the spread by disabling email systems and isolating infected machines from networks. The worm's ability to delete files or cause system crashes complicated the cleanup process, making recovery a lengthy and resource-intensive process.

Law enforcement agencies and cybersecurity professionals launched investigations to trace the origin of the Sircam worm, but no definitive source was identified. The widespread nature of the attack and the anonymity provided by the Internet made it difficult to pinpoint the individuals responsible. Nevertheless, the incident served as a wake-up call for organizations to strengthen their email security protocols and educate users about the dangers of opening unsolicited attachments.

Assessing the Impact

The immediate impact of the Sircam worm was significant, particularly due to the privacy concerns it raised. Many businesses and individuals found that sensitive or confidential documents had been sent to random email contacts, leading to potential breaches of privacy and intellectual property. This aspect of Sircam set it apart from other worms, as the threat of data leaks added a new dimension of risk for affected organizations. The financial losses were substantial, as businesses faced downtime, lost productivity, and the cost of recovering from the worm's effects.

Operationally, the worm caused widespread disruption to email systems and corporate networks. Many organizations temporarily shut down email services to prevent further spread, disrupting communication and business operations. The potential for the worm to delete files or crash systems also created a long-term risk, as infected machines required thorough scanning and potential reinstallation to ensure full recovery.

In the long term, the Sircam worm impacted how organizations approached email security and data protection. The incident highlighted the dangers of social engineering and the importance of user awareness in preventing malware infections. It also underscored the need for businesses to implement stronger email filtering and antivirus protections to detect and block threats before they could spread across networks.

Lessons Learned and Takeaways

The Sircam worm provided several critical lessons for the cybersecurity community. One of the most important takeaways was the need for robust email security practices. The worm spread through email attachments, exploiting users' trust in familiar subject lines and attachments, emphasizing the importance of educating users on the dangers of opening unsolicited files. In response, many organizations implemented stricter policies around email attachments and improved filtering mechanisms to block potentially harmful emails.

Another key lesson was the importance of network security. Sircam's ability to spread through shared network drives demonstrated the need for organizations to secure their internal networks and limit access to sensitive files. This attack also highlighted the need for better encryption and data protection strategies to prevent sensitive information from being leaked in the event of a malware infection.

Finally, the Sircam worm underscored the value of timely patch management and regular system updates. While the worm did not exploit a specific vulnerability in operating systems, the widespread use of outdated antivirus software contributed to its success. Ensuring systems were equipped with the latest security patches and protections could have mitigated the attack's impact.

Case Study Summary

The Sircam worm of 2001 stands out as a unique and dangerous malware attack due to its ability to leak sensitive documents and cause widespread disruption to email systems. Its rapid spread through email and *continued* network shares and the risk of data leaks made it one of the most concerning threats of the early 2000s. Key takeaways from this case include the need for stronger email security protocols, better user education, and improved network security measures to prevent the spread of similar threats.

Reflecting on the broader impact of the Sircam worm, it served as a reminder of the growing complexity of cyber threats and the importance of staying vigilant against evolving attack vectors. The lessons learned from this case continue to inform modern cybersecurity practices, particularly in email security, data protection, and user awareness. The Sircam worm highlighted the importance of proactive defense strategies to mitigate the risks of sophisticated malware attacks.

CHAPTER CONCLUSION

The early 2000s saw a dramatic rise in sophisticated malware and viruses, with each new attack offering distinct challenges and lessons for the cybersecurity community. The common themes that emerge from these case studies include the importance of user awareness, the need for proactive defense mechanisms, and the rapid evolution of attack methods. One major takeaway is the constant race between attackers exploiting vulnerabilities and defenders responding to incidents after they unfold. In many circumstances, as I've noted throughout these case studies, information regarding response and detection has been extrapolated from media reports and other sources because direct accounts from affected organizations were often limited or unavailable.

The lessons from these attacks remain highly relevant for today's cybersecurity professionals. Many of the vulnerabilities exploited by these early viruses—such as unpatched systems, weak email security, and social engineering—still pose significant threats. Cyber defenders must stay ahead of attackers by implementing layered defenses, focusing on timely patch management, and educating users about evolving threats. The rise of polymorphic malware underlines the need for advanced detection methods beyond traditional antivirus solutions. Modern threat actors are more agile and adaptive and so must be the defenders.

Looking forward, cybersecurity professionals must prioritize rapid detection and response, proactive threat hunting, and user education. Many of the attacks in this chapter exploited human weaknesses—whether through curiosity, trust, or lack of awareness about malware risks. Strengthening human defenses and technical measures like intrusion detection systems, network segmentation, and robust patch management will help prevent future large-scale incidents. Moreover, the collaborative response between cybersecurity firms, law enforcement, and affected organizations, which became more common after these early attacks, is now a foundational part of modern incident response.

Ultimately, the evolution of malware and viruses in the early 2000s laid the groundwork for today's cybersecurity landscape. The lessons from these incidents highlight that while attackers' tools and techniques evolve, many of the core vulnerabilities—human behavior, outdated systems, and unpatched software—remain constant. For cybersecurity professionals, the challenge is to anticipate these threats, stay ahead of attackers, and foster a security culture that recognizes the ongoing and dynamic nature of cyber threats. The past is a powerful reminder that vigilance, adaptability, and collaboration are essential to navigating today's complex threat landscape.

3

WORMS AND THEIR RAPID SPREAD

Ah, worms—those lovely little digital critters that bring joy to IT departments and endless amusement to cybersecurity professionals everywhere. Unlike the garden variety that ruins your lawn, these digital worms can bring down networks, disrupt entire industries, and leave a trail of chaos in their wake. If you have ever wanted to see what happens when a single line of code gets loose and decides to cause a global meltdown, you are in the right place. But do not worry, there is no need for pesticides here—just good cybersecurity practices and maybe stronger coffee.

Jokes aside, worms represent one of the most dangerous categories of malware due to their ability to spread autonomously and quickly across networks. From the infamous SQL Slammer to the ever-resilient Conficker, worms have left an indelible mark on the history of cybersecurity. While each attack we have examined in this book unfolded differently, they all shared a common theme: exploiting known vulnerabilities, preying on unpatched systems, and leveraging the interconnected nature of modern networks to spread their reach. Understanding how these worms worked, what weaknesses they exploited, and the damage they caused is vital for today's cybersecurity professionals since these historical attacks continue to offer valuable lessons on vulnerability management, detection, and response (see Figure 3.1).

I've had to extrapolate details about response efforts and detection strategies from media reports and available sources in many of these case studies. These attacks were often so rapid and overwhelming that detailed, accurate accounts of real-time responses were either unavailable or incomplete. Despite this, the general patterns we can observe offer critical insights into the flaws that allowed these worms to spread so effectively. Even in cases where perfect information does not exist, the lessons remain clear: failure to patch

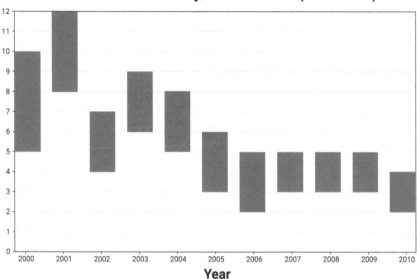

Figure 3.1   Major worm attacks (*source*: Google)

vulnerabilities, weak passwords, and insufficient network segmentation were all key enablers of these attacks.

This chapter aims to explore these infamous worm attacks in depth, not just to understand how they happened but to extract actionable lessons that can help us prevent similar incidents in the future. By analyzing the methods used, the vulnerabilities exploited, and the varying response efforts, we can arm today's cybersecurity professionals with the knowledge needed to avoid past mistakes. Whether it is staying on top of patch management, adopting better password policies, or implementing network segmentation, the history of worms shows us that proactive security measures are the best defense against these rapidly spreading threats.

WHAT ARE WORMS?

Worms are a type of malicious software designed to self-replicate and spread across networks without the need for human intervention. Unlike viruses, which require a host file to propagate, worms exploit vulnerabilities in operating systems, software, or network protocols to infect multiple systems rapidly. Once a worm infiltrates a network, it can spread from one device to another by copying itself, using up system resources, slowing down networks, and causing widespread disruption. Over the years, famous worms like Morris Worm (1988) and Conficker (2008) have caused significant damage, illustrating the persistent threat posed by these self-replicating programs (see Figure 3.2).

The attack mechanism of a worm typically involves exploiting security flaws in networked systems. Worms spread through open ports, unsecured network shares, or unpatched software vulnerabilities. Once a worm enters a system, it replicates and transmits itself across the network. Some worms carry payloads that can install backdoors for later exploitation, steal sensitive data, or enable other types of malware like ransomware or spyware. For example, the SQL Slammer worm (2003) used a buffer overflow vulnerability in the Microsoft SQL Server to spread rapidly across the Internet, causing massive disruptions by overwhelming network traffic.

To protect against worms, organizations and individuals must implement a range of security measures. First and foremost, patching software and operating systems is crucial since worms often exploit known vulnerabilities that could have been fixed with updates. Firewalls and intrusion detection systems can block unauthorized access attempts, limiting the ability of worms to infiltrate and spread across a network. Additionally, practicing good network segmentation ensures that even if a worm infects one part of the network, it cannot easily spread to the entire infrastructure.

Another critical defense is using endpoint security solutions that monitor and block suspicious activity. Email filtering and web gateways can also

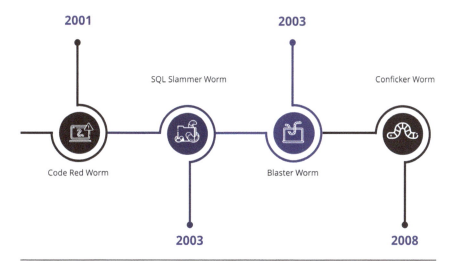

Figure 3.2   The timeline of attacks discussed in this chapter

prevent worms from entering systems through phishing or malicious downloads. In more advanced scenarios, behavioral analysis and machine learning-based tools can detect anomalies in network traffic that indicate the presence of a worm. Regular network monitoring and incident response planning are also essential in quickly identifying and containing worm infections before they cause widespread damage. Organizations can significantly reduce the risk of worm-related attacks by combining proactive patch management, robust network security, and continuous monitoring.

CODE RED WORM (2001)

The Code Red worm, which first appeared in July 2001, became one of the most infamous and destructive worms of the early twenty-first century. Targeting vulnerabilities in Microsoft's Internet Information Services (IIS) web server software, the worm rapidly infected hundreds of thousands of computers, causing widespread disruption. Code Red was unique because it was designed to exploit a buffer overflow vulnerability, allowing attackers to take control of infected machines. The worm was named *Code Red* after the Code Red Mountain Dew soft drink that the researchers analyzing the worm were drinking at the time.

The growing reliance on web servers and networked systems created fertile ground for cyberattacks like Code Red. The worm took advantage of this technological landscape, where many organizations were slow to apply security patches, leaving their systems vulnerable to exploitation. Its ability to spread rapidly without requiring user interaction made it particularly dangerous, affecting both large enterprises and smaller organizations.

Key stakeholders involved in the attack included government agencies, private companies, and individual users whose systems relied on IIS web servers. The U.S. government was especially concerned about the attack since it targeted both public and private sectors, raising alarms about the potential damage to national security and critical infrastructure.

Unfolding the Attack

The Code Red worm spread by exploiting a buffer overflow vulnerability in Microsoft's IIS web server software. From the information I was able to put together, I assume the worm initially infected a vulnerable web server and replicated itself by sending requests to random Internet Protocol (IP) addresses, seeking other vulnerable servers to infect. Once the worm found another target, it would exploit the same vulnerability, allowing it to spread rapidly across the Internet. This method of propagation enabled Code Red to infect over 350,000 systems within just a few hours of its initial release on July 19, 2001.

The worm was designed to operate in phases. In the first phase, it scanned for additional vulnerable servers to infect. In the second phase, it launched a denial-of-service (DoS) attack on a specific target, attempting to bring down the White House's web servers by overwhelming them with traffic. Fortunately, U.S. government officials could mitigate the attack by changing the targeted IP address before significant damage was done. The worm's final phase involved creating a *backdoor* in infected systems, leaving them vulnerable to further exploitation.

One of the most alarming aspects of the Code Red worm was its ability to spread without user intervention. Unlike previous viruses and worms that relied on users opening infected attachments or files, Code Red propagated automatically by exploiting server vulnerabilities. This allowed the worm to spread unprecedentedly, with infected machines continuing to search for new targets in a self-replicating cycle.

Detection and Response Efforts

The Code Red worm was detected relatively quickly due to the high volume of traffic it generated and the noticeable disruption to web servers worldwide. Information technology (IT) administrators and cybersecurity professionals immediately recognized the signs of a large-scale attack as their servers became overwhelmed with traffic. I assume the initial response focused on identifying the exploited vulnerability and developing a patch to prevent further infections.

Microsoft released a patch for the IIS vulnerability a month before the worm's release, but many organizations failed to apply it, exposing their systems. Once the worm was identified, Microsoft and cybersecurity firms urged organizations to immediately update their systems with the patch to stop the spread of the worm. However, the rapid propagation of Code Red meant that even those who acted quickly experienced significant disruptions.

The U.S. government and private cybersecurity firms worked together to mitigate the impact of the worm. Emergency response teams were mobilized to address the DoS attack aimed at the White House while law enforcement agencies investigated the attack's origin. Despite these efforts, the worm spread for several weeks, with new variants of Code Red emerging, further complicating response efforts.

Assessing the Impact

The immediate impact of the Code Red worm was widespread, affecting hundreds of thousands of systems worldwide. The financial losses were estimated to be in the billions, as businesses and government agencies faced downtime, lost productivity, and the costs associated with cleaning and securing infected systems. The DoS attack on the White House, while ultimately unsuccessful, underscored the potential for cyberattacks to target critical government infrastructure and created a heightened sense of urgency around cybersecurity at the national level.

Operational disruptions were significant for businesses relying on web servers for their operations. Many companies experienced outages and slowdowns as their servers were overwhelmed with traffic from the worm. Infected systems also remained vulnerable to future attacks due to the backdoor created by the worm, raising concerns about long-term security risks. The worm's rapid spread and ability to target random IP addresses made it difficult for organizations to predict or prevent infection.

In the long term, the Code Red worm profoundly impacted the cybersecurity landscape. It exposed the dangers of unpatched known vulnerabilities, prompting many organizations to adopt more rigorous patch management practices. It also highlighted the need for better coordination between government and private sectors in responding to large-scale cyberattacks, setting the stage for future cybersecurity collaborations. The worm's success in exploiting a single vulnerability demonstrated how a seemingly small oversight could lead to massive disruptions on a global scale.

Lessons Learned and Takeaways

The Code Red worm highlighted the critical importance of timely patch management. Despite Microsoft releasing a patch for the IIS vulnerability before the attack, many organizations failed to apply it, leaving their systems open to infection. This incident underscored the need for businesses and government agencies to prioritize security updates and ensure that all known vulnerabilities are addressed before they can be exploited.

Another key takeaway was the importance of robust incident response plans. The worm's rapid spread and the DoS attack on the White House demonstrated the need for organizations to have contingency plans for responding to large-scale cyberattacks. Many businesses were unprepared for the disruption caused by Code Red, and the incident prompted a reevaluation of how organizations approach disaster recovery and cybersecurity defense.

Finally, the Code Red worm emphasized the dangers of automated, self-propagating malware. The worm's ability to spread without user interaction made it dangerous and difficult to contain. In response, cybersecurity firms began to develop more sophisticated intrusion detection systems and network monitoring tools to better identify and mitigate such threats in the future.

Case Study Summary

The Code Red worm of 2001 was a significant milestone in the evolution of cyber threats, demonstrating the destructive potential of automated, self-propagating malware. Its rapid spread and ability to exploit a single vulnerability in Microsoft's IIS web server software caused widespread disruption and financial losses while underscoring the importance of timely patch management and incident response planning. Key takeaways from this case include the need for organizations to stay vigilant in applying security updates, the importance of robust cybersecurity defenses, and the ongoing threat posed by automated cyberattacks.

Reflecting on the broader impact of the Code Red worm, it played a crucial role in shaping modern cybersecurity practices. The incident led to greater awareness of the need for collaboration between public and private sectors in responding to cyber threats, and it prompted organizations to adopt more proactive approaches to vulnerability management and network security. The lessons learned from Code Red continue to guide best practices in defending against large-scale cyberattacks and ensuring the resilience of critical infrastructure in the face of evolving threats.

SQL SLAMMER WORM (2003)

In early 2003, the world witnessed one of the fastest-spreading worms in internet history: the SQL Slammer worm. This attack profoundly affected the technological landscape, demonstrating the far-reaching impact of security vulnerabilities. At the time, the Internet was growing rapidly, and organizations increasingly relied on connected systems and networks. Despite this growth, security practices were not keeping pace, leaving many systems vulnerable to threats that could propagate with incredible speed.

The SQL Slammer worm primarily targeted Microsoft SQL Server 2000 systems. These servers were widely used in enterprise environments for managing databases, therefore making them an attractive target for attackers looking to cause widespread disruption. The attack, while not directly malicious in terms of data destruction or theft, exploited a vulnerability that allowed the worm to spread uncontrollably, saturating network bandwidth and causing widespread DoS.

Key stakeholders in this incident included organizations running the vulnerable SQL Server software, internet service providers (ISPs), and government agencies that relied on the affected systems for critical operations. The worm's ability to turn off vital services—sometimes within minutes—highlighted the interconnectedness of global networks and the necessity of strong security measures.

Unfolding the Attack

The SQL Slammer worm spread with unparalleled speed, infecting thousands of systems within minutes of its release on January 25, 2003. The worm exploited a buffer overflow vulnerability in Microsoft SQL Server 2000, specifically in handling User Datagram Protocol (UDP) packets on port 1434. By sending a single packet crafted to exploit this vulnerability, the worm could propagate without user interaction, making it particularly dangerous.

The information shows that the attack began in South Korea before rapidly spreading across the globe, though the exact origin of the worm remains uncertain. Within 10 minutes of its release, the worm had infected 75,000 systems, causing significant slowdowns across the Internet. Due to the nature of UDP and the worm's replication, infected systems bombarded networks with traffic, leading to widespread outages and DoS.

Once inside a system, SQL Slammer did not have a payload designed to steal or corrupt data. Instead, its primary function was replication. This lack of a destructive payload might have initially made detection more challenging, as organizations were not facing data loss but overwhelming network congestion. The worm's ability to replicate rapidly in memory also meant it was short-lived on individual systems, further complicating efforts to trace its origins.

Detection and Response Efforts

Detecting the SQL Slammer worm was challenging due to its speed and the fact that it did not leave traditional indicators of compromise, such as altered files or stolen data. The first signs of the worm's presence were significant slowdowns in network traffic and outright failures of key internet services. Organizations running Microsoft SQL Server 2000 systems began noticing severe operational disruptions within minutes of the attack beginning, with many being forced offline as their systems struggled to cope with the network load.

The information shows that many organizations were slow to react since the worm exploited a vulnerability for which a patch had already been available for six months. Despite this, many systems were not updated, highlighting the critical importance of timely patch management. Incident response teams and cybersecurity firms worked tirelessly to identify the cause of the network outages, but the worm had already caused substantial damage by the time it was detected.

The response to the attack involved a coordinated effort between affected organizations, ISPs, and security firms. Network administrators scrambled to block traffic on UDP port 1434, the worm's entry point, to stem the spread. Additionally, Microsoft issued guidance to customers on how to protect their systems from further infection. Unfortunately, when these efforts were implemented, much of the damage had already been done.

Assessing the Impact

The SQL Slammer worm's impact was immediate and far-reaching. Within minutes of the worm's release, internet traffic slowed significantly, rendering several critical systems and services unusable. Major financial institutions, airlines, and government agencies were among those affected. For example, Bank of America's ATM network was taken offline, causing inconvenience to customers and significant reputational damage. In South Korea, the attack brought down internet access for millions of users.

In terms of financial loss, the attack is estimated to have caused over one billion dollars in damages, primarily through operational disruption. The worm's rapid spread and the subsequent network congestion resulted in widespread service outages, leading to lost revenue, reputational damage, and a wake-up call for organizations regarding the importance of patch management.

The long-term consequences of the attack were equally significant. Organizations began to reevaluate their patch management practices and network security postures. This event also prompted discussions about the responsibility of software vendors like Microsoft to ensure that vulnerabilities are addressed before they can be exploited. Moreover, the SQL Slammer worm exposed the broader industry's lack of preparedness for rapid, large-scale cyber threats.

Lessons Learned and Takeaways

The SQL Slammer worm taught the cybersecurity industry several important lessons, many of which remain relevant today. First and foremost, the attack underscored the importance of timely patch management. Despite a patch being available six months before the attack, many organizations failed to implement it, leading to widespread vulnerability. Organizations must develop robust patch management programs to mitigate such risks in the future.

Another critical lesson from this incident is the importance of network segmentation and monitoring. The worm's rapid spread was facilitated by unsegmented networks, which allowed it to propagate unhindered. By implementing network segmentation, organizations can limit the impact of such attacks by isolating infected systems from the rest of the network.

Finally, the SQL Slammer worm demonstrated the need for better coordination and communication between vendors, security firms, and organizations during a cybersecurity crisis. The industry's slow response to the worm highlighted gaps in incident response and the need for real-time collaboration to mitigate the effects of such fast-spreading threats. Changes in patch management policies, network segmentation, and the development of early warning systems were among the long-term adjustments that came from the aftermath of this attack.

Case Study Summary

The SQL Slammer worm of 2003 was a watershed moment in cybersecurity history, highlighting the dangers represented by worms and the need for rapid response capabilities. The attack unfolded rapidly, infecting systems across the globe within minutes, and caused widespread disruption despite having no destructive payload. Key lessons from this case include timely patch management, network segmentation, and coordinated response efforts during a crisis.

By analyzing this attack, we gain valuable insights into the weaknesses in cybersecurity at the time and the steps that have since been taken to address those weaknesses. The SQL Slammer worm serves as a reminder that even the simplest vulnerabilities, when left unpatched, can lead to widespread chaos in today's interconnected digital world.

BLASTER WORM (2003)

In August 2003, the Blaster worm, also known as the Lovesan worm, quickly became a global cybersecurity concern by targeting vulnerabilities in Microsoft's Windows operating systems. The worm primarily exploited a vulnerability in the Distributed Component Object Model Remote Procedure Call (RPC) service that had been identified and patched by Microsoft just a month before the attack. However, despite the availability of a patch, many systems remained vulnerable, illustrating the widespread challenge of timely patch management.

At the time of the Blaster worm outbreak, the Internet was still expanding rapidly, and many organizations were beginning to grasp the importance of robust cybersecurity practices. This worm was notable for its aggressive spread and its design to trigger a DoS attack against Microsoft's website, targeting the company itself in what appeared to be an attempt to hold them accountable for the vulnerability. Key stakeholders affected by this worm included businesses, government agencies, and individual users running unpatched versions of Microsoft Windows, particularly Windows XP and Windows 2000.

The technological landscape in 2003 was defined by the growing reliance on networked systems and the increasing importance of securing these systems against rapidly evolving threats. Unfortunately, the Blaster worm's rapid spread highlighted significant gaps in organizational cybersecurity readiness, particularly in patch management and system updates.

Unfolding the Attack

The Blaster worm's spread began on August 11, 2003, exploiting a vulnerability in the RPC service by allowing remote code execution on unpatched systems. Once inside a system, the worm would initiate a DoS attack against the Microsoft website (windowsupdate.com) as part of its payload. The worm's self-propagation allowed it to spread rapidly across networks, compromising systems without requiring any user interaction. From the available data, it appears that the worm's primary goal was disruption rather than data theft or destruction, focusing on spreading as quickly as possible and crippling targeted systems.

The worm's initial infection vector involved scanning random IP addresses for vulnerable systems. Once it found a vulnerable host, the worm would exploit the RPC vulnerability to copy itself to the system and execute its payload. In many cases, users experienced sudden system crashes and reboots, often without any indication of what was happening, making the initial detection even more challenging.

The timeline of the Blaster worm's spread was extraordinarily fast. Hundreds of thousands of systems had been infected within days, and the worm's presence was felt globally. The attack also began a new wave of worms that sought to cause large-scale disruptions, often with political or protest-driven motivations. From the information available, it is clear that the Blaster worm's success was largely due to the failure of organizations and individuals to apply the necessary patch in time.

Detection and Response Efforts

Detecting the Blaster worm was difficult due to the worm's ability to operate silently and propagate rapidly. Most users realized something was wrong when their systems crashed unexpectedly or exhibited strange behavior, such as repeated reboots. Initial reports from organizations and ISPs pointed to widespread outages, with some networks becoming so congested with worm traffic that they were rendered inoperable.

Once the worm's activity was identified, Microsoft and cybersecurity firms moved quickly to inform internet users how to protect vulnerable systems. The solution involved applying the patch that had been released a month prior and temporarily disabling the vulnerable RPC service to prevent further exploitation. Antivirus and intrusion detection systems also started issuing updates to detect and block the worm, though these measures were reactive rather than proactive.

Regarding response efforts, many organizations had to work closely with ISPs and external cybersecurity firms to contain the spread of the worm within their networks. However, the speed at which the worm spread and its exploitation of a widely used service made it difficult to contain immediately. In some cases, law enforcement agencies became involved as the worm's origin was traced back to a young programmer in Minnesota, illustrating the growing role of legal and governmental bodies in responding to cyberattacks.

Assessing the Impact

Infected systems experienced continuous crashes and reboots, severely disrupting business operations and critical services. In some cases, entire networks were brought down by the sheer volume of worm-generated traffic, leading to operational losses that were difficult to recover from in the short term. From the information available, I assume that Blaster worm's total financial impact likely reached hundreds of millions of dollars, including both direct damages and indirect costs related to system recovery and lost productivity.

One of the more notable long-term consequences of the Blaster worm was its role in pushing the importance of regular patch management into the spotlight. Organizations that had been slow to implement patches were forced to confront the risks of not keeping systems up to date. The worm also had a notable impact on Microsoft, prompting the company to reconsider its approach to releasing patches and communicating the importance of updates to its users.

The reputational damage to organizations heavily affected by the Blaster worm was significant. Customers and partners expected these organizations to have better protections in place, and the widespread system outages led to a loss of trust in their ability to safeguard critical services. In the long term, the worm also had a broader impact on the cybersecurity industry, reinforcing the need for proactive defenses against rapidly spreading threats.

Lessons Learned and Takeaways

The Blaster worm highlighted several critical lessons for organizations and cybersecurity professionals. First and foremost, the importance of timely patch management cannot be overstated. From the available data, I assume that if more organizations had applied the patch for the RPC vulnerability when it was initially released, the scale of the attack could have been significantly mitigated. This incident is a powerful reminder of the dangers of delayed patching in the face of known vulnerabilities.

Another key takeaway from the Blaster worm is the need for robust network monitoring and traffic analysis. The worm's spread could have been detected and mitigated earlier if organizations had implemented better network monitoring tools to identify abnormal traffic patterns. This is especially important when dealing with self-propagating malware that relies on unchecked network communication to spread.

Finally, the Blaster worm reinforced the necessity of incident response planning and collaboration. Organizations that had established relationships with cybersecurity firms and governmental agencies were better positioned to respond to the attack. The importance of having a coordinated, well-prepared response plan became evident as organizations without one struggled to contain the damage.

Case Study Summary

The Blaster worm of 2003 is a cautionary tale about the risks posed by unpatched vulnerabilities and the need for proactive cybersecurity measures. The worm exploited a known vulnerability in Microsoft Windows, affecting hundreds of thousands of systems and causing widespread operational disruptions. Key lessons from this case include timely patch management, robust network monitoring, and coordinated incident response planning.

By analyzing the Blaster worm attack, we can draw valuable insights into the evolving nature of cyber threats and the critical need for organizations to remain vigilant. The worm's rapid spread and global impact demonstrate the importance of staying ahead of vulnerabilities and maintaining a proactive cybersecurity posture.

CONFICKER WORM (2008)

In November 2008, the Conficker worm, also known as Downadup, emerged as one of the most complex and widespread worms of its time. Conficker exploited a vulnerability in Microsoft Windows, specifically in the Server Service, which allowed the worm to spread rapidly across networks and infect millions of machines globally. The vulnerability, identified as CVE-2008-4250, was patched by Microsoft a month before the worm's release. However, as with many previous incidents, many systems had not been updated, leaving them vulnerable to the attack.

The Conficker worm targeted businesses, governments, and individual users alike, and its ability to disable security services and create a resilient botnet made it a serious threat. The technological landscape was becoming increasingly connected at the time, with consumer and enterprise systems relying on network services. The worm exploited this interconnectivity to spread quickly, and its ability to evolve with new variants made it particularly difficult to eradicate.

Key stakeholders responding to the Conficker outbreak included Microsoft, security firms, governments, and the broader cybersecurity community. The widespread nature of the infection led to the formation of the Conficker Working Group, a coalition of experts tasked with containing and mitigating the worm's impact.

Unfolding the Attack

The Conficker worm began spreading in November 2008, shortly after Microsoft released a patch for the vulnerability it exploited. The available information shows that the worm used multiple techniques to propagate, including exploiting the Windows vulnerability, infecting removable drives, and leveraging weak administrative passwords to compromise systems. Once inside a system, Conficker disabled security services and blocked access to websites that could be used to remove it, making it difficult to detect and clean.

The worm evolved, with new variants (Conficker A, B, and C) emerging to enhance its capabilities. These variants added features like peer-to-peer communication, allowing infected machines to stay connected even if external control servers were taken down. From the information I researched, I assume that this ability to self-sustain made Conficker one of the most resilient worms ever created, as it could survive efforts to disrupt its command-and-control infrastructure.

The timeline of Conficker's spread saw rapid infection rates, with estimates suggesting that by early 2009, the worm had compromised up to 15 million systems worldwide. The worm's ability to create a large botnet of infected machines raised concerns that it could be used for malicious purposes, such as launching distributed DoS attacks or spreading further malware. However, despite these fears, Conficker's true purpose remained unclear for a significant period, leaving many to speculate about its endgame.

Detection and Response Efforts

Detection of the Conficker worm was complicated by its ability to turn off security tools and prevent access to websites that provided removal instructions. Organizations and individuals first became aware of the infection when their systems exhibited strange behavior, such as disabling automatic updates or blocking access to security websites. Many infected systems also experienced performance degradation due to the worm's background activity, further signaling that something was amiss.

The cybersecurity community, led by Microsoft and several other key players, quickly responded to the Conficker outbreak by issuing guidance on detecting and removing the worm. Microsoft offered a patch (MS08-067) for the vulnerability and provided tools to remove Conficker from infected systems. Despite these efforts, the worm continued to spread due to the large number of unpatched systems and its ability to exploit weak passwords and removable media.

The formation of the Conficker Working Group in early 2009 marked a significant step in coordinating the response to the worm. This group included representatives from major technology companies, government agencies, and security firms, all working to mitigate the worm's impact. Law enforcement agencies also became involved, as there was a growing fear that Conficker's botnet could be used for large-scale cyberattacks. However, from the available information, the worm's creator(s) never fully activated the botnet for any specific purpose, leaving the cybersecurity community on a heightened alert for months.

Assessing the Impact

The impact of the Conficker worm was substantial, both in terms of its immediate and long-term effects. Conficker infected millions of systems in the short term, causing widespread operational disruptions across businesses, government agencies, and even military networks. The worm's ability to disable security services and block access to remediation tools made recovery difficult for many organizations, prolonging the disruption caused by the infection.

From the available data, I assume that the financial cost of Conficker was enormous, both in terms of direct recovery expenses and lost productivity. The worm also raised significant concerns about the potential for future cyberattacks, given its ability to create a massive botnet of compromised systems. While Conficker itself did not deliver a destructive payload or steal sensitive data, its sheer scale and potential for misuse made it one of the most feared worms of its time.

In the long term, the Conficker outbreak profoundly impacted the cybersecurity landscape. It exposed patch management and password security weaknesses and highlighted the need for better coordination between private industry and government entities in responding to large-scale cyber threats. Conficker also spurred the development of more advanced detection and mitigation tools as the cybersecurity community sought to prevent similar incidents in the future.

Lessons Learned and Takeaways

The Conficker Worm provided several key lessons for organizations and the cybersecurity community. One of the most critical takeaways was the importance of timely patch management. Despite Microsoft releasing a patch for the vulnerability a month before the worm's release, many systems remained unpatched, illustrating organizations' ongoing challenges in keeping their systems updated. From this case, it is clear that regular patching and vulnerability management are essential to reducing the risk of widespread infections.

Another lesson from the Conficker worm is the importance of strong password policies. The worm's ability to spread using weak administrator passwords underscored the need for organizations to implement more robust password security measures. This includes using complex passwords, regularly updating them, and avoiding default or easily guessed credentials.

The Conficker worm also highlighted the value of collaboration in combating large-scale cyber threats. The creation of the Conficker Working Group demonstrated how coordinated efforts between private companies, governments, and security experts can help mitigate the impact of major cyber incidents. The group's success in containing Conficker, even without fully understanding its purpose, is a testament to the power of collaboration in cybersecurity.

Case Study Summary

The Conficker worm of 2008 was one of the most significant cyber threats of its time, infecting millions of systems and creating a vast botnet with the potential for misuse. Key lessons from this case include the critical importance of patch management, password security, and collaborative efforts in responding to large-scale cyber incidents. Despite its widespread reach, the true purpose of the Conficker worm remains unclear, leaving cybersecurity experts to speculate on its ultimate intent.

By analyzing the Conficker worm, we gain valuable insights into the evolving nature of cyber threats and the steps organizations must take to protect their systems from rapidly spreading malware. This case serves as a reminder that even when the immediate danger of a worm or virus is contained, the underlying vulnerabilities that allowed it to spread must be addressed to prevent future incidents.

CHAPTER CONCLUSION

The case studies explored in this chapter demonstrate the significant impact that rapidly spreading worms can have on organizations, governments, and individuals. A recurring theme in these attacks is the exploitation of known vulnerabilities, often for which patches had been available long before the worms were unleashed. Despite the availability of solutions, the failure to apply patches and update systems left countless machines vulnerable to attack, allowing these worms to propagate alarmingly. This points to a key takeaway for cybersecurity professionals: timely patch management is critical to minimizing exposure to cyber threats, especially in an age of increasingly automated and self-replicating malware.

In addition to patch management, another common theme across these worm attacks is the importance of strong network segmentation and robust monitoring. Many worms spread rapidly within networks because organizations lack sufficient isolation between systems, allowing malware to hop from one vulnerable device to another without much resistance. In each case study, detection often lagged behind the initial infection, resulting in widespread damage before adequate response measures could be taken. While some of the detection and response details in these cases have been extrapolated from media reports and available information, it's clear that faster detection and better segmentation could have limited the spread and impact of these worms.

For today's cybersecurity professionals, these historical incidents offer valuable lessons. One of the most important is the need for proactive rather than reactive security measures. In many of these cases, organizations only realized they were under attack after the damage had already been done. Developing automated detection tools, engaging in regular network traffic analysis, and ensuring timely vulnerability assessments are crucial to staying ahead of future threats. Additionally, the rise of more sophisticated worms like Conficker, which leveraged weak passwords and resilient command-and-control networks, underscores the importance of adopting strong password policies, conducting regular security audits, and ensuring systems are resilient to internal and external threats.

Looking forward, cybersecurity professionals should focus on building a culture of security awareness, ensuring that every part of an organization—from the IT team to leadership—is committed to maintaining a proactive defense posture. The rapid evolution of malware, the persistence of unpatched vulnerabilities, and the growing sophistication of attacks mean that organizations cannot afford to be complacent. By learning from these past worm attacks and adopting a forward-thinking approach, cybersecurity professionals can mitigate the risks posed by future threats and help protect their organizations from the next wave of rapidly spreading cyber incidents.

4

DATA BREACHES AND
THEIR IMPACT

If data breaches were an Olympic event, some of the companies in this chapter would be standing proudly on the podium, clutching their medals of embarrassment. From social media giants to financial institutions, it seems no industry is immune to the ever-growing digital pickpockets. Remember MySpace? If the 2008 data breach did not convince you to delete your old account, maybe you are just waiting to see if hackers can bring back your old emo profile playlist. In many cases, these breaches read like crime thrillers, where cybercriminals stay several steps ahead while organizations scramble to figure out what went wrong.

But behind the humor lies a serious reality. Data breaches can devastate organizations financially, damage reputations, and cause severe stress for millions of affected users. The breaches outlined in this chapter—from Target to Capital One—reveal the widespread problem and highlight the glaring vulnerabilities across industries. This chapter aims to examine these incidents in detail and provide cybersecurity professionals with valuable insights into where things went wrong, what could have been done differently, and how to prevent these incidents in the future.

In some cases, the information about how breaches were detected or responded to is not fully available in the public domain. I have extrapolated certain details from media reports and industry sources, filling in the gaps where direct information does not exist. By analyzing patterns across various breaches, we can infer common weaknesses in detection and response strategies. These extrapolations are based on known cybersecurity practices of the time. While they may not be 100 percent accurate, they provide a reasonable framework for understanding how these organizations might have handled—or mishandled—such attacks.

Ultimately, this chapter is a call to action for cybersecurity professionals. The breaches described here are more than historical events; they are lessons in cyber threats' dynamic and evolving nature. The hope is that by examining these incidents, professionals can gain a deeper understanding of the mistakes that led to these breaches and apply that knowledge to better secure their systems and data. The digital world is constantly changing, and as attackers get smarter, so must the defenders. The stakes are high, and the consequences of inaction could be catastrophic.

WHAT IS A DATA BREACH?

A data breach occurs when unauthorized individuals access sensitive, confidential, or protected information, leading to the data's exposure, theft, or compromise. These breaches can affect individuals, organizations, or governments, and the compromised data often includes personal details, financial information, intellectual property, or business secrets. Data breaches are one of the most significant and damaging types of cyberattacks because they can lead to financial losses, legal consequences, reputational damage, and identity theft for affected individuals (see Figure 4.1). Notable breaches, such as those involving Equifax (2017) and Yahoo (2014), have highlighted the profound consequences of these attacks on a global scale.

Data breaches typically happen through a variety of methods. Attackers may exploit vulnerabilities in software, launch phishing attacks to deceive employees into revealing login credentials, or use social engineering to manipulate individuals into providing access. Once inside a system, hackers may escalate their privileges, allowing them to access and exfiltrate large amounts of data. SQL injection attacks—where malicious code is inserted into a vulnerable website or application—can also be used to extract sensitive data directly from databases. In some cases, insiders with malicious intent or weak security controls can expose critical data, as seen in the Facebook-Cambridge Analytica scandal.

Preventing data breaches requires a multifaceted approach that combines technical defenses, employee training, and strong data governance. Encryption is one of the most effective methods for protecting sensitive data in transit and at rest. Even if attackers manage to breach a system, encryption

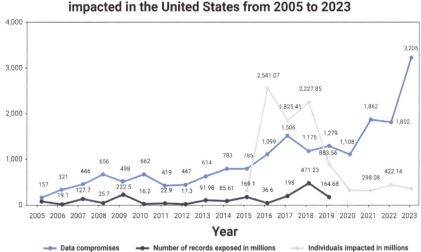

Figure 4.1 The impact of data breaches (*source*: Statista Search Department)

ensures the stolen data remains unreadable without the decryption keys. Multifactor authentication (MFA) and strong password policies add an extra layer of security, making it more difficult for attackers to access systems, even if they manage to steal credentials. Regular vulnerability assessments and patch management are essential for closing off security gaps that attackers might exploit.

Another critical protection method is data minimization, which involves reducing the amount of sensitive data stored and ensuring it is only retained for as long as necessary. Network segmentation also helps limit the potential damage from a breach by isolating sensitive areas of a network from general access. Additionally, organizations must implement comprehensive incident response plans and train employees to recognize and respond to potential threats. By combining these proactive measures, organizations can significantly reduce the likelihood of a data breach and minimize the impact if one does occur.

The following chart illustrates the timeline associated with the attacks that will be examined in this chapter (see Figure 4.2).

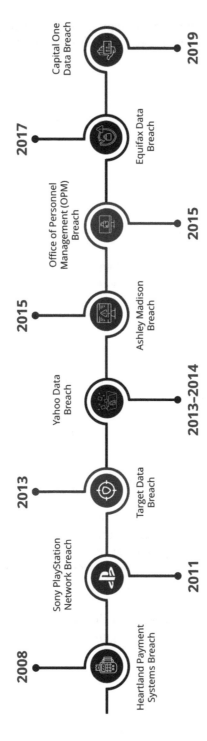

Figure 4.2   The timeline of attacks discussed in this chapter

HEARTLAND PAYMENT SYSTEMS BREACH (2008)

The Heartland Payment Systems breach of 2008 is one of the financial industry's largest and most consequential data breaches. Heartland Payment Systems, a major payment processing company, handled credit and debit card transactions for thousands of businesses across the United States. With millions of transactions processed daily, the company was responsible for securing vast amounts of sensitive payment card information. Heartland was considered a significant player in the industry at the time of the breach, but its security measures proved insufficient to protect against the ensuing sophisticated attack.

In 2008, the technological landscape was increasingly focused on digitization and electronic payment systems. However, many companies, including Heartland, were still adapting to the evolving cybersecurity threats that targeted payment systems. Encryption practices and monitoring technologies were not as advanced, leaving many systems vulnerable to attacks. The key stakeholders involved in this breach included Heartland's leadership, financial institutions, businesses relying on Heartland's services, and millions of consumers whose payment card data was compromised.

Unfolding the Attack

The Heartland breach began with a sophisticated malware attack that infiltrated the company's payment processing system. From the information available, I assume that the attackers gained access by exploiting vulnerabilities in Heartland's network through SQL injection attacks—a common method used to penetrate databases by injecting malicious code into the system. The initial compromise likely occurred months before the breach was discovered, allowing the attackers to install malware that captured sensitive payment card information in real time as transactions were processed.

The attack timeline reveals that Heartland's systems were compromised for several months, with attackers silently harvesting credit and debit card data during that time. The malware allowed the attackers to intercept card numbers, expiration dates, and cardholder names as the payment system processed them. This data was then exfiltrated and sold on the black market, leading to one of the largest known cases of credit card fraud. The prolonged nature of the breach highlights the dangers of undetected, persistent threats in payment processing environments.

Detection and Response Efforts

The breach was discovered in January 2009 when Visa and MasterCard notified Heartland of suspicious activity linked to transactions processed by the company. Before this notification, Heartland had been unaware that its systems were compromised, indicating the company's security monitoring and detection measures were insufficient. Once the breach was confirmed, Heartland worked with forensic cybersecurity firms and law enforcement agencies to assess the damage and secure the affected systems.

Heartland's initial response was swift once the breach was identified, but the extent of the damage had already been done. From the available information, I assume Heartland lacked a well-developed incident response plan for dealing with an attack of this scale, which delayed some aspects of the response. The company immediately began efforts to notify affected customers and financial institutions while cooperating with law enforcement to investigate the breach. The involvement of external cybersecurity firms helped Heartland identify the scope of the compromise and implement more robust security measures to prevent future attacks.

Assessing the Impact

The impact of the Heartland Payment Systems breach was severe, both financially and reputationally. The breach exposed approximately 130 million credit and debit card numbers, making it one of the largest data breaches ever recorded at that time. Financial institutions that issued the compromised cards faced significant costs related to fraud prevention and issuing new cards to affected customers. Heartland was held financially responsible for much of the fallout, including settlements with major credit card companies and affected businesses.

The long-term consequences of the breach were equally damaging. Heartland faced multiple lawsuits from financial institutions and class-action suits from affected consumers. The company also suffered reputational damage, as trust in its ability to protect sensitive payment data was shaken. This breach led to regulatory scrutiny, fines, and changes in the Payment Card Industry (PCI) Data Security Standard (DSS), which governs the security of payment card transactions. The breach highlighted the critical importance of encryption and robust security monitoring in payment processing systems.

Lessons Learned and Takeaways

One of the most significant lessons from the Heartland breach is the importance of using end-to-end encryption to protect payment card data. At the time of the breach, Heartland's systems did not fully encrypt data as it moved through the payment process, leaving it vulnerable to interception. This case underscores the need for businesses handling sensitive financial information to adopt the strongest encryption technologies and regularly update their systems to mitigate emerging threats.

Another key takeaway is the necessity of robust monitoring and detection mechanisms. From the information I was able to gather, I assume Heartland's inability to detect the breach for several months was due to inadequate monitoring tools. This prolonged the attack and allowed more data to be compromised. Continuous network monitoring and anomaly detection are essential for identifying suspicious activities before they can escalate into full-scale breaches.

In response to the breach, Heartland implemented significant security improvements, including end-to-end encryption and the adoption of tokenization to protect payment data. These measures and increased oversight helped the company regain some of its lost trust. For the broader payment industry, the Heartland breach warned about the risks posed by advanced, persistent cyber threats and the need for continual security enhancements.

Case Study Summary

The Heartland Payment Systems breach of 2008 is a stark reminder of the vulnerabilities within the payment processing industry and the need for stronger security measures. The breach, which compromised 130 million credit and debit card numbers, exposed weaknesses in encryption practices and detection capabilities. Key takeaways include the necessity of end-to-end encryption, continuous network monitoring, and timely incident response. The broader implications of the breach led to changes in PCI DSS standards and increased awareness of cybersecurity risks in financial transactions.

SONY PLAYSTATION NETWORK BREACH (2011)

The Sony PlayStation Network (PSN) breach of 2011 was one of the largest cyberattacks in the gaming industry, affecting millions of users worldwide. At the time, the PSN was a major online gaming service, allowing users to play games, stream content, and interact with others. The breach led to the unauthorized access of personal and financial data belonging to over 77 million users, forcing Sony to shut down the service for several weeks. The attack raised critical concerns about the security of online gaming platforms and the responsibility of large corporations to protect user data.

The increasing popularity of online services marked the technological landscape in 2011, but it was also a period where many companies were still developing comprehensive security frameworks. Sony's PSN was a target due to the vast amount of personal data being stored, including credit card information and personal details. The key stakeholders in this case included Sony's leadership, its information technology and security teams, law enforcement, affected users, and regulatory bodies that later became involved in investigating the breach.

Unfolding the Attack

The PSN breach began in mid-April 2011 when attackers exploited Sony's network infrastructure vulnerabilities. I assume the attackers used a combination of techniques, including exploiting outdated software, to gain access to the network. The entry point may have been a vulnerability in a web application or through weak access controls, though the exact method was never fully disclosed. Once inside, the attackers accessed Sony's servers, where they could extract personal information, including names, email addresses, login credentials, and potentially credit card information.

The timeline of the attack is crucial, as Sony did not immediately detect the breach. From April 17–19, attackers could extract data without raising alarms. It wasn't until April 20 that Sony became aware of the unauthorized access and took action by shutting down the PSN. The delay in detection allowed the attackers to steal a significant amount of sensitive data, and Sony's decision to take the entire network offline for investigation indicated the breach's severity.

Detection and Response Efforts

Sony's detection of the breach was delayed, and by the time the company responded, the attackers had already compromised millions of user accounts. Once Sony identified the breach on April 20, it took swift action by shutting down the PSN entirely, which would last 23 days. From the available information, I assume Sony's incident response plan was reactive rather than proactive, as the company had to scramble to assess the full extent of the breach and secure its systems.

In the wake of the breach, Sony worked with external cybersecurity firms and law enforcement agencies to investigate the attack and identify the exploited vulnerabilities. Public notification of the breach came several days after the shutdown, sparking criticism from users and regulators who believed the company should have been more transparent and quicker in addressing the issue. Sony offered affected users free credit monitoring services and enhanced its security protocols to prevent future incidents, but the delayed response and prolonged downtime damaged its reputation significantly.

Assessing the Impact

The financial and reputational impact of the PSN breach was immense. Sony estimated that the breach cost the company around 171 million dollars, including compensation to users, legal fees, and overhauling its security systems. The downtime also affected Sony's revenue stream, as the PSN was a critical part of its gaming ecosystem, and users could not make purchases or access content for nearly a month. Additionally, Sony faced class-action lawsuits from users who claimed the company had not done enough to protect their personal information.

The long-term consequences of the breach included a significant loss of consumer trust. Sony's failure to detect and respond to the breach in a timely manner led to public outrage, and many users were hesitant to return to the platform even after it was restored. Regulatory bodies, including the U.S. Congress and the UK's Information Commissioner's Office, launched investigations into Sony's handling of the breach, leading to fines and further scrutiny of its data protection practices. The breach also set a precedent for how gaming companies should handle cybersecurity and user privacy.

Lessons Learned and Takeaways

One of the most important lessons from the Sony PSN breach is keeping software and systems current. From the available information, I infer that Sony's failure to patch known vulnerabilities in its network infrastructure contributed to the attack's success. This highlights the critical importance of regular security audits and timely updates to prevent attackers from exploiting known weaknesses. Companies handling sensitive user data must prioritize cybersecurity as part of their business operations rather than viewing it as an afterthought.

Another key takeaway is the need for robust incident detection and response systems. The fact that Sony did not detect the breach until days after the initial attack allowed the attackers to steal more data than they might have otherwise. This underscores the importance of real-time monitoring and intrusion detection systems that can help companies identify and respond to threats before significant damage occurs. Additionally, Sony's delayed communication with its user base revealed the importance of transparency during a breach because users expect timely updates and clear action plans in such situations.

In the aftermath, Sony made substantial changes to its security protocols, including enhanced encryption of user data, two-factor authentication, and improved network monitoring. These changes reflected a broader shift in the industry toward more secure online platforms, especially in the gaming sector, where user data is often a prime target for attackers. The broader implications of the breach were felt across the industry, leading other companies to strengthen their security practices to avoid similar incidents.

Case Study Summary

The Sony PSN breach of 2011 is a stark reminder of the risks posed by outdated security systems and the importance of robust cybersecurity practices. The breach, which compromised the personal information of over 77 million users, exposed weaknesses in Sony's network infrastructure and highlighted the need for real-time monitoring and timely patching of vulnerabilities. Key takeaways include the critical importance of system updates, strong incident detection mechanisms, and clear communication with affected users. The broader impact of the breach reshaped how the gaming industry approaches cybersecurity, setting new standards for protecting user data on online platforms.

TARGET DATA BREACH (2013)

The 2013 Target data breach was one of the most significant and widely publicized cybersecurity incidents of the early twenty-first century. Not to mention the first breach in which my own credit card information was stolen. Target, one of the largest retail chains in the United States, was responsible for processing millions of transactions daily, making it an attractive target for cybercriminals. This breach highlighted vulnerabilities in large-scale retail systems, especially third-party access and security oversight. The breach resulted in the theft of personal and financial information of over 40 million customers, underscoring the need for robust security measures in large organizations.

At the time, Target was using systems that, while considered standard, were not fully equipped to deal with sophisticated cyberattacks. Point-of-sale (POS) systems and third-party vendor access created a large attack surface. The key stakeholders in this incident included Target's leadership, IT and security teams, law enforcement, third-party vendors, and the millions of customers whose information was compromised. This breach ultimately set new standards for how companies should handle cybersecurity and vendor relationships in a retail setting.

Unfolding the Attack

The Target data breach began with a compromised third-party vendor, which provided HVAC services to the retailer. From the information I collected, I assume the attackers gained access to Target's network by stealing the vendor's login credentials. This initial compromise occurred in late November 2013, with the attackers using the vendor's credentials to infiltrate Target's internal systems. Once inside, they moved laterally through the network, targeting the POS systems where credit card data was processed.

The malware used in the attack was designed to scrape credit and debit card information from Target's POS terminals. This information included card numbers, expiration dates, and cardholder names, all of which were collected by the attackers for several weeks. During Target's busy holiday shopping season, the attack continued undetected through December 2013. The timing of the attack allowed the cybercriminals to collect a vast amount of customer data before the breach was discovered.

Detection and Response Efforts

Target's internal security tools detected the suspicious activity early in the breach, but the alerts were not immediately acted upon. From the available information, I assume that Target's security team may not have fully understood the severity of the threat at first, allowing the attackers to continue their operation for weeks. It was not until a third-party security firm alerted Target in mid-December that the company fully realized the extent of the breach. By then, millions of records had already been compromised.

Once the breach was confirmed, Target took steps to mitigate the damage. The company shut down the compromised systems and began working with law enforcement and cybersecurity firms to investigate the attack. Public notification of the breach occurred later in December, but the delay in addressing the issue drew criticism from customers and security experts. Target also offered free credit monitoring services to affected individuals to regain customer trust. Though comprehensive once initiated, the response revealed gaps in the company's initial incident response.

Assessing the Impact

The immediate financial impact of the Target data breach was substantial. The company faced lawsuits, regulatory fines, and the cost of compensating customers affected by the breach. Estimates put the breach's total cost at over 200 million dollars, including settlements with banks, payment processors, and consumers. Target's stock price took a hit in the aftermath, and the company's sales dropped as customers lost trust in its ability to protect sensitive data. The breach also led to the resignation of several senior executives, including the CEO and CIO.

In the long term, the breach had wide-reaching consequences for Target's reputation and the retail industry. The breach spurred changes in how companies manage third-party vendors, with many adopting stricter security standards for accessing internal systems. It also led to improvements in the PCI DSS, particularly regarding encryption and monitoring of POS systems. For Target, rebuilding customer trust took years, and the incident remains a key example of how a single vulnerability in vendor management can lead to a massive breach.

Lessons Learned and Takeaways

One of the key lessons from the Target breach is the importance of securing third-party vendor access. From the available information, I infer that Target's failure to properly monitor and restrict the vendor's access to its internal network was critical to the attack's success. This case emphasizes the need for organizations to implement strong authentication methods, such as multifactor authentication, and to limit vendor access to only what is necessary for their work.

Another critical lesson is the need for effective incident detection and response mechanisms. Target's internal security tools flagged suspicious activity early in the breach, but the company's failure to act on those alerts escalated the attack. This underscores the importance of having a well-trained and proactive security team that can recognize and respond to threats in real time. Additionally, the breach highlighted the importance of timely communication with affected customers to minimize damage and preserve trust.

Target implemented several security improvements post-breach, including end-to-end payment data encryption and enhanced third-party access monitoring. These changes helped the company regain some of the trust it lost. Still, the broader lesson for the industry is clear: companies must prioritize cybersecurity at all levels, from third-party management to internal monitoring.

Case Study Summary

The Target data breach of 2013 is a powerful example of how vulnerabilities in vendor management and internal security can lead to massive data compromises. The breach, which affected over 40 million customers, exposed weaknesses in how large organizations protect payment information and respond to cyber threats. Key takeaways include securing third-party access, improving incident response, and ensuring timely communication with affected stakeholders. The broader impact of the breach led to changes in industry standards and highlighted the critical need for continuous improvement in cybersecurity practices.

YAHOO DATA BREACH (2013-2014)

The Yahoo data breach, spanning from 2013 to 2014, remains one of the largest data breaches in history, affecting all three billion user accounts managed by the company. At the time, Yahoo was a major Internet service provider, offering email, search, and other services to a vast global audience. This breach exposed sensitive information, including names, email addresses, phone numbers, dates of birth, and hashed passwords. However, financial information, such as payment card data, was reportedly not compromised. The breach highlighted severe security vulnerabilities at Yahoo, which was in the process of being acquired by Verizon at the time the full scope of the incident became public.

The technological landscape during the breach saw a rise in cloud services and increasing internet connectivity, making user data a highly valuable commodity for cybercriminals. Despite this, Yahoo's security infrastructure was insufficient to prevent or detect such a massive breach. The key stakeholders included Yahoo executives, its IT and security teams, Verizon (as the acquiring company), law enforcement, and the billions of affected users worldwide. The breach also underscored the importance of cybersecurity in mergers and acquisitions.

Unfolding the Attack

The Yahoo data breach began with a spear-phishing attack, where attackers targeted Yahoo employees to gain access to privileged internal systems. From the information, I assume that attackers used social engineering techniques to compromise employee credentials, giving them access to Yahoo's user databases. The initial compromise occurred in 2013, with the attackers exploiting weak security controls to access and steal vast amounts of user data over an extended period.

Once inside Yahoo's systems, the attackers moved laterally to target more sensitive areas of the network, including user-account databases. They were able to extract significant portions of user data without being detected. The stolen data, which included hashed passwords using the outdated MD5 algorithm, was vulnerable to cracking. The attackers also accessed security questions and answers, further jeopardizing users' online accounts. Yahoo initially detected the breach in 2014, but the full scale of the breach wasn't disclosed until 2016, raising serious questions about the company's detection and response mechanisms.

Detection and Response Efforts

Yahoo's detection of the breach was delayed, and even when the company became aware of the compromise, it failed to comprehend or fully disclose the incident's scope. From the available data, I infer that Yahoo's security monitoring was insufficient to detect the breach in real time, allowing the attackers to operate undetected for an extended period. Yahoo discovered the breach in late 2014 but did not report it publicly until 2016 when Verizon acquired the company.

Once the breach was made public, Yahoo faced widespread criticism for its slow response and lack of transparency. The company initially reported that only 500 million accounts were affected, but this figure was later revised to three billion, encompassing all Yahoo user accounts. Yahoo collaborated with law enforcement and hired cybersecurity firms to investigate the breach further. However, the delayed response and the massive scale of the breach severely damaged the company's reputation. Verizon, acquiring Yahoo at the time, reduced its offer by 350 million dollars due to the breach's disclosure.

Assessing the Impact

The immediate impact of the Yahoo breach was significant, both financially and reputationally. Yahoo faced numerous class-action lawsuits, regulatory scrutiny, and a loss of user trust. The company's stock price was affected, and its acquisition by Verizon was notably devalued. The settlement costs for the breach amounted to approximately 117.5 million dollars in 2019. Yahoo also faced a 35 million dollar fine from the U.S. Securities and Exchange Commission for failing to disclose the breach promptly.

Beyond the financial fallout, Yahoo suffered long-term reputational damage. The breach eroded consumer confidence in the company's ability to protect sensitive information. Yahoo had long been a trusted Internet service provider for many users, and this breach highlighted severe weaknesses in its security infrastructure. The breach also had broader implications for the cybersecurity industry, emphasizing stronger encryption practices, particularly regarding password hashing, and improved breach detection systems.

Lessons Learned and Takeaways

One of the most critical lessons from the Yahoo breach is the importance of timely breach detection and disclosure. From accessible data, I assume that Yahoo's failure to detect the breach in real time and its subsequent delay in reporting the incident caused significant damage. Organizations must invest in real-time monitoring and detection tools to quickly identify potential breaches. Additionally, transparency in the aftermath of a breach is essential for maintaining user trust and complying with regulatory standards.

Another key takeaway is the need for robust encryption practices. Yahoo's use of the outdated MD5 hashing algorithm left user passwords vulnerable to cracking, which allowed attackers to gain access to other accounts. The case underscores the importance of using strong, modern encryption standards, such as bcrypt or Argon2, to protect sensitive information. Furthermore, MFA should be a standard practice for protecting user accounts, adding a layer of security if credentials are compromised.

Yahoo's failure to implement adequate security measures ultimately reshaped how companies approach user data protection. In response to the breach, the industry has moved toward stronger encryption methods, better incident response plans, and stricter regulations governing data breach notifications. The breach highlighted severe operational and leadership failures in Yahoo's cybersecurity management.

Case Study Summary

The Yahoo data breach of 2013–2014 remains one of history's largest and most consequential. Affecting all three billion of the company's user accounts, the breach exposed significant weaknesses in Yahoo's security infrastructure, including outdated encryption and inadequate breach detection systems. Key takeaways include the critical importance of real-time monitoring, strong encryption methods, and the need for timely disclosure of breaches. The broader implications of the breach reshaped industry standards and emphasized the importance of proactive cybersecurity measures in protecting sensitive user data.

ASHLEY MADISON BREACH (2015)

The Ashley Madison breach of 2015 was a significant and controversial data breach that exposed sensitive information about millions of users of the online dating site known for facilitating extramarital affairs. Ashley Madison, owned by the parent company Avid Life Media, had millions of users worldwide, many of whom had entrusted the platform with highly sensitive personal information, including email addresses, payment details, and explicit messages. The attack exposed this data and created a firestorm of media coverage, causing massive reputational damage to the company and its users. Also, it is widely believed that this was the first time a demand was sent with the accompanying music of AC DC's "Thunderstruck."

At the time of the breach, online platforms like Ashley Madison faced increasing scrutiny around data security, particularly given the sensitive nature of the stored information. Despite these concerns, Ashley Madison's security measures were insufficient to defend against a motivated cyberattack. The key stakeholders involved included Avid Life Media executives, the platform's users, law enforcement agencies, and the hackers who called themselves *The Impact Team*, responsible for the breach. The incident raised critical questions about privacy, online security, and ethical business practices.

Unfolding the Attack

The Ashley Madison breach began when a hacker collective—The Impact Team—accessed the company's internal systems. From the information, I assume the attackers initially infiltrated Ashley Madison's systems through stolen credentials or an inside source, allowing them to bypass external defenses. Once inside, they copied vast amounts of user data, including personally identifiable information, financial transactions, and private messages. The attackers left a message demanding that Avid Life Media permanently shut down Ashley Madison, or they would publicly release the data.

The timeline of the attack spanned several months, with the breach first occurring in July 2015. The attackers issued their demands shortly after gaining access to the company's systems, and when those demands were not met, they followed through on their threat in August 2015. The leaked data exposed the identities of millions of users, many of whom were married or had used the site under the assumption of anonymity. The attack's public nature and the morally charged context of the site's purpose made this breach particularly damaging on both a personal and corporate level.

Detection and Response Efforts

Ashley Madison and its parent company, Avid Life Media, were slow to respond to the initial infiltration. The breach was not detected internally, and the company only became aware of the attack when The Impact Team publicly posted a warning. From the available data, I assume that Avid Life Media lacked robust monitoring systems capable of detecting unusual activity within their networks. Once the attackers issued their ultimatum, Avid Life Media sought to mitigate the damage by strengthening security and negotiating behind the scenes, but these efforts were ultimately unsuccessful.

Avid Life Media was forced to respond publicly when the hackers released the stolen data. The company issued a statement condemning the attack and worked with law enforcement agencies and cybersecurity firms to investigate the breach. However, the response was reactive rather than proactive, as the company had not implemented sufficient preventative measures. Public notification of the breach came after the data leaked, exposing millions of users without warning.

Assessing the Impact

The Ashley Madison breach had immediate and far-reaching consequences for the company and its users. Financially, Avid Life Media faced significant losses, both in terms of revenue and legal costs. The breach led to multiple lawsuits from affected users, claiming negligence in the company's data protection efforts. Additionally, the company faced a reputational crisis, with its brand forever associated with the scandal. The immediate effects were felt by Avid Life Media and its customers, many of whom suffered personal and professional fallout due to the exposure.

The breach had broader implications for data privacy and cybersecurity in the long term. The incident highlighted the vulnerabilities inherent in platforms that store sensitive personal information, prompting consumers and businesses to reevaluate their security practices. Avid Life Media faced regulatory scrutiny and fines, and while the company attempted to rebrand and recover, the breach had an indelible impact on its reputation. The event also sparked debates around the ethical responsibility of companies that handle morally sensitive data and whether stronger consumer protections were needed.

Lessons Learned and Takeaways

One of the key lessons from the Ashley Madison breach is the importance of safeguarding sensitive user data, particularly when that data is tied to services that deal with sensitive or confidential personal matters. From the available information, I infer that Ashley Madison failed to implement basic security measures, such as encrypting sensitive user information. The company's lack of attention to encryption allowed attackers to access and expose data in a way that caused maximum harm. This case underscores the need for strong encryption and regularly updating security practices to meet evolving threats.

Another critical takeaway is the need for robust detection and response mechanisms. Ashley Madison's failure to detect the breach early on and the subsequent delay in notifying affected users worsened the overall damage. Businesses must implement comprehensive monitoring systems to detect unauthorized access immediately and establish clear incident response protocols. Additionally, companies must communicate breaches transparently and quickly, offering support to affected users to minimize the personal and professional impact of the breach.

In the aftermath, Avid Life Media was forced to implement stronger security practices, including better encryption and improved access controls. However, the broader implications of the breach extended to the entire online service industry, which faced increasing pressure to adopt higher security standards for protecting sensitive user data. The Ashley Madison breach warns companies about the importance of security, privacy, and ethical responsibility in the digital age.

Case Study Summary

The Ashley Madison breach in 2015 was a major cybersecurity incident that exposed millions of users' personal and financial data. The breach, carried out by a hacker group known as The Impact Team, revealed weaknesses in Ashley Madison's security practices and highlighted the ethical and privacy challenges of storing sensitive user information. Key takeaways include the importance of encryption, strong access controls, and early detection of breaches. The broader impact of the breach reshaped discussions on data privacy and security in online services, particularly those handling highly sensitive user data.

OFFICE OF PERSONNEL MANAGEMENT BREACH (2015)

The 2015 U.S. Office of Personnel Management (OPM) breach is regarded as one of a federal government agency's most significant and damaging cyberattacks.

OPM is responsible for maintaining records on current and former federal employees, handling sensitive data such as social security numbers, addresses, employment histories, and, in some cases, background check information for security clearances. With millions of federal employees relying on OPM to safeguard their personal information, this breach revealed critical weaknesses in the cybersecurity measures of a vital government agency.

In 2015, OPM's technological landscape was outdated and underfunded, making it a prime target for an advanced persistent threat (APT). The attack, which exposed the personal data of more than 21.5 million people, underscored the growing vulnerability of government systems to sophisticated cyberattacks. The breach also highlighted serious gaps in how government agencies handled cybersecurity, from patch management to access control. The key stakeholders in this case included federal employees, government agencies, and contractors—all of whom had sensitive information stored in OPM's databases.

Unfolding the Attack

The OPM breach is believed to have started as early as 2014, when attackers first gained access to the agency's network. It is safe to assume the attackers used phishing emails targeting specific OPM employees to gain initial entry into the network. These phishing emails likely contained malicious links or attachments that, when clicked, installed malware capable of granting the attackers unauthorized access. Once inside, the attackers moved laterally through the network, escalating privileges and evading detection.

The attackers spent several months carefully navigating OPM's systems, likely utilizing custom malware to maintain persistence. Their primary goal was to access the agency's sensitive databases, particularly personnel records and security clearance information. I assume the attackers were highly skilled and operated with the precision of an APT group, systematically exfiltrating large volumes of data without triggering immediate alarms. The most devastating part of the breach involved data theft from background check forms (SF-86), which included detailed personal and financial information that could be used for identity theft or espionage.

Detection and Response Efforts

OPM discovered the breach in April 2015 after a contractor working on security improvements detected unusual activity on the agency's network. It was later revealed that OPM had been the target of multiple attacks over the previous year, with varying degrees of success. Once the breach was confirmed,

OPM immediately began working with the Department of Homeland Security, the Federal Bureau of Investigation (FBI), and private cybersecurity firms to assess the scope of the intrusion and mitigate further damage.

From the available timeline, it is clear that OPM's response was swift once the breach was detected, but the attackers had already exfiltrated a vast amount of data. The organization disconnected affected systems and focused on bolstering its network defenses. It is assumed that OPM took immediate steps to revoke compromised credentials and patch known vulnerabilities. Public notification of the breach came in June 2015, when OPM disclosed that millions of federal employees and contractors had their personal information compromised. OPM offered credit monitoring services to those affected and worked closely with federal agencies to manage the breach's aftermath.

Assessing the Impact

The immediate impact of the OPM breach was widespread panic among federal employees and contractors, many of whom feared identity theft and the misuse of their data. The breach also led to significant operational disruptions as OPM worked to rebuild and secure its systems. Financially, the breach cost OPM millions of dollars in remediation efforts, including offering credit monitoring services and enhancing its cybersecurity infrastructure. The agency also faced congressional hearings, where lawmakers criticized OPM for its lack of preparedness and failure to address known cybersecurity weaknesses.

The long-term consequences of the OPM breach were equally severe. Beyond the immediate financial costs, the breach led to a loss of trust in the government's ability to safeguard sensitive information. Many speculated that the stolen data could be used for espionage, particularly given the highly sensitive nature of the information contained in the background check forms. For federal employees with security clearances, the breach raised concerns about foreign actors using their personal information for coercion or blackmail. The reputational damage to OPM and the federal government was profound, leading to a renewed focus on cybersecurity at the highest levels of government.

Lessons Learned and Takeaways

The OPM breach exposed critical weaknesses in the federal government's approach to cybersecurity. One of the most significant lessons from this incident is the importance of updating and maintaining secure systems. At the time of the breach, OPM was operating on outdated infrastructure, with known vulnerabilities that had not been adequately patched. The attack highlighted the need for continuous monitoring, regular updates, and implementing modern cybersecurity practices to mitigate the risk of a breach.

Another key takeaway is the importance of MFA and privileged access management. From the available information, I assume the attackers could escalate privileges using compromised credentials, which allowed them to access sensitive databases. If stronger access controls, such as MFA, had been in place, it could have significantly reduced the attackers' ability to move freely through the network. The breach also underscored the need for better employee training on phishing and social engineering attacks, as the initial compromise likely occurred through a phishing email.

Post-attack, OPM substantially changed its cybersecurity posture, modernizing its IT infrastructure and implementing more robust access controls. The breach also led to broader government reforms, with increased funding for cybersecurity initiatives and the creation of the Federal Cybersecurity Enhancement Act, which aimed to strengthen federal networks. For the cybersecurity community, the OPM breach was a stark reminder of the consequences of neglecting basic security hygiene and the importance of remaining vigilant in the face of persistent threats.

Case Study Summary

The 2015 OPM breach remains one of the most impactful cyberattacks on a federal government agency, affecting millions of federal employees and contractors. The attack exposed critical weaknesses in OPM's cybersecurity defenses and led to significant financial, operational, and reputational damage. The key lessons from this case include updating infrastructure, implementing strong access controls, and providing ongoing employee training to defend against phishing and other social engineering attacks. The broader impact of the OPM breach extended beyond the agency, leading to government-wide reforms and increased investment in cybersecurity at the federal level.

EQUIFAX DATA BREACH (2017)

The 2017 Equifax data breach was one of the most significant cybersecurity incidents of the decade, impacting the personal information of approximately 147 million individuals. Equifax, one of the three major credit reporting agencies in the United States, held vast amounts of sensitive data, including Social Security numbers, birth dates, and credit histories. This data breach exposed critical flaws in Equifax's security practices and raised concerns about protecting personal information held by large institutions. The breach demonstrated how a single vulnerability could be exploited to devastating effect, leading to one of the largest known data breaches in history.

At the time of the breach, the technological landscape was marked by increasing awareness of cybersecurity threats. Still, many organizations, including Equifax, had not fully adopted the necessary practices to defend against sophisticated attacks. Despite being a custodian of highly sensitive information, Equifax failed to implement timely security updates, ultimately leading to the breach. The key stakeholders included Equifax's executives, IT and security teams, law enforcement, regulatory bodies, and the millions of individuals affected by the breach.

Unfolding the Attack

The Equifax data breach began with a vulnerability in Apache Struts, an open-source web application framework used by Equifax. From the material I collected, I assume the attackers exploited this vulnerability after Equifax failed to apply a security patch that had been available for months. The initial entry point was likely through an unpatched server, which allowed the attackers to move laterally across the network and gain access to critical databases.

The timeline of the attack is crucial to understanding how the breach unfolded. Attackers gained access in May 2017, and over several weeks, they exfiltrated large amounts of personal information. It was not until July 29, 2017, that Equifax discovered the unauthorized access. By that time, the damage had already been done, and the attackers had successfully compromised data belonging to millions of people. The breach highlighted the importance of timely patching and the risks associated with using outdated software.

Detection and Response Efforts

Equifax's breach detection was delayed, allowing attackers to remain within the system for months. The breach was detected on July 29, 2017, but the company did not publicly disclose the incident until September 7, 2017, drawing widespread criticism for the delay. From the available information, I infer that Equifax's internal monitoring systems were insufficient, as they failed to detect the breach in real time. The extended time between the initial attack and its detection allowed the attackers to exfiltrate massive amounts of data without being noticed.

Once the breach was discovered, Equifax took steps to contain the damage, including hiring external cybersecurity firms to investigate the attack.

However, the company's delayed response and lack of clear communication with the public worsened the situation. Equifax initially offered credit monitoring services to affected individuals, but the response was seen as inadequate, given the scale of the breach. Regulatory bodies, including the Federal Trade Commission (FTC) and the U.S. Congress, launched investigations into Equifax's incident handling, resulting in further scrutiny and legal ramifications.

Assessing the Impact

The immediate financial impact of the Equifax data breach was severe. The company faced a significant drop in its stock price, multiple lawsuits from affected individuals, and regulatory fines. In 2019, Equifax settled with the FTC, agreeing to pay up to 700 million dollars in restitution, including compensation for consumers affected by the breach. The breach also led to class-action lawsuits and further legal action, adding to the financial burden on the company. The operational disruption was immense, as Equifax had to overhaul its security infrastructure and rebuild trust with the public.

The long-term consequences of the breach extended beyond financial losses. Equifax suffered lasting reputational damage, with many consumers losing trust in its ability to safeguard their personal information. The breach also exposed systemic weaknesses in how large organizations handle sensitive data, prompting calls for stronger regulations and more rigorous security practices. The incident served as a wake-up call for the entire industry, emphasizing the need for robust cybersecurity measures and proactive incident response strategies.

Lessons Learned and Takeaways

One of the critical lessons from the Equifax breach is the importance of timely patching and software updates. From available data, I assume Equifax's failure to patch a known vulnerability in Apache Struts allowed attackers to exploit a weakness publicly disclosed months earlier. This highlights the need for organizations to prioritize security updates and ensure that all systems are regularly patched to mitigate known vulnerabilities. Regular security audits and automated patch management systems could have prevented the attack.

Another key takeaway is the need for real-time detection and response mechanisms. Equifax's delayed detection allowed the attackers to operate undetected for months, significantly increasing the damage. Organizations must invest in advanced monitoring tools that detect unauthorized access early and respond before attackers can exfiltrate large amounts of data. Additionally, the breach underscored the importance of transparency and clear communication with affected individuals. Equifax's delayed public notification further eroded trust, demonstrating the need for prompt and transparent disclosure during cybersecurity incidents.

In response to the breach, Equifax implemented several security improvements, including stronger encryption, enhanced monitoring, and better access controls. However, the broader implications of the breach extended to the entire industry, leading to increased regulatory scrutiny and greater emphasis on data protection and cybersecurity governance.

Case Study Summary

The Equifax data breach of 2017 is a landmark case that exposed the vulnerabilities in large organizations handling sensitive personal data. The breach, which compromised the personal information of 147 million individuals, highlighted the dangers of failing to apply timely security patches and the need for stronger monitoring and response systems. Key takeaways include the importance of regular software updates, real-time detection, and transparent communication with the public. The broader impact of the breach reshaped the cybersecurity landscape, leading to increased regulatory oversight and greater awareness of the risks associated with data breaches.

CAPITAL ONE DATA BREACH (2019)

The Capital One data breach of 2019 was one of the largest financial data breaches in recent history, affecting over 100 million customers in the United States and Canada. At the heart of the attack was the exposure of sensitive personal and financial information, including Social Security numbers, credit card details, and banking information. Capital One, a major player in the banking and financial services sector, had adopted cloud computing as a core component of its infrastructure. The breach exploited a vulnerability in their cloud setup, underscoring the growing risks associated with cloud environments, especially in sectors that handle vast amounts of sensitive data.

Capital One had a reputation for being at the forefront of digital transformation in the banking sector. The company's early adoption of cloud computing, primarily through partnerships with major cloud providers, was seen as a progressive move to enhance scalability, flexibility, and security. However, this transition increased reliance on third-party systems and configurations, introducing potential supply chain and cloud security risks. At the time of the breach, many organizations were grappling with the complexities of cloud security, as traditional security approaches were often inadequate for the dynamic and shared nature of cloud environments.

The breach also highlighted the vulnerabilities in modern cybersecurity defenses. From the outset, Capital One was well-equipped with sophisticated security tools and resources. Yet, as the breach unfolded, it became apparent that even large organizations with dedicated cybersecurity teams could fall victim to sophisticated attacks exploiting misconfigurations in cloud environments. Key stakeholders in this breach included Capital One's customers, the company's leadership, and regulatory authorities, all of whom faced significant challenges in the aftermath of the incident.

Unfolding the Attack

The Capital One data breach began when Paige Thompson, a former Amazon Web Services (AWS) employee, exploited a misconfiguration in a Capital One-supplied web application firewall (WAF) in its cloud infrastructure. From the information available, I assume the misconfiguration allowed unauthorized access to sensitive data stored on Capital One's AWS cloud servers. Thompson's initial entry point was through the aforementioned poorly configured firewall, which allowed her to obtain credentials and infiltrate the system, granting her access to large amounts of customer data.

The attack's timeline indicates that it began in March 2019, but it was not detected until July 2019, when Thompson boasted about her exploits on social media, which ultimately led to her arrest. During this period, she accessed over 140,000 Social Security numbers, 1 million Canadian Social Insurance numbers, and 80,000 bank account numbers. Her methods combined basic hacking techniques with knowledge of cloud architecture vulnerabilities—particularly focusing on exploiting server misconfigurations.

Thompson used AWS command-line tools to interact with Capital One's cloud infrastructure. She could escalate her access privileges and extract large datasets by identifying the WAF misconfiguration. The breach demonstrated the complex nature of cloud security, where a simple misconfiguration could lead to a massive data breach. It also emphasized the need for stronger security practices when handling sensitive data in the cloud.

Detection and Response Efforts

The Capital One data breach was not detected by internal security measures but by an external party who noticed Thompson's bragging online and reported it. Once Capital One was made aware of the breach in July 2019, they immediately launched an investigation and notified law enforcement, leading to Thompson's arrest by the FBI shortly after. This delayed detection raised questions about the effectiveness of Capital One's internal monitoring and incident response processes, especially in detecting unauthorized activities in its cloud environment.

Upon detecting the breach, Capital One's initial response was swift. They publicly disclosed the breach within days, acknowledging the scale of the data exposed and informing affected customers. Their cybersecurity team, alongside external forensic investigators, worked to contain the breach and secure the cloud infrastructure by fixing the WAF misconfiguration that had been exploited. Capital One also engaged with AWS and cybersecurity firms to assess the extent of the damage and ensure their cloud security practices were up to industry standards.

External cybersecurity experts and law enforcement involvement were crucial in the incident response. This collaborative effort helped identify the attacker, secure the compromised systems, and mitigate further risks. However, the breach highlighted the importance of proactive detection mechanisms, which could have shortened the response time and potentially minimized the damage.

Assessing the Impact

The impact of the Capital One breach was both immediate and long-lasting. In the short term, the company faced intense scrutiny from regulators, customers, and the media. The financial costs of the breach were significant, with Capital One estimating that the total price, including legal fees, remediation efforts, and customer compensation, could exceed 150 million dollars. Beyond financial costs, the breach severely damaged Capital One's reputation, losing customer trust and confidence in its ability to protect sensitive data.

In the long term, Capital One faced legal and regulatory consequences. The company was hit with multiple lawsuits from affected customers and was eventually fined 80 million dollars by U.S. regulators for failing to secure its cloud environment. This penalty reminded all organizations of the high stakes in maintaining cloud security, particularly in sectors dealing with sensitive personal information. The breach also raised concerns among stakeholders about the security of cloud-based services and the responsibilities of cloud service providers in preventing such incidents.

The breach exposed personal and financial information for the customers, putting them at risk of identity theft and fraud. Capital One offered free credit monitoring services to affected individuals, but the breach's broader implications for customer privacy and data security were undeniable. The attack also had a ripple effect across the financial services industry, with other organizations reevaluating their cloud security practices and tightening their cybersecurity protocols.

Lessons Learned and Takeaways

The Capital One data breach offers several critical lessons for improving cloud security and preventing future supply chain attacks. One of the most important takeaways from this incident is the need for organizations to assess and secure their cloud configurations rigorously. While seemingly minor, misconfigurations can create significant vulnerabilities that attackers can exploit. Organizations must ensure their cloud environments are properly configured and regularly audited to avoid such breaches.

Another lesson is the importance of robust monitoring and detection mechanisms. In this case, Capital One relied heavily on traditional security measures, which were insufficient to detect the breach early. Implementing advanced threat detection tools, particularly those tailored for cloud environments, could have helped detect the anomaly sooner. Additionally, the breach underscores the importance of incident response preparedness. Having a rapid, coordinated response plan is essential in minimizing the damage of a breach once it occurs.

Capital One made several changes post-breach, including enhancing its cloud security practices, improving its firewall configurations, and increasing oversight of its cloud infrastructure. The broader implications of this breach extend beyond Capital One, as organizations across industries have taken note of the risks associated with cloud adoption and have implemented stricter security measures to protect their cloud environments.

Case Study Summary

The Capital One data breach of 2019 is a stark reminder of the vulnerabilities that can arise in cloud environments. The breach exposed sensitive data for millions of customers, leading to significant financial, legal, and reputational consequences for the company. This case study shows the importance of cloud configuration management, proactive threat detection, and rapid incident response. The broader impact of this attack resonates throughout the financial services industry and serves as a valuable lesson for all organizations navigating the complexities of cloud security.

CHAPTER CONCLUSION

The data breaches discussed in this chapter, from Heartland in 2008 to the Capital One incident in 2019, illustrate several recurring themes and highlight critical cybersecurity challenges that persist today. One of the most significant patterns is the reliance on outdated security protocols, such as weak encryption algorithms and inadequate password protection, which made many of these breaches possible. Many companies failed to implement strong encryption standards, allowing attackers to exploit vulnerabilities once they easily gained access to sensitive data. This is a vital reminder for cybersecurity professionals today that maintaining up-to-date encryption and security protocols is nonnegotiable, as even minor lapses can result in widespread data exposure.

Another major theme is the importance of real-time detection and response capabilities. Across multiple cases, such as the Yahoo incident, the delayed detection of breaches allowed attackers to remain within systems for months or even years, extracting data without being noticed. The response efforts were often reactive rather than proactive, further exacerbating the damage. Although details on how some breaches were detected and mitigated are not always publicly available, from the information that exists, I have extrapolated that many organizations lacked the necessary monitoring tools or processes to detect these incidents early. For cybersecurity professionals today, the key lesson is the critical need for continuous monitoring, real-time threat detection, and automated alert systems to identify and mitigate breaches before significant damage is done.

The human element also plays a critical role in many of these breaches, particularly in compromised credentials, phishing, or social engineering cases. In the Capital One incident, attackers gained access to sensitive systems through compromised employee credentials, highlighting the need for stronger access controls and MFA. Training employees on security awareness and enforcing policies around credential management are essential to minimizing the risk of human error leading to significant breaches. For today's cybersecurity professionals, balancing technological defenses with education and human factors is critical for maintaining a secure environment.

Finally, these case studies underscore the broader responsibility of cybersecurity professionals to not only secure current systems but to anticipate future threats and address legacy vulnerabilities. As seen with the Yahoo breach, legacy systems that are no longer actively maintained can become a major liability. Professionals must adopt a holistic approach to security, where continuous audits, regular updates, and retirement of outdated infrastructure are integral parts of the strategy. In conclusion, the lessons drawn from these major breaches are not simply historical footnotes but serve as a framework for future action. Cybersecurity professionals must remain vigilant, continually evolve their practices, and implement proactive measures to stay ahead of evolving threats.

5

NATION-STATE ATTACKS

Imagine a world where the phrase *going to war* no longer conjures up images of tanks and soldiers but rather a group of people huddled over keyboards, furiously typing lines of code. Instead of air raids, we have distributed denial-of-service (DDoS) attacks, and instead of spies with secret cameras, we have malware quietly infiltrating networks. It sounds like a plot straight out of a sci-fi movie, but for modern nation-states, this is reality. Cyberattacks have become one of the most effective tools in a nation's arsenal, providing a stealthy, scalable, and often deniable means to disrupt, degrade, or even dismantle the digital infrastructure of a rival. While it is easy to joke about hackers in hoodies taking over the world, the consequences of nation-state cyberattacks are anything but funny.

This chapter explores a few of the most prominent examples of nation-state cyberattacks, examining how these digital conflicts unfolded and what we can learn from them. From the Russian cyberattacks on Estonia in 2007 to the sabotage of Iran's nuclear program via Stuxnet, these cases reveal the growing power and sophistication of cyber warfare. These incidents illustrate how fragile our interconnected systems can be and how quickly they can become battlegrounds in geopolitical struggles. As I analyze each attack, it is important to note that in many cases, I have had to extrapolate information about how the attacks were detected and how organizations responded since specific details are often not made public.

What is most unsettling about nation-state attacks is how hard they are to trace back to their perpetrators. These attacks often involve layers of deception, with the culprits covering their tracks through proxy servers, botnets, and compromised machines spread across the globe. Where factual accounts were unavailable, I have pieced together a narrative based on media reports and expert analysis, giving readers an informed yet cautious interpretation of how these attacks were handled.

Ultimately, this chapter is not just a history lesson—it is a warning and a guide for cybersecurity professionals. Nation-state attacks are no longer rare anomalies but are now part of the global political landscape. As professionals defending against these threats, we must learn from these past incidents to better prepare for the future. Understanding the strategies used in these attacks and their broader implications is critical for staying one step ahead. Let's dive in, but do not worry, we will not need night-vision goggles—just a keen eye for detecting cyber threats.

WHAT IS A NATION-STATE ATTACK?

A nation-state attack is a cyberattack by or on behalf of a government or state-sponsored group to advance that nation's strategic, political, or economic interests. Unlike traditional cybercriminal activities that often focus on financial gain, nation-state attacks are driven by a broader geopolitical agenda. These attacks are usually sophisticated, well-resourced, and persistent while targeting critical infrastructure, military operations, government agencies, and even private corporations that play key roles in national security or international influence. While espionage and intelligence gathering are common objectives, some nation-state attacks aim to sabotage, disrupt, or manipulate public opinion (see Figure 5.1).

What makes nation-state attacks particularly concerning is their complexity and scale. These operations are often carried out over extended periods, using advanced techniques such as zero-day exploits (where attackers leverage undiscovered flaws to gain access), phishing, and malware to avoid detection. Nation-state attackers can invest significant resources into reconnaissance, ensuring they understand their target's infrastructure, vulnerabilities, and defenses before launching an attack. This contrasts with more opportunistic cyberattacks that might be designed to exploit random, poorly defended systems. The involvement of state resources means that these attacks are often more sophisticated and persistent than those carried out by independent hackers or cybercriminal groups.

One of the defining characteristics of a nation-state attack is its often-deniable nature. Attackers typically operate through proxy servers, botnets,

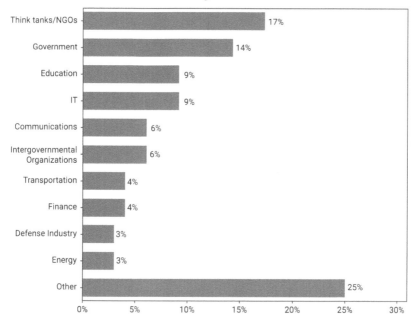

Figure 5.1   European industries targeted by nation-state cyber threats (*source*: Statista Search Department)

or compromised networks in neutral countries, making it difficult to attribute the attack directly to the sponsoring government. This plausible deniability allows the attacking nation to avoid direct consequences while achieving its espionage, disruption, or influence goals. For instance, attacks like the Estonian cyberattacks may involve circumstantial evidence pointing to specific state actors, but definitive attribution remains elusive. These operations reveal the strategic use of cyber warfare to influence geopolitical outcomes without engaging in open conflict.

The following chart illustrates the timeline associated with the attacks that will be explored in this chapter (see Figure 5.2).

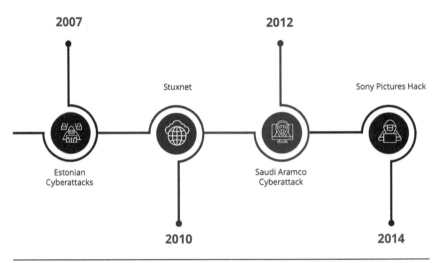

Figure 5.2   The timeline of attacks discussed in this chapter

ESTONIAN CYBERATTACKS (2007)

In 2007, Estonia, a small but digitally advanced Baltic nation, became the target of one of the first large-scale cyberattacks against a nation's infrastructure, often regarded as a watershed moment in the history of cyber warfare. These attacks occurred against a backdrop of increasing political tension between Estonia and Russia, with the immediate cause tied to Estonia's decision to relocate a Soviet-era war monument from its capital, Tallinn. This decision sparked protests among the country's ethnic Russian minority and condemnation from Moscow, escalating into a *digital* conflict that soon followed.

At the time, Estonia had invested heavily in digitizing its government services, earning it the reputation of being one of the most digitally dependent nations in the world. Services such as online banking, government communication, and media networks all relied on a robust, centralized digital infrastructure. The country had embraced technology to such an extent that digital vulnerability became a critical national security concern. Estonia's reliance on internet-based systems made it a prime target, and it would soon face unprecedented disruption.

Key stakeholders included the Estonian government, public and private sector institutions, and international bodies such as NATO, which would later offer assistance. The scale and sophistication of the attacks quickly revealed that this was not merely the work of amateur hackers but a coordinated effort, leading many to suspect involvement from nation-state actors, specifically from Russia. While Moscow denied involvement, the attacks bore the hallmarks of politically motivated cyber warfare.

Unfolding the Attack

The cyberattacks unfolded over several weeks, starting on April 27, 2007. The initial wave of attacks began with DDoS attacks, which aimed to overwhelm Estonia's internet infrastructure by flooding targeted servers with massive traffic. These attacks crippled websites and online services, particularly those belonging to government agencies, banks, and media outlets. For several days, crucial websites were either down or functioning erratically, cutting off access to essential services for Estonia's citizens and businesses.

From the information available, it can be assumed that the attackers used botnets and large networks of compromised computers to launch DDoS attacks. This method allowed them to generate traffic from millions of devices worldwide, making it difficult to trace the origin or the entity controlling the attack. According to some cybersecurity experts, the attackers likely used a combination of social engineering and malware to infiltrate systems and expand their botnet.

The timeline of events reveals a methodical escalation. After the initial DDoS attacks, the cyber onslaught became more sophisticated, targeting specific government systems and databases. This shift suggests that the attackers tested the Estonian government's resilience before launching more focused assaults. By early May, the attacks had peaked, with several major offline or severely disrupted services.

Detection and Response Efforts

Estonia's detection and response efforts were quick but initially overwhelmed by the sheer scale of the attack. The first indication that something was amiss came when government websites became inaccessible due to the DDoS attacks. Estonian officials quickly realized they were under a coordinated cyber assault and moved to isolate critical systems to prevent further breaches. However, due to the distributed nature of the attack, it took time to pinpoint the exact entry points and methods used by the attackers.

The response involved local cybersecurity teams and external assistance from NATO and the European Union. Estonia's close integration with international cyber defense alliances proved crucial in containing the attacks. Cybersecurity firms worldwide also became involved, assisting in mitigating the ongoing threat by helping reroute traffic and identifying compromised systems.

From the available information, it seems likely that Estonia employed rapid countermeasures to block traffic from suspicious IP addresses and worked to restore key services while preventing further disruption. The attacks were a wake-up call, exposing the nation's vulnerabilities and prompting a swift and comprehensive response. Although the attack lasted several weeks, by mid-May, the Estonian government had regained control of most of its online services, though the scars of the attack would linger.

Assessing the Impact

The immediate impact of the Estonian cyberattacks was significant, as much of the nation's digital infrastructure was brought to a standstill. Government agencies, financial institutions, and media outlets all suffered major disruptions, and for a time, Estonia's reputation as a digitally advanced nation appeared under threat. The attacks eroded public trust in the security of online services, with many questioning whether Estonia had moved too quickly into the digital age without sufficient safeguards.

The financial cost of the attacks was substantial, though exact figures vary. In addition to the direct economic losses from disrupted services, the Estonian government had to invest heavily in bolstering its cyber defenses in the aftermath. Internationally, the attack served as a stark reminder of the vulnerabilities associated with digital dependence, prompting other nations to reconsider their cybersecurity strategies.

Long-term consequences for Estonia included a renewed focus on cybersecurity at the national and international levels. Estonia became a vocal advocate for stronger global cybersecurity protocols, culminating in establishing NATO's Cooperative Cyber Defence Centre of Excellence in Tallinn later that year. While the attack was disruptive, it ultimately strengthened Estonia's cybersecurity posture, catalyzing its role as a cyber defense leader.

Lessons Learned and Takeaways

The Estonian cyberattacks offer several critical lessons for both nation-states and private organizations. First and foremost, the attacks highlighted the importance of resilience in the face of digital threats. Estonia's response, though initially overwhelming, demonstrated the value of international collaboration in defending against cyberattacks. By leveraging support from NATO and external cybersecurity experts, Estonia was able to regain control and mitigate the damage.

Another key lesson is the importance of diversified infrastructure. Estonia's heavy reliance on centralized online services made it an attractive target, and the attackers exploited this vulnerability. Since the attacks, Estonia and other nations have worked to decentralize critical infrastructure and build redundancies into their systems to withstand similar attacks in the future.

From a broader perspective, the attacks underscored the evolving nature of warfare in the digital age. Cyberattacks can now significantly damage national infrastructure without firing a single shot. Governments must treat cybersecurity as a core element of national defense alongside more traditional military capabilities. Additionally, this case reinforced the need for public-private partnerships to build robust cybersecurity defenses, as private entities own and operate much of the world's critical infrastructure.

Case Study Summary

The 2007 Estonian cyberattacks are a crucial example of how nation-states can wield cyber weapons to achieve political objectives. Though the attackers' identities were never definitively confirmed, the attacks fit the profile of state-sponsored cyber warfare. This case illustrates the potential for cyberattacks to paralyze a country's infrastructure, disrupt essential services, and erode public trust.

The key takeaways from this case study include the importance of rapid detection and response, the value of international cooperation, and the need for ongoing investments in cybersecurity. While the Estonian attacks were a crisis, they also became a turning point for the global conversation around cyber defense. Estonia's experience has informed cybersecurity practices worldwide, demonstrating that vigilance, resilience, and collaboration are the keys to mitigating the growing threat of nation-state cyberattacks.

STUXNET (2010)

The Stuxnet attack in 2010 is one of modern history's most significant and sophisticated cyberattacks. It marked the first known instance of a cyber weapon being used to cause physical damage to critical infrastructure, particularly targeting Iran's nuclear program. The target of the attack was the Natanz uranium enrichment facility, which was a crucial component of Iran's nuclear development efforts. Stuxnet was designed to sabotage the facility by infecting the industrial control systems (ICS) that operated the centrifuges used for uranium enrichment.

During the Stuxnet attack, an increasing reliance on digital control systems within critical infrastructure characterized the technological landscape. Once isolated from external networks, industrial systems became more integrated with corporate and external networks, creating new vulnerabilities. Stuxnet exploited these vulnerabilities, taking advantage of the interconnectedness of industrial control systems and the absence of adequate security measures in such environments.

The key stakeholders in this attack included the Iranian government, international actors suspected to have developed the Stuxnet malware (believed to be a joint effort by the United States and Israel), and Siemens, whose industrial control systems were targeted. While neither the United States nor Israel has officially claimed responsibility for the creation and deployment of Stuxnet, many experts attribute the attack to these nations due to their geopolitical interest in delaying Iran's nuclear ambitions.

Unfolding the Attack

The Stuxnet attack began with the deployment of a highly specialized piece of malware that targeted Siemens' programmable logic controllers (PLCs), which were used to operate the centrifuges at the Natanz facility. The malware was introduced through infected USB drives, a method likely chosen because the target facility was air-gapped from external networks, meaning it had no direct internet connection. From the information available, I assume the initial compromise was facilitated either by insiders or by exploiting a supply chain vulnerability, where infected software updates or devices reached the facility.

Once inside the system, Stuxnet acted with precision. It did not immediately cause disruptions but lay dormant for a time, collecting information and identifying the specific systems it was designed to attack. The malware was programmed to alter the speed of the centrifuges, causing them to spin at irregular rates while reporting normal operation back to monitoring systems. This delayed detection and prolonged the sabotage, gradually degrading the effectiveness of Iran's uranium enrichment efforts without triggering immediate suspicion.

The attack unfolded over months, and by the time it was discovered, Stuxnet had reportedly destroyed approximately 1,000 of the 5,000 centrifuges at the Natanz facility. Its sophisticated design targeted specific configurations, minimizing the risk of collateral damage to other industrial systems outside of the intended target. The malware's code exploited multiple zero-day vulnerabilities in Windows systems, making it one of the most technically advanced cyber weapons ever created.

Detection and Response Efforts

Stuxnet remained undetected for a significant time, primarily because it was designed to operate covertly and mislead operators at the Natanz facility into believing their systems were functioning correctly. The first signs of Stuxnet were detected in mid-2010 by cybersecurity researchers at Virus-BlokAda. This Belarusian security company noticed the unusual behavior of the malware in systems far removed from the Iranian nuclear program. This discovery sparked a global investigation into the malware's origin, behavior, and purpose.

From the data I obtained, it is evident that the Iranian government and the operators at the Natanz facility were unaware of the attack's full scope until much later. Initial response actions included isolating infected systems and attempting to remove the malware from the compromised networks. However, Stuxnet's complexity and modular nature made it difficult to eradicate. Its ability to propagate through removable media and network shares meant that even systems thought to be secure could be reinfected.

Internationally, cybersecurity firms like Symantec and Kaspersky Lab have become involved in analyzing malware. Their investigations revealed Stuxnet's sophisticated targeting of Siemens' PLCs and the use of multiple zero-day vulnerabilities. Law enforcement and intelligence agencies were also drawn into the investigation due to the suspected involvement of nation-states. Despite these efforts, the damage to the Natanz facility had already been done, and the malware had effectively accomplished its goal of delaying Iran's nuclear program.

Assessing the Impact

The immediate impact of the Stuxnet attack was significant, as it caused a serious setback to Iran's nuclear program. The destruction of nearly 1,000 centrifuges effectively delayed Iran's ability to enrich uranium to levels necessary for developing atomic weapons. Although the exact financial cost to Iran is difficult to quantify, the operational disruption was substantial, forcing the country to replace equipment and reinforce its cybersecurity measures.

The long-term consequences of the Stuxnet attack extended beyond Iran's nuclear program. The attack demonstrated the potential for cyber weapons to cause physical damage, a previously more theoretical than practical concept. This new precedent raised concerns among nations worldwide about the vulnerability of critical infrastructure, such as power plants, water treatment facilities, and manufacturing plants, to similar attacks. As a result, countries began reevaluating their cybersecurity strategies, particularly concerning industrial control systems and the security of air-gapped networks.

The global response to Stuxnet also included increased cooperation in the cybersecurity field. Organizations like the International Atomic Energy Agency became more involved in discussions around nuclear security and the potential role of cyber threats. Additionally, cybersecurity firms and national governments emphasized detecting and mitigating zero-day vulnerabilities that could be exploited in future attacks.

Lessons Learned and Takeaways

Stuxnet provided several critical lessons for both nation-states and the cybersecurity industry. First and foremost, it highlighted the vulnerability of ICS and supervisory control and data acquisition systems, which were not originally designed with cybersecurity in mind. The attack revealed that even air-gapped systems that were long considered secure from external threats could be compromised through physical access or supply chain vulnerabilities.

Another key lesson is the value of layered security. The information shows that the lack of robust security measures in the Natanz facility's internal network allowed Stuxnet to spread undetected. The implementation of a combination of security controls, such as network segmentation, anomaly detection, and stronger access controls, could have mitigated the damage caused by the malware. This case underscored the importance of not relying on a single security mechanism but instead adopting a defense-in-depth approach.

The broader implications of the Stuxnet attack for the cybersecurity industry include the need for increased vigilance regarding zero-day vulnerabilities. Stuxnet exploited such vulnerabilities in widely used software, raising questions about how prepared organizations are to defend against unknown threats. In the years following Stuxnet, there was a marked increase in investment in zero-day detection and response capabilities and a greater focus on securing industrial systems.

Case Study Summary

The Stuxnet cyberattack represents a turning point in the history of cyber warfare, as it was the first known instance of a cyber weapon being used to cause physical destruction to a nation's infrastructure. The key takeaways from this case study include the importance of securing industrial control systems, the need for defense-in-depth strategies, and the risks posed by zero-day vulnerabilities.

continued

Stuxnet's impact extended beyond the immediate damage to Iran's nuclear program, influencing global cybersecurity practices and raising awareness of the potential dangers of cyber warfare. The attack demonstrated that cyber threats are not limited to data breaches or espionage but can have real-world, physical consequences. As the first of its kind, Stuxnet remains a case study with enduring lessons for cybersecurity professionals, policymakers, and governments worldwide.

SAUDI ARAMCO CYBERATTACK (2012)

In August 2012, one of the largest oil companies in the world, Saudi Aramco, fell victim to a devastating cyberattack that disrupted its operations and caused widespread damage to its information technology (IT) infrastructure. This attack, later known as the *Shamoon* attack—after the malware that was used—was a significant escalation in cyber warfare against a major national asset. Saudi Aramco, a state-owned enterprise, plays a vital role in the global energy market and is critical to Saudi Arabia's economy, making it an attractive target for politically motivated cyberattacks.

At the time, the technological landscape in the Middle East, particularly in Saudi Arabia, was rapidly evolving. Companies were increasingly dependent on digital infrastructure to manage operations, communications, and financial transactions. Saudi Aramco was no exception, and its IT systems were integral to managing its vast operations, including oil production, supply chains, and financial management. However, this growing digital dependence also meant that any vulnerabilities in these systems could have far-reaching consequences.

The key stakeholders involved in this attack included the Saudi Aramco management team, cybersecurity teams, and the Saudi government, given the company's importance to national security. Externally, the attack was attributed to nation-state actors or groups with geopolitical motivations, with fingers pointed at Iran as part of a broader cyber conflict. Though the Iranian government denied involvement, the timing and targets suggest that this was a state-sponsored attack aimed at destabilizing Saudi Arabia's oil industry.

Unfolding the Attack

The Saudi Aramco cyberattack unfolded on August 15, 2012, when an estimated 30,000 workstations across the company's network were infected with the Shamoon malware. The attack began with a breach in the company's network, which, from the information available, I assume was likely facilitated through spear-phishing emails or social engineering techniques targeting employees. Once inside the network, the malware spread rapidly, designed to overwrite the master boot records of the infected machines, rendering them unusable.

Shamoon was particularly destructive, not only disabling thousands of workstations but also replacing files with an image of a burning U.S. flag, a clear indication that the attack had a political or ideological motivation. The timeline of the attack indicates that the malware had been designed to activate and spread across the network during a specific window, suggesting a high level of planning and coordination. This would support the theory that the attackers had conducted reconnaissance on Saudi Aramco's internal systems long before the actual execution of the attack.

The entry point and initial compromise remain speculative, but attackers likely gained access through weak internal security protocols, possibly by exploiting vulnerable devices or privileged user accounts. Once inside, Shamoon leveraged these weaknesses to propagate quickly and efficiently across the network. The malware was designed to cause maximum disruption to the company's day-to-day operations by targeting its core IT infrastructure, which underscores the strategic nature of the attack.

Detection and Response Efforts

Saudi Aramco's response to the attack was swift, though initially overwhelmed by the sheer scale of the disruption. The malware's destructive payload was designed to overwrite critical system files, making recovery difficult. The available information shows that the attack was detected shortly after it began, as systems across the company started failing simultaneously. Working with external cybersecurity firms, Saudi Aramco's IT team quickly moved to isolate the affected systems to prevent further damage.

The company's priority was ensuring critical oil production operations were unaffected. Fortunately, the malware primarily targeted the corporate IT network, sparing the operational technology (OT) systems controlling oil production and distribution processes. This allowed Saudi Aramco to continue its core operations, though the attack disrupted internal communications and day-to-day business functions. The company temporarily disconnected its corporate network from the Internet to contain the malware's spread.

External parties, including cybersecurity firms and government agencies, were brought in to assist with the recovery process. Given the geopolitical implications of the attack, law enforcement and intelligence agencies from Saudi Arabia and allied nations also became involved. Saudi Aramco's response included a massive effort to replace the damaged workstations and rebuild its

IT infrastructure. Despite the substantial recovery cost, the company restored most of its systems within two weeks.

Assessing the Impact

The immediate impact of the Saudi Aramco cyberattack was significant, both in terms of financial loss and operational disruption. While the company's core oil production operations remained intact, the attack crippled its corporate IT network, disrupting internal communications, financial transactions, and supply chain management. The destruction of 30,000 workstations forced the company to spend millions of dollars on hardware replacement and system recovery. Additionally, the company's public image took a hit as the attack raised questions about its cybersecurity preparedness.

The long-term consequences of the attack extended beyond the financial cost. For Saudi Aramco, the attack highlighted critical weaknesses in its cybersecurity infrastructure, particularly in protecting its corporate network from targeted attacks. In the years following the attack, Saudi Aramco significantly strengthened its cybersecurity defenses, implemented more robust security protocols, and worked with international cybersecurity experts to prevent future incidents.

The geopolitical impact of the attack was also profound. It escalated tensions between Saudi Arabia and Iran, as many suspected that the attack was part of a broader cyber campaign by Iranian actors. This case demonstrated the potential for cyberattacks to be used as a tool of geopolitical conflict, targeting critical infrastructure to achieve strategic objectives without conventional military engagement. The attack also served as a wake-up call for other regional nations to bolster their defenses against similar cyber threats.

Lessons Learned and Takeaways

Several critical lessons emerged from the Saudi Aramco cyberattack for the company and the broader cybersecurity community. One of the most important lessons was the need for stronger internal security protocols to prevent initial compromises. From the information available, it seems likely that weak access controls or poor employee awareness of phishing risks contributed to the attackers gaining a foothold in the network. After the attack, strengthening internal defenses and employee training on cybersecurity risks became a top priority for Saudi Aramco.

Another key lesson was the importance of network segmentation. While the attack caused widespread damage to the company's corporate network, the operational systems controlling oil production were largely unaffected.

This separation of IT and OT systems helped prevent a complete shutdown of Saudi Aramco's operations. Going forward, organizations learned the value of isolating critical infrastructure from less secure networks to limit potential cyberattack damage.

The attack also highlighted the growing role of cyber warfare in geopolitical conflicts. The use of cyberattacks to disrupt critical infrastructure has become an increasingly common tactic in nation-state conflicts, and the Saudi Aramco incident was one of the first large-scale examples of this trend. The case underscored the need for stronger international collaboration in cybersecurity and the development of more advanced defensive capabilities to counter future cyber threats.

Case Study Summary

The Saudi Aramco cyberattack of 2012 represents a pivotal moment in the evolution of cyber warfare because it demonstrated the ability of cyberattacks to disrupt critical national infrastructure on a massive scale. The key takeaways from this case study include the importance of internal security protocols, network segmentation, and the growing role of cyberattacks in geopolitical conflicts.

While Saudi Aramco recovered from the attack relatively quickly, the incident served as a stark reminder of the vulnerabilities in digital infrastructures. The attack prompted significant changes in the company's cybersecurity posture and influenced global cybersecurity practices, particularly in the energy sector. As a case study, the Saudi Aramco attack remains a valuable example of how nation-state actors can use cyberattacks to achieve strategic objectives, and it provides important lessons for improving cybersecurity resilience in the face of growing threats.

SONY PICTURES HACK (2014)

In November 2014, Sony Pictures Entertainment, one of the world's leading entertainment companies, fell victim to a devastating cyberattack that had widespread implications across the entertainment industry, international politics, and cybersecurity. The attack, carried out by a group calling itself the *Guardians of Peace*, crippled the company's IT infrastructure, leaked sensitive data, and led to public embarrassment for Sony. The attack is believed to have been motivated by the release of *The Interview*, a comedy film depicting a fictional assassination attempt on North Korean leader Kim Jong-un. The North

Korean government condemned the film, and many experts attributed the attack to a North Korean state-sponsored group known as the *Lazarus Group*.

At the time of the attack, Sony Pictures had substantial digital assets, including intellectual property, confidential communications, and sensitive personal information. Like many organizations, it relied heavily on digital infrastructure to manage its global operations, making it a prime target for cyberattacks. The attack was one of the first to cross over from the digital to the political, with the attackers threatening violence if the film was not pulled from theaters. This event highlighted the growing role of nation-state actors in using cyberattacks to achieve political objectives.

Key stakeholders included Sony Pictures' executives, employees, partners, the broader entertainment industry, and government officials concerned about the implications of such an attack on freedom of expression. The incident also drew in international governments, particularly the United States and North Korea, adding a geopolitical dimension to what began as a corporate cybersecurity breach.

Unfolding the Attack

The Sony Pictures hack began to unfold in late November 2014 when employees at Sony discovered that their computers were displaying ominous messages from the group calling itself Guardians of Peace. These messages demanded that Sony halt the release of *The Interview* and threatened to leak sensitive data if their demands were unmet. The hackers made good on their threats, releasing a trove of sensitive information, including confidential emails, employee salaries, unreleased films, and personal details of Sony employees.

It seems likely that the attackers gained access through phishing attacks targeting Sony employees, although the exact entry point has not been confirmed. Once inside the network, the attackers navigated Sony's systems undetected for months, planting malware designed to destroy data and steal information. The attackers used a form of malware known as a wiper, which rendered many of Sony's systems inoperable, further crippling the company's ability to respond.

The attack timeline suggests that the hackers had been inside Sony's network for an extended period before launching their final destructive phase. After months of reconnaissance and exfiltration of sensitive data, the group launched its public campaign, releasing damaging information in waves and crippling Sony's ability to operate. The attackers also threatened physical violence against theaters planning to show *The Interview*, escalating the attack from a corporate security breach to a matter of public safety.

Detection and Response Efforts

The Sony hack was detected when the attackers made their presence known by displaying messages on employees' screens. However, by that time, the attack was underway and damage had been done. Sony Pictures' IT teams scrambled to respond, but the sophisticated nature of the attack made recovery difficult. The malware deployed by the attackers had effectively wiped large portions of Sony's data, forcing the company to take many of its systems offline.

Sony quickly called in external cybersecurity firms to assist in the response and recovery efforts. The U.S. Federal Bureau of Investigation (FBI) also became involved since the attack appeared to be linked to a nation-state actor, specifically North Korea. With help from cybersecurity experts and law enforcement, Sony worked to isolate the malware and begin the arduous process of restoring its systems. Despite these efforts, the company struggled to mitigate the immediate fallout, as sensitive data, including private emails between executives, continued to be leaked to the public.

The involvement of the FBI and other government agencies highlighted the geopolitical nature of the attack. The U.S. government ultimately attributed the attack to North Korea, with President Obama publicly condemning the attack as an assault on free speech. This official attribution underscored the complexity of the attack, which was not only a breach of corporate security but also a politically motivated strike against a major U.S. corporation.

Assessing the Impact

The immediate impact of the Sony Pictures hack was devastating. The company's operations were severely disrupted, and significant financial losses were suffered from the breach and the ensuing fallout. The leaked emails exposed embarrassing internal conversations between executives, leading to public relations crises and the resignation of some high-profile employees. Unreleased films and other intellectual property were also leaked, causing further damage to the company's bottom line.

Long-term consequences included reputational damage and reevaluating cybersecurity practices for Sony and the entertainment industry. The attack demonstrated that no industry is immune to nation-state cyberattacks, and it highlighted the need for stronger cybersecurity defenses in sectors beyond finance and government. While successfully restoring operations, Sony's response showed how difficult it can be to recover from a sophisticated, politically motivated cyberattack.

The geopolitical impact of the attack was also significant. The U.S. government's public attribution of the attack to North Korea increased tensions between the two nations. It highlighted the growing use of cyberattacks as international influence and intimidation tools. The incident also raised concerns about the vulnerability of corporations to state-sponsored attacks, particularly those involving politically sensitive content.

Lessons Learned and Takeaways

The Sony Pictures hack provides several important lessons for cybersecurity professionals and organizations. One of the key takeaways is the importance of proactive security measures, including stronger access controls and employee training to prevent phishing attacks, which are often the entry point for these types of breaches. From the information available, it seems likely that the attackers gained access through relatively simple phishing tactics, demonstrating the need for robust defenses against social engineering attacks.

Another critical lesson is the importance of incident response preparedness. Sony's recovery was slow and painful, highlighting the need for organizations to have well-developed incident response plans before an attack occurs. The complexity and scope of the Sony attack also underscored the value of public-private partnerships in cybersecurity, as the involvement of external firms and law enforcement was crucial in managing the response and attributing the attack to North Korea.

The broader implications for the cybersecurity industry include recognizing that politically motivated cyberattacks can target any organization, regardless of industry. Cybersecurity professionals must be prepared to defend against financially motivated attacks and those driven by geopolitics, particularly as nation-states increasingly use cyber operations as tools of influence. The Sony hack serves as a reminder that the consequences of a breach can extend far beyond financial losses, affecting national security, public safety, and freedom of expression.

Case Study Summary

The 2014 Sony Pictures hack represents a watershed moment in the evolution of cyberattacks, as it demonstrated the ability of nation-states to use cyber operations to achieve political objectives on a global stage. The key takeaways from this case study include the importance of robust cybersecurity measures, the need for incident response preparedness, and the growing threat of politically motivated cyberattacks that target private corporations.

continued

As cybersecurity professionals continue to defend against increasingly sophisticated attacks, the Sony hack serves as a cautionary tale about the potential consequences of cyber warfare. The incident also highlights the need for a coordinated response involving private and public sectors and strong cybersecurity practices across all industries. The Sony Pictures hack was more than just a corporate breach—it was a global event that changed how the world views cyber threats and their impact on international relations.

CHAPTER CONCLUSION

The nation-state cyberattacks discussed in this chapter underscore digital warfare's evolving and sophisticated nature in the modern age. From the Russian cyberattacks on Estonia in 2007 to the infamous Stuxnet malware, each case reveals a common theme: cyberattacks have become a critical tool in geopolitical conflict. These attacks are not isolated incidents but part of larger strategies that nation-states use to achieve political and economic objectives without conventional warfare. Understanding these types of attacks is essential for today's cybersecurity professionals, as they represent some of the most complex and coordinated threats organizations may face.

A recurring element across all the cases is the attackers' ability to exploit vulnerabilities in digital infrastructure—whether through social engineering, unpatched systems, or weak network defenses. The attackers often rely on advanced persistent threat techniques, where they infiltrate systems, establish long-term footholds, and exfiltrate data over extended periods. One of the key takeaways is the importance of continuous monitoring and rapid detection capabilities. In many instances, attackers could remain undetected for months, significantly amplifying the damage caused by their actions.

These historical incidents serve as warnings and guides for today's cybersecurity professionals. The evolving threat landscape requires technical expertise and a strategic approach to defending critical infrastructure. Cybersecurity teams must prioritize proactive measures, such as regular vulnerability assessments, the implementation of robust access controls, and the development of incident response plans tailored to large-scale attacks. Investing in cybersecurity training for employees, strengthening public-private partnerships, and fostering international collaboration are all critical to mitigating the risks of nation-state actors. While the attacks discussed in this chapter were devastating, they have also improved how organizations and governments think about and implement cybersecurity strategies.

The lessons learned from these attacks often stem from extrapolated data where specifics about detection and response were not publicly disclosed. This emphasizes the challenge cybersecurity professionals face today: defending against threats whose true scale and impact may not always be clear. Adapting to an ever-changing threat landscape and a deeper understanding of nation-state tactics will be crucial for the next generation of cybersecurity defenders. Ultimately, staying vigilant, continuously improving defenses, and preparing for the unexpected are the best safeguards in an increasingly complex world of digital conflict.

6

ADVANCED PERSISTENT THREATS

If *Cyber Threats* was a horror movie, an advanced persistent threat (APT) would be the slow-moving villain you can't shake off, lurking in the shadows, biding its time, and making its presence known only when it is too late. While ransomware might get the headlines with its quick, attention-grabbing demands, an APT is more like the espionage thriller that keeps you on edge—calculated, patient, and persistent. These APT attackers do not want to lock you out; they want to sneak in, rifle through your most sensitive data quietly, and then disappear without a trace. So, while some might see picture hackers as hoodie-clad criminals hammering away at keyboards, the reality is that APTs are more akin to secret agents, executing sophisticated, covert operations over months or even years.

But jokes aside, APTs represent some of the most dangerous and complex challenges facing cybersecurity professionals today. These state-sponsored actors often target critical sectors like healthcare, defense, and technology, seeking to steal intellectual property and sensitive information or to disrupt critical infrastructure. The case studies in this chapter explore some of the most infamous APT campaigns, from the Chinese APT1 operations to the Shadow Brokers' leak of National Security Agency (NSA) tools. These examples reveal the methods used by attackers and the often frustrating gaps in detection and response efforts. Where official documentation on responses was lacking, I have had to extrapolate from media reports and industry insights to create a complete picture of how these events unfolded.

This chapter aims to give cybersecurity professionals a deeper understanding of how APTs operate and, more important, how organizations have responded—or failed to respond—in the face of such threats. By analyzing these historical incidents, we can draw valuable lessons about how today's defenders can better protect their networks. Whether it is improving vulnerability management, investing in advanced detection systems, or preparing for the worst through robust incident response plans, these case studies offer critical insights into the ongoing battle against APTs.

Ultimately, this chapter serves as a reminder that APTs are not a one-time threat but an ongoing risk that requires constant vigilance. As cybersecurity professionals, we must stay ahead of the curve because, as these case studies show, the adversary is always adapting. The information presented here is a mix of documented facts and, where details were scarce, informed extrapolation. This approach ensures we can learn as much as possible from these incidents, even if every aspect of the response was not made public. So, buckle up—this is the long game, and every move counts in the world of APTs.

WHAT IS AN ADVANCED PERSISTENT THREAT?

An APT is a sophisticated and methodical cyberattack, typically carried out by highly skilled, often state-sponsored groups. In this chapter, an APT is defined by its ability to infiltrate networks stealthily, remain undetected for extended periods, and methodically extract valuable information or carry out destructive actions. Unlike common cyber threats that aim for immediate financial gain or disruption, APTs are patient and precise, focusing on long-term goals such as espionage, intellectual property theft, or strategic political objectives. What makes APTs particularly dangerous is their persistence— once inside a network, they employ advanced tactics to maintain access, move laterally across systems, and cover their tracks to avoid detection.

APTs often begin with spear-phishing or exploiting zero-day vulnerabilities and then evolving and adapting to an organization's defenses. In many cases discussed in this chapter, such as APT1 or APT41, the attackers demonstrated the ability to operate undetected for months or even years, gathering intelligence or laying the groundwork for more significant actions. These operations are usually backed by nation-states, giving APT groups access to resources that allow them to develop custom malware, manipulate human behavior through social engineering, and precisely target organizations.

In the context of this chapter, APTs are the focus because they represent the most dangerous, resource-intensive, and hard-to-counter threats in the cybersecurity landscape. Each case study in this chapter—from the Dark-Hotel campaign to the Shadow Brokers' leak of NSA tools—illustrates how APTs operate, how organizations have responded, and the devastating impact these attacks can have. Understanding APTs requires technical knowledge of how they infiltrate networks and strategic insight into their objectives, ranging from corporate espionage to national security threats. For cybersecurity professionals, recognizing and defending against APTs is not just about responding to immediate threats but staying one step ahead of adversaries continually evolving in their tactics and objectives.

The following chart illustrates the timeline associated with the attacks that will be explored in this chapter (see Figure 6.1).

DARKHOTEL APT (2007–2020)

The DarkHotel APT campaign, active from 2007 to 2020, was a highly targeted cyber espionage operation focused on high-profile business executives, government officials, and other key individuals during their stays at luxury hotels. This group gained notoriety for exploiting vulnerabilities in hotel Wi-Fi networks to carry out their attacks, making them one of the most persistent and elusive threats over a decade. The exact origin of the DarkHotel group remains unclear. However, many security experts believe it may have ties to East Asia, given the attacks' geography and the targets' nature.

At the time of the first discovered attacks in the late 2000s, business and government travel were heavily dependent on hotel infrastructure for secure communications, and many of these networks were not designed to withstand sophisticated cyber threats. Key stakeholders in the DarkHotel attacks included business executives, government officials, hotel chains, and cybersecurity firms that played a significant role in detecting and mitigating these threats.

Unfolding the Attack

The DarkHotel campaign unfolded through a multilayered attack strategy. The attackers initially gained access to hotel networks, often exploiting weak or outdated network security systems to deliver Wi-Fi to guests. From the information available, it is assumed that the attackers would position themselves on the same network as the target or even compromise hotel infrastructure ahead of the target's arrival. Once the victim connected to the compromised network, the attackers used phishing and malware-laced software updates to infiltrate their devices.

One hallmark of DarkHotel's tactics was the delivery of fake software updates, which appeared legitimate and were tailored to the specific software running on the victim's device. I assume that once the victim unknowingly installed the malicious software, attackers could escalate privileges, steal credentials, and install keyloggers, effectively gaining full control of the target's

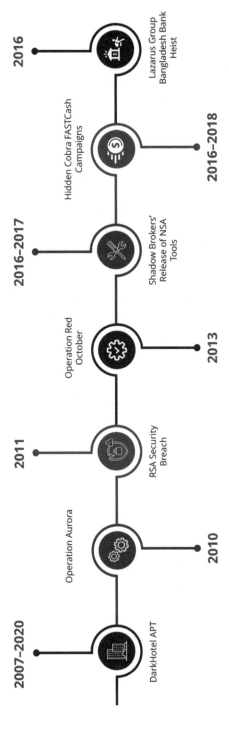

Figure 6.1 The timeline of attacks discussed in this chapter

system. The level of targeting indicated that the group had done extensive reconnaissance, often deploying these tactics only for short windows during the victim's hotel stay.

Detection and Response Efforts

The detection of DarkHotel's activities began in 2014 when the cybersecurity firm Kaspersky Lab uncovered the group's operations. Kaspersky's investigation revealed that the attacks had been ongoing for years and were extremely selective, targeting executives and government officials from regions including the United States, South Korea, and Japan. The information shows that the attack was detected when cybersecurity researchers observed unusual network activity linked to hotel Wi-Fi systems. The sophisticated nature of the attacks made them difficult to detect since the attackers carefully limited their exposure by targeting only a few individuals and wiping their traces after the operation.

Once discovered, Kaspersky and other cybersecurity firms worked to isolate the malware used in the DarkHotel campaigns and provided tools to detect and remove the malicious software. Law enforcement agencies were also involved, though attributing the attacks proved challenging due to the group's use of encrypted communications and proxy servers. Hotels affected by the breach were informed, and efforts were made to update security protocols for their networks to prevent further incidents.

Assessing the Impact

The immediate impact of the DarkHotel campaign was felt by business and government officials targeted during their travels. The stolen information often included sensitive corporate data, credentials for secure systems, and confidential communications, raising significant concerns about the security of international business dealings and diplomatic relations. While the exact financial losses associated with DarkHotel remain difficult to quantify, the theft of intellectual property and trade secrets likely had significant financial and strategic repercussions for affected organizations.

In the long term, the DarkHotel campaign served as a wake-up call for the hospitality industry, which had largely neglected to invest in cybersecurity. Hotel chains were forced to rethink their network security protocols, with many upgrading their Wi-Fi systems and implementing stronger encryption methods to protect guests' data. The campaign also heightened awareness among business travelers and government officials about the risks of using public or semipublic networks. This led to an increased adoption of virtual private networks (VPNs) and other security measures while traveling.

The DarkHotel attacks also impacted the broader cybersecurity community, prompting a reevaluation of how targeted APTs operate and how they can exploit seemingly innocuous systems such as hotel Wi-Fi networks. For cybersecurity firms, the attack demonstrated the need for continuous monitoring and developing more sophisticated detection tools to identify and counter advanced threats.

Lessons Learned and Takeaways

The DarkHotel campaign highlighted several critical lessons for the cybersecurity community, particularly around the vulnerabilities of public networks and the importance of securing communication channels. One key lesson from this case is the need for more stringent network security measures in industries like hospitality, where business travelers often rely on potentially insecure Wi-Fi networks. From the information available, it is clear that hotels were not adequately prepared to defend against a targeted APT campaign, demonstrating the importance of regular security audits and updates to network infrastructure.

Another important takeaway is the value of secure personal practices. Executives and government officials targeted by DarkHotel could have mitigated the damage by employing security tools such as VPNs and multifactor authentication (MFA), reducing the attackers' ability to steal credentials or intercept communications. Training employees and officials about the risks associated with using public networks and how to identify phishing attempts is essential in reducing the effectiveness of attacks like DarkHotel.

The DarkHotel campaign also underscored the importance of threat intelligence sharing between the public and private sectors. The discovery of the attacks by cybersecurity firms like Kaspersky was pivotal in limiting the spread of the malware and raising awareness of the risks associated with using unsecured networks. Collaboration between hotel chains, cybersecurity experts, and governments will be critical in preventing similar incidents in the future.

Case Study Summary

The DarkHotel APT campaign (2007–2020) is a stark reminder of the risks associated with using unsecured public networks, particularly for high-profile individuals traveling for business or government purposes. The highly targeted nature of the attacks, combined with the exploitation of hotel

continued

Wi-Fi networks, exposed critical vulnerabilities in the hospitality industry and raised awareness about the need for stronger cybersecurity measures. Key takeaways from this case include securing public networks, educating individuals about the risks of targeted phishing and malware, and improving collaboration between private industry and cybersecurity experts to defend against advanced persistent threats. The lessons learned from DarkHotel continue to influence cybersecurity practices for travelers and the hospitality sector.

OPERATION AURORA (2010)

Operation Aurora, uncovered in January 2010, was a highly sophisticated cyber espionage campaign targeting major corporations, including Google, Adobe Systems, and over 20 other companies. The attack—believed to be orchestrated by state-sponsored actors—specifically targeted intellectual property and sensitive information within these organizations. Google's disclosure of the attack was particularly significant because it marked one of the first times a major corporation publicly acknowledged being a victim of an advanced cyber operation.

At the time of the breach, the technological landscape was characterized by rapid advancements in cloud computing, web applications, and online services. Many companies began expanding their digital footprints, relying more heavily on remote services and interconnected systems, which inherently expanded the attack surface for cybercriminals. The key stakeholders in Operation Aurora included the affected companies, particularly Google, whose search engine and cloud-based services were integral to millions of users worldwide. The attack also had broader implications for governments and industries that relied on the targeted corporations for technological innovations and services.

Unfolding the Attack

Operation Aurora reportedly began in mid-2009, though it was not publicly disclosed until January 2010. The attackers utilized a combination of zero-day vulnerabilities in Microsoft's Internet Explorer and social engineering techniques to compromise targeted companies' networks. From the data I was able to obtain, I assume that the attackers sent phishing emails to key employees containing malicious links that exploited a previously unknown vulnerability in Internet Explorer. Once clicked, the malware embedded itself in the system, enabling the attackers to gain a foothold in the victim's network.

Once inside, the attackers moved laterally by escalating privileges and siphoning off sensitive data. The attackers focused primarily on intellectual property, source code from targeted companies, and information regarding human rights activists connected to Google. Data exfiltration occurred over several months, and it seems the attackers carefully avoided detection by blending into legitimate network traffic. Google's eventual decision to reveal the attack to the public was driven in part by the sensitive nature of the targeted data, especially related to the email accounts of Chinese human rights activists.

Detection and Response Efforts

Operation Aurora was detected in December 2009 when Google noticed unusual activity on its network. Google's internal security team investigated the anomalies and uncovered the broader scope of the attack, including the involvement of multiple other companies. Upon identifying the breach, Google promptly enhanced its security measures, disconnected compromised systems, and launched a detailed investigation into the attack. The company also worked with external cybersecurity firms to analyze the malware used and trace the attack's origins.

In January 2010, Google publicly announced the attack, revealing that it had been targeted by what appeared to be a state-sponsored group originating from China. This disclosure was significant, as it signaled a shift in how companies approached cyberattacks—opting for transparency rather than secrecy. Other companies targeted in the attack, such as Adobe, also initiated response efforts, but none were as vocal as Google regarding public disclosure. Law enforcement agencies, including the Federal Bureau of Investigation (FBI) and private cybersecurity firms who worked to analyze the attack vectors and mitigate further damage, were involved.

Assessing the Impact

The immediate impact of Operation Aurora was far-reaching, affecting not only the companies targeted but also their clients and the broader public. For Google, the breach prompted significant internal changes in handling security and privacy. Financially, the attack increased costs for incident response, remediation, and security upgrades. The breach also raised concerns among

Google's users about the safety of their data, particularly given the involvement of human rights activists' email accounts.

Operation Aurora's long-term impact was profound because it underscored the vulnerability of major corporations to state-sponsored cyber espionage. The attack resulted in the loss of valuable intellectual property and geopolitical implications. Google's public response to the attack, including its decision to stop censoring search results in China, strained relations between the company and the Chinese government. For the other companies affected, the attack highlighted critical weaknesses in their security infrastructure, prompting a reevaluation of cybersecurity strategies.

The broader implications of Operation Aurora extended to the entire tech industry as companies worldwide began to realize that even the most advanced security systems were susceptible to sophisticated, well-funded adversaries. Governments, too, became more involved in addressing cybersecurity risks as the attack demonstrated the increasing role of state-sponsored actors in cyber operations.

Lessons Learned and Takeaways

Operation Aurora highlighted several key lessons for the cybersecurity community, the most significant of which was the importance of transparency in addressing cyberattacks. Google's decision to publicly disclose the attack was a turning point for how organizations approach cybersecurity incidents. This level of transparency allowed other companies and governments to take proactive measures to protect their systems from similar threats.

From a technical perspective, the attack underscored the need for companies to update and patch their systems regularly. The zero-day vulnerability in Internet Explorer used in Operation Aurora had gone undetected for some time, allowing attackers to infiltrate multiple companies' networks. This breach emphasized the importance of regular vulnerability assessments and advanced detection systems that can identify abnormal behavior patterns within networks.

Operation Aurora also highlighted the increasing involvement of state-sponsored actors in cyber espionage, leading to greater collaboration between private companies and government agencies to counter such threats. Companies affected by the attack implemented more stringent access controls, encryption protocols, and employee training programs to mitigate the risk of future attacks.

Case Study Summary

Operation Aurora remains one of the most significant examples of state-sponsored cyber espionage targeting major corporations. The attack exposed critical weaknesses in corporate cybersecurity and demonstrated the risks posed by zero-day vulnerabilities and sophisticated adversaries. Key takeaways from this case include the importance of transparency, the need for regular system updates, and the role of collaboration between public and private sectors in addressing cyber threats. Operation Aurora's legacy continues to influence cybersecurity strategies today as organizations across the globe work to stay ahead of increasingly complex threats.

RSA SECURITY BREACH (2011)

In 2011, RSA Security, a globally recognized leader in encryption and security technologies, fell victim to a sophisticated cyberattack that significantly impacted its reputation and the broader cybersecurity landscape. RSA is best known for its SecurID two-factor authentication tokens, which are widely used by corporations, governments, and institutions worldwide to secure sensitive systems and data. At the time of the breach, RSA was considered a cornerstone in digital security, trusted by millions of users and organizations globally. This placed the company at the center of a rapidly evolving technological landscape where data breaches and cyber threats were becoming more complex and targeted.

The technological environment in 2011 was one of increasing reliance on cloud services, remote access, and advanced encryption for securing digital assets. RSA's SecurID tokens were a key component of many organizations' defenses, using a combination of time-based codes and PINs to authenticate users. However, despite the strength of their technology, RSA became the target of what appeared to be an APT, a form of cyberattack characterized by prolonged and targeted efforts aimed at infiltrating high-value systems. The breach would later reveal vulnerabilities in RSA's defenses and the broader industry reliance on SecurID tokens for authentication security.

Unfolding the Attack

The RSA Security breach began with phishing emails sent to small groups of RSA employees. These emails contained malicious Excel files, exploiting a zero-day vulnerability in Adobe Flash embedded within the Excel file. This marked the initial compromise, allowing the attackers to plant malware that enabled remote access to RSA's systems. From the information available, it is assumed that the attackers had mapped RSA's internal network beforehand, carefully selecting their targets for maximum impact. Once inside the network, the attackers methodically escalated privileges and moved laterally across RSA's systems, eventually gaining access to the SecureID system.

The attack unfolded over several stages, with the adversaries persistently working to exfiltrate sensitive data over an extended period. The most significant element stolen during the breach was information related to RSA's SecurID tokens, including the seed values used to generate the authentication codes. This breach created a ripple effect as high-profile clients, including defense contractors, financial institutions, and government agencies, used these tokens. The attackers captured highly sensitive details about RSA's key security product, which could later be used to compromise the systems that relied on these tokens for user authentication.

Detection and Response Efforts

RSA first detected unusual activity in its network in March 2011, although the attack had likely been ongoing for weeks before it was uncovered. The organization quickly mobilized its internal cybersecurity team to assess the breach and limit further damage. Initial response efforts involved disconnecting compromised systems from the network and conducting a forensic analysis to determine the extent of the data exfiltration. From the information I acquired, I assume RSA engaged third-party cybersecurity firms and law enforcement agencies early in the investigation to help contain the breach and manage communication with affected clients.

The timeline of the response was rapid, given the potential implications of the breach. RSA decided to notify its clients within days of discovering the extent of the attack, issuing a public statement that acknowledged the compromise of its SecurID technology. The notification was coupled with guidance to customers on additional security measures, such as hardening their two-factor authentication systems and being on alert for targeted attacks. The U.S. Department of Homeland Security and other government agencies were also involved, particularly due to the sensitive nature of the organizations using RSA's authentication technology.

Assessing the Impact

The immediate impact of the RSA breach was far-reaching, with consequences rippling through RSA's client base and the broader cybersecurity industry. The breach significantly damaged RSA's reputation as a trusted security solutions provider. The company faced financial losses in remediation costs and the potential loss of clients who were now questioning the reliability of their flagship product, SecurID. One of the most visible effects of the breach came when major RSA clients, such as defense contractor Lockheed Martin, reported targeted cyberattacks using compromised SecurID tokens, further illustrating the seriousness of the breach.

In the long term, RSA invested heavily in restoring trust, including offering to replace or reissue SecurID tokens for its affected customers at no cost. Legal ramifications followed as RSA faced lawsuits from clients who alleged negligence in securing their critical assets. More broadly, the RSA breach raised serious concerns about the security of two-factor authentication systems based on tokens, driving many organizations to reassess their reliance on such technologies. The breach highlighted the importance of the technology and the processes around managing and securing those technologies from increasingly sophisticated cyberattacks.

Lessons Learned and Takeaways

One of the critical lessons from the RSA Security breach is the importance of securing the entire supply chain in cybersecurity. As a critical component of many organizations' security infrastructures, RSA became a target for attackers seeking to compromise *multiple* organizations in one well-coordinated attack. The breach demonstrated that even the most secure and trusted security providers can be vulnerable to advanced, persistent adversaries. It also underscored the need for organizations to employ a layered security approach and not rely solely on one form of defense, such as two-factor authentication.

The attack also highlighted the need for better phishing detection and user education. The initial compromise occurred through a well-crafted phishing email, showing how even well-trained employees can fall victim to social engineering tactics. The broader industry learned the importance of regularly updating and patching software to protect against zero-day vulnerabilities since the attackers exploited an unpatched vulnerability in Flash to gain their initial foothold.

Following the attack, RSA made several changes to its policies and practices, focusing on improving its internal security processes and offering better guidance to clients on managing authentication systems. The breach also prompted the broader cybersecurity community to examine two-factor authentication more critically and seek more robust, adaptive security measures that could protect against similar compromises in the future.

Case Study Summary

The 2011 RSA Security breach illustrates the danger of APTs, which lever-age prolonged, targeted attacks to compromise high-value targets. For RSA, the breach was a watershed moment that challenged the trust clients had in its security products and drove significant changes in how organi-zations view two-factor authentication. The key takeaways from this case include the importance of securing the supply chain, maintaining vigilance against phishing attacks, and adopting a multilayered security approach to mitigate the risks posed by increasingly sophisticated adversaries.

OPERATION RED OCTOBER (2013)

Operation Red October, discovered in 2013 by Kaspersky Lab, is one of the most sophisticated and long-running cyber espionage campaigns ever uncovered. The operation began around 2007 and lasted for at least five years, targeting high-profile organizations, including diplomatic missions, governmental agencies, and scientific research institutions across Europe, Central Asia, and North America. The attackers aimed to collect sensitive geopolitical intelligence, credentials, and classified information from various targets, demonstrating the scale and precision of nation-state-sponsored cyber espionage.

The cyber espionage campaign was named after the Tom Clancy novel and film "The Hunt for Red October," reflecting the clandestine nature of the operation. By the time it was uncovered, Red October had infiltrated networks across multiple sectors with extensive tools and techniques that allowed attackers to remain undetected for years. The technological landscape during this period was transitioning, with a growing emphasis on cyber espionage, nation-state hacking, and the vulnerabilities of interconnected networks.

Key stakeholders in the Red October operation included the targeted governments, research institutions, and cybersecurity firms like Kaspersky Lab, which played a critical role in uncovering the attack. The incident also highlighted the growing threat of APTs, where attackers persistently target organizations over long periods using highly specialized malware and social engineering tactics.

Unfolding the Attack

The Red October cyber espionage campaign was marked by its stealth and persistence. Attackers used various methods to infiltrate target networks, often relying on spear-phishing emails containing malicious attachments or links. These emails appeared legitimate, luring victims to click on the links or open documents that would then download the malware onto their systems. Once installed, the malware enabled attackers to establish a foothold in the network and escalate their privileges over time.

Red October's attack toolkit was highly modular, allowing it to adapt to different operating systems and devices. The malware could infect Windows-based machines, mobile devices, and network equipment. The attackers also could reinfect machines that had been previously compromised, ensuring that they maintained long-term access to critical systems. Their malware could steal sensitive data, including credentials for diplomatic communications, scientific research, and classified government information.

The timeline of events stretched over several years, with Red October infiltrating networks as early as 2007. The attack remained undetected due to its highly sophisticated nature. The malware was customized for specific targets, and the attackers employed encrypted communication channels to exfiltrate data back to their command-and-control servers. By the time the campaign was discovered, the attackers had already collected vast amounts of sensitive data, raising alarms about the vulnerability of diplomatic and governmental networks worldwide.

Detection and Response Efforts

The detection of Operation Red October was a landmark moment in cybersecurity. In late 2012, Kaspersky Lab began investigating suspicious activity related to a cluster of infections in high-profile networks. In early 2013, after months of research, Kaspersky uncovered the full scope of the Red October campaign, identifying its modular malware, the network of command-and-control servers, and the extensive list of targets. Given the duration and scale of the campaign, the discovery sent shockwaves through the cybersecurity community.

Once the attack was identified, immediate steps were taken to mitigate the damage and prevent further data theft. Kaspersky collaborated with affected organizations and governments to patch the vulnerabilities that allowed Red October to persist. Their malware analysis led to a deeper understanding of the tools used by the attackers, which in turn helped cybersecurity teams develop countermeasures. However, because of the campaign's persistence and complexity, it took significant time to eradicate the malware from compromised systems completely.

In the wake of the discovery, various cybersecurity firms and law enforcement agencies worldwide were involved in tracking down the origins of Red

October. While the attribution of the attack was never conclusively tied to a specific nation-state, many cybersecurity analysts speculated that the operation was backed by a sophisticated actor, likely with geopolitical motives. The complexity of the malware and the types of data targeted strongly indicated nation-state involvement, though the exact sponsor of the operation remains unclear.

Assessing the Impact

The immediate impact of Operation Red October was the realization that sensitive diplomatic, governmental, and scientific data had been compromised over a sustained period. While it is difficult to quantify the exact financial loss or operational disruption caused by the campaign, the attackers' access to such critical information posed significant security risks for the affected organizations. The breach of diplomatic communications and geopolitical intelligence could have altered the strategic landscape for several governments.

The long-term consequences of the attack included reputational damage for the compromised organizations, especially those that handled sensitive government and scientific data. The discovery of such a prolonged and widespread campaign eroded trust in the cybersecurity measures of the targeted entities. Moreover, the incident underscored the need for governments and institutions to reevaluate their approach to cyber defense, particularly against APTs, which could operate undetected for years.

Operation Red October also had significant legal and geopolitical implications. The difficulty attributing the attack to a specific nation-state hindered international cooperation in cybersecurity enforcement. This incident served as a wake-up call for governments worldwide, pushing them to strengthen their cybersecurity frameworks and consider new strategies for combating APTs. The attack also increased scrutiny of how diplomatic and scientific institutions handle and secure sensitive data.

Lessons Learned and Takeaways

Operation Red October provided critical lessons for the cybersecurity community and targeted organizations. First and foremost, it demonstrated the persistence and sophistication of modern cyber espionage campaigns. The attackers' ability to operate undetected for years using modular malware and reinfection tactics underscored the necessity for continuous monitoring and advanced detection capabilities within targeted networks.

One key weakness the attackers exploited was the human element, particularly through spear-phishing emails. The campaign highlighted the need for stronger security awareness training since even the most advanced technical defenses can be undermined by social engineering. Additionally, the attack revealed gaps in the cyber defense strategies of diplomatic and governmental organizations, pushing these institutions to adopt more robust security frameworks and regularly update their defensive measures.

The Red October incident reaffirmed the importance of information sharing and collaboration between private cybersecurity firms and government entities for the broader industry. Kaspersky Lab's role in discovering the attack and coordinating the response demonstrated how private companies could play a crucial part in defending against state-sponsored cyber threats. The case also underscored the need for international cooperation in addressing the challenges posed by APTs, given their potential to operate across borders and target a wide range of institutions.

Case Study Summary

The discovery of Operation Red October in 2013 marked a pivotal moment in the history of cyber espionage. This sophisticated APT campaign targeted high-profile diplomatic, governmental, and scientific research organizations across the globe while operating undetected for more than five years. The attackers used a modular, highly adaptive malware toolkit to collect sensitive data, including geopolitical intelligence and government credentials. The operation's scale, persistence, and stealth underscored the growing threat posed by nation-state-sponsored cyber espionage.

Key takeaways from this case include the importance of continuous monitoring for advanced threats, the vulnerability of human factors to spear-phishing attacks, and the need for stronger international collaboration in combating APTs. The Red October incident highlighted the evolving nature of cyber threats and the necessity for organizations to adopt more sophisticated defense strategies to protect sensitive data. This case is a stark reminder of the complexities of defending against state-sponsored cyber espionage and the critical importance of remaining vigilant in an increasingly connected world.

SHADOW BROKERS' RELEASE OF NSA TOOLS (2016-2017)

In 2016, a mysterious group known as the *Shadow Brokers* began releasing hacking tools allegedly stolen from the U.S. NSA. These tools, many of which were linked to the NSA's elite hacking unit known as the Equation Group, included a variety of sophisticated exploits designed to compromise computer systems worldwide. The most infamous release occurred in 2017, when the group made public a cache of powerful vulnerabilities, including the EternalBlue exploit, which was later used in the devastating WannaCry ransomware attack. The release of these tools sent shockwaves through the cybersecurity community and raised significant concerns about the security of state-developed cyber weapons.

The technological landscape at the time was characterized by increasing reliance on cloud services, digital transformation, and interconnected systems. The exposure of NSA-developed tools had the potential to cause widespread damage, especially since many of the tools targeted unpatched vulnerabilities in popular software and operating systems. The key stakeholders involved included the NSA, global cybersecurity firms, affected companies and governments, and the broader public, as cybercriminals and nation-state actors quickly adopted the tools to carry out attacks.

Unfolding the Attack

The Shadow Brokers first appeared in August 2016, when the group announced that it had obtained tools from the NSA and offered them for auction. Over the following months, the group released several batches of tools, but it was not until April 2017 that the most dangerous exploits were made public. From the information available, it is assumed that the Shadow Brokers either obtained the tools through a direct breach of the NSA or via an insider leak. However, the exact method of acquisition remains unclear.

The group's release of the EternalBlue exploit in April 2017 marked a turning point. EternalBlue exploited a vulnerability in the Server Message Block (SMB) protocol used by Windows systems. Despite the NSA allegedly informing Microsoft of the vulnerability before the release, many systems remained unpatched, exposing them to attacks. I assume the attackers likely knew that releasing these tools into the public domain would lead to widespread exploitation by cybercriminals and other state-sponsored groups.

The Shadow Brokers' release was notable for the tools and the group's mocking tone, issuing cryptic messages that taunted the U.S. government and cybersecurity community. Their actions highlighted the risks of stockpiling cyberweapons, which, when leaked, can be turned against both government and civilian targets.

Detection and Response Efforts

Cybersecurity researchers detected the release of NSA hacking tools by the Shadow Brokers almost immediately, who then began analyzing the tools and determining the potential damage they could cause. One of the most pressing concerns was the EternalBlue exploit, which, if leveraged, could enable attackers to execute remote code on vulnerable systems without requiring user interaction. From the available information, it is clear that the cybersecurity community responded swiftly, with Microsoft issuing a patch for the SMB vulnerability in March 2017, just before the Shadow Brokers' release.

However, many systems worldwide remained unpatched, and within weeks of the release, the EternalBlue exploit was used in the WannaCry ransomware attack, which affected hundreds of thousands of systems across more than 150 countries. Governments, law enforcement agencies, and private sector companies scrambled to contain the ransomware spread, with some organizations suffering critical disruptions to their operations, particularly in the healthcare sector. The U.S. government and NSA did not officially acknowledge the leak at that time. Still, it was widely understood that the tools were part of a stockpile of cyberweapons developed for offensive purposes.

Cybersecurity firms worked closely with affected organizations to patch vulnerabilities, mitigate the impact of the tools, and prevent further exploitation. The involvement of law enforcement agencies, such as the FBI, was critical in investigating the origin of the Shadow Brokers and tracing the use of the stolen tools in subsequent cyberattacks.

Assessing the Impact

The immediate impact of the Shadow Brokers' release of NSA tools was felt across multiple sectors. The exposure of advanced state-developed exploits caused significant disruptions, particularly in organizations that had not yet patched their systems. The WannaCry ransomware attack, which leveraged the EternalBlue exploit, was one of the most damaging incidents linked to the Shadow Brokers' release, causing an estimated four billion dollars in damages globally. Hospitals, businesses, and government agencies were paralyzed as the ransomware locked users out of their systems and demanded payment in cryptocurrency for the decryption of files.

Beyond the financial cost, the reputational damage to the NSA was severe. The leak raised questions about the security of state-developed cyber weapons and the risks associated with stockpiling exploits that, if exposed, could be weaponized by adversaries. Additionally, the leak had long-term consequences for the cybersecurity landscape, as many of the tools released by the Shadow Brokers continued to be used in subsequent attacks, including the NotPetya ransomware incident.

For governments and organizations, the breach forced a reevaluation of their cybersecurity posture, particularly regarding patch management and vulnerability disclosure. The release of these tools demonstrated the dangers of relying on outdated or unpatched systems, as even a single vulnerability could lead to widespread damage if exploited.

Lessons Learned and Takeaways

The Shadow Brokers' release of NSA tools highlighted several critical lessons for the cybersecurity community. One of the most important takeaways is the need for timely patching of vulnerabilities. The information shows that many systems affected by the EternalBlue exploit were left vulnerable due to delayed or incomplete patching. Organizations must prioritize updating their systems to address known vulnerabilities, particularly those that could be exploited by advanced tools.

Another key lesson is the importance of transparency and responsible disclosure. The fact that the NSA had been aware of the SMB vulnerability before the Shadow Brokers' release raised concerns about the ethical implications of stockpiling cyberweapons. Governments and security agencies must balance the need for offensive capabilities with the potential risks to global cybersecurity. The fallout from the leak demonstrated the consequences of failing to secure and manage these tools properly.

Finally, the case underscored the need for stronger international cooperation in cybersecurity. The global impact of the WannaCry attack and other incidents tied to the Shadow Brokers' release highlighted the interconnected nature of modern cyber threats. Governments, private sector companies, and cybersecurity firms must collaborate to share intelligence, coordinate response efforts, and develop frameworks for mitigating the risks posed by state-sponsored and criminal cyber actors.

Case Study Summary

The Shadow Brokers' release of NSA hacking tools in 2016 and 2017 had profound implications for global cybersecurity. The exposure of sophisticated state-developed exploits, particularly EternalBlue, led to widespread damage, including the devastating WannaCry ransomware attack. Key takeaways from this case include the importance of timely patching, the ethical considerations of stockpiling cyberweapons, and the need for international collaboration to address the growing threat of advanced cyberattacks. The legacy of this incident continues to shape how governments and organizations approach vulnerability management and cybersecurity strategies in the face of increasingly sophisticated threats.

HIDDEN COBRA—FASTCASH CAMPAIGNS (2016–2018)

Between 2016 and 2018, the North Korean state-sponsored hacking group *Hidden Cobra*, or Lazarus Group, launched the FASTCash campaigns, manipulating financial messaging systems to enable fraudulent automated teller machine (ATM) cashouts globally. These attacks targeted financial institutions, primarily in developing nations with weaker cybersecurity defenses, allowing the hackers to withdraw millions of dollars in cash from ATMs across multiple countries in hours. The FASTCash campaigns represent a sophisticated and well-coordinated cyberattack, exploiting weaknesses in banking systems that process financial transactions, particularly those involving the international financial messaging system, SWIFT.

At the time of the attacks, the global financial sector was increasingly digitized, with ATMs and electronic transaction processing systems becoming key targets for cybercriminals. The reliance on financial messaging networks and outdated security systems in certain institutions made them vulnerable to large-scale attacks. The primary stakeholders involved in the FASTCash campaigns were the financial institutions affected, the cybersecurity firms investigating the breaches, law enforcement agencies, and international governments concerned with the threat posed by North Korean cyber operations.

Unfolding the Attack

The FASTCash campaigns unfolded through a meticulous and well-planned series of actions designed to exploit vulnerabilities in the financial messaging systems used by targeted banks. Hidden Cobra began their attack by infiltrating the banks' networks through spear-phishing emails or exploiting known vulnerabilities in outdated software. From the information available, it is assumed that the attackers used malware to access the banks' internal networks and manipulate the payment switch applications that facilitate ATM transactions. Once inside these systems, they could intercept and manipulate transaction approval messages, allowing unauthorized cash withdrawals from ATMs.

The attackers' ability to bypass the financial institutions' security protocols was critical to the attack. From the information available, it appears that Hidden Cobra gained control over the systems responsible for approving or denying ATM transactions, creating fraudulent approvals that enabled accomplices stationed at ATMs in various countries to withdraw cash. The timeline of the FASTCash campaigns indicates that Hidden Cobra spent weeks, if not months, in the victim networks, preparing for the coordinated cashout events. On the day of the attack, they executed simultaneous withdrawals from multiple ATMs, often overwhelming the banks' systems before the fraud could be detected.

Detection and Response Efforts

The FASTCash campaigns went undetected due significantly to the attackers' sophisticated techniques and deep understanding of banking systems. Financial institutions typically became aware of the attack only after the fraudulent ATM withdrawals were underway. It is fair to assume that the campaign was initially detected by anomalies in transaction processing and alerts raised by ATM networks showing unusual cash withdrawals across multiple countries in a short period.

Once detected, affected institutions worked swiftly to halt the fraudulent withdrawals, but millions of dollars had already been stolen when the attacks were fully mitigated. Cybersecurity firms like FireEye and law enforcement agencies like the U.S. Secret Service and Interpol became involved in the investigation. These organizations worked together to trace the source of the attacks and uncover the tools and malware used by Hidden Cobra. The response included patching vulnerabilities in financial messaging systems and issuing warnings to financial institutions worldwide about the methods employed in the FASTCash campaigns.

Assessing the Impact

The immediate impact of the FASTCash campaigns was the loss of millions of dollars in fraudulent ATM withdrawals, causing significant financial damage to the affected banks. Beyond the financial loss, these campaigns exposed critical weaknesses in the security of financial messaging systems, particularly in banks with outdated infrastructure. The global nature of the attacks also raised concerns about the vulnerability of international financial systems, prompting banks worldwide to reevaluate their security measures.

The long-term consequences of the FASTCash campaigns included reputational damage to the affected institutions, which had to reassure customers and regulators that they were addressing the vulnerabilities exploited by the attackers. For North Korea, the attacks were believed to be part of a broader strategy to generate revenue for the regime amid international sanctions, thus highlighting the growing use of cybercrime as a tool of statecraft. The campaigns also intensified efforts by governments and cybersecurity organizations to defend critical financial infrastructure against similar attacks in the future.

Lessons Learned and Takeaways

The FASTCash campaigns highlight important lessons for the financial sector and cybersecurity professionals. One of the key takeaways is the need for financial institutions to regularly update and secure their systems, especially those handling sensitive financial transactions. The information shows that many banks targeted by Hidden Cobra had outdated software and insufficient security protocols, making them vulnerable to sophisticated attacks. Implementing stronger authentication mechanisms, encryption, and regular security audits can help prevent similar incidents in the future.

Another important lesson is the value of proactive monitoring and anomaly detection in financial systems. The FASTCash campaigns could have been mitigated if banks had more robust real-time monitoring systems to detect unusual transaction patterns and respond to them quickly. Furthermore, the global nature of these attacks underscores the importance of international cooperation between law enforcement agencies, financial institutions, and cybersecurity firms in sharing intelligence and responding to emerging threats.

The FASTCash campaigns also serve as a reminder of the growing threat posed by state-sponsored cybercrime. As nation-states increasingly turn to cyberattacks to achieve financial and political goals, organizations must be prepared to defend against highly sophisticated APT groups with significant resources. For cybersecurity professionals, the lessons learned from the FAST-Cash campaigns are crucial for developing strategies to protect financial systems and prevent future large-scale cyber heists.

Case Study Summary

The Hidden Cobra FASTCash campaigns (2016–2018) represent one of the most audacious examples of cybercrime targeting the global financial system. By manipulating financial messaging systems, the attackers orchestrated coordinated ATM cashouts, stealing millions of dollars and exposing critical vulnerabilities in banking infrastructure. Key takeaways from this case include the importance of securing financial messaging systems, implementing proactive monitoring and anomaly detection, and strengthening international collaboration to combat state-sponsored cybercrime. The lessons learned from these attacks continue to shape how financial institutions and cybersecurity professionals approach the defense of critical financial infrastructure.

LAZARUS GROUP—BANGLADESH BANK HEIST (2016)

In February 2016, the world witnessed one of the most audacious and sophisticated cyberattacks in modern history when the *Lazarus Group*, a North Korean state-sponsored hacking group, attempted to steal nearly one billion dollars from the Bangladesh Bank via fraudulent SWIFT transactions. The group ultimately succeeded in transferring 81 million dollars before their activity was discovered, making this one of the largest cyber heists to date. The stolen funds were transferred to accounts in the Philippines and eventually laundered through casinos, making the recovery of the money exceptionally difficult. The attack exposed critical vulnerabilities in the international banking system, particularly the SWIFT network, which facilitates secure financial messaging between banks.

At the time, the Bangladesh Bank operated with standard security measures, but like many financial institutions, it relied heavily on trust in the security of the SWIFT network. The heist sent shockwaves through the global economic system, as it raised concerns about the security of transactions facilitated by the infrastructure meant to ensure the safe transfer of billions of dollars daily. The key stakeholders included the Bangladesh Bank, the SWIFT network, the Federal Reserve Bank of New York (which processed fraudulent transactions), law enforcement agencies, and global financial institutions.

Unfolding the Attack

The Bangladesh Bank heist unfolded over several months, beginning with the initial compromise of the bank's network. From the information available, it is assumed that the Lazarus Group gained access through a phishing attack that targeted key individuals within the bank. The attackers used this foothold to install malware, which allowed them to monitor the bank's operations for weeks, studying how the SWIFT messaging system was used and gathering the necessary credentials to initiate fraudulent transactions. Going by the data I obtained, I can assume the Lazarus Group meticulously planned their attack, understanding the precise mechanics of how large international transfers were processed.

The heist occurred in early February 2016, when the hackers sent 35 fraudulent transfer requests to the Federal Reserve Bank of New York, attempting to transfer nearly one billion dollars from the Bangladesh Bank's account. Due to a typographical error in one of the requests and the intervention of financial institutions in the Philippines and Sri Lanka, only five of the requests were processed, totaling 81 million dollars. The stolen funds were transferred to accounts in the Philippines, where they were quickly laundered through local casinos. The rest of the requests were flagged and halted, sparing the bank from losing the full amount.

Detection and Response Efforts

The detection of the heist was delayed, as the attackers had carefully timed the fraudulent transfers to occur over a weekend when banking activity would be minimal. From what I could gather, the Bangladesh Bank first noticed the missing funds when its internal systems flagged the discrepancy in its SWIFT transaction logs. As previously stated, by the time the bank realized the extent of the breach, the attackers had already transferred 81 million dollars out of their accounts. Immediate attempts to recall the funds were unsuccessful since much of the money had already been laundered through casinos in the Philippines.

Once the breach was identified, the Bangladesh Bank contacted the SWIFT network, the Federal Reserve Bank of New York, and local law enforcement agencies to initiate an investigation. The recovery process proved difficult because the attackers had exploited loopholes in local financial systems that allowed the funds to be rapidly withdrawn and laundered. International law enforcement agencies, including Interpol and the FBI, became involved, though recovering the stolen funds was complicated by the involvement of unregulated financial systems in the Philippines. Meanwhile, the Bangladesh Bank faced intense scrutiny over its cybersecurity measures, leading to reforms and strengthened security protocols within the institution.

Assessing the Impact

The immediate impact of the Bangladesh Bank heist was both financial and reputational. The loss of 81 million dollars was a devastating blow to the bank, which had relied on the security of the SWIFT network to protect its assets. The heist also exposed weaknesses in the global financial system, particularly the ease with which attackers could exploit vulnerabilities in one part of the world to steal funds from another. The attack highlighted the need for stronger security measures and protocols for SWIFT to prevent unauthorized access to its messaging systems.

Beyond the financial loss, the Bangladesh Bank heist had far-reaching consequences for the global banking industry. Many financial institutions were forced to reevaluate their security protocols, particularly in relation to the SWIFT network. SWIFT implemented a series of security upgrades, requiring member banks to adopt stronger cybersecurity measures. The attack also raised concerns about the role of state-sponsored hacking groups since the

Lazarus Group was linked to North Korea's broader efforts to fund its regime through illicit activities, including cybercrime.

Lessons Learned and Takeaways

The Bangladesh Bank heist offers critical lessons for the cybersecurity and financial communities. One of the key takeaways is the importance of securing not just internal systems but also the interfaces with external networks, such as SWIFT. From the information available, it is clear that the attackers were able to exploit weaknesses in both the bank's internal cybersecurity and the broader SWIFT infrastructure. Ensuring that all access points are protected with MFA, stronger encryption, and regular monitoring is essential for preventing similar incidents in the future.

Another important lesson from this attack is the need for proactive monitoring and anomaly detection. The fraudulent SWIFT transactions could have been detected earlier if the bank had used more robust monitoring tools to flag unusual transaction patterns. Additionally, the timing of the attack, which took advantage of weekend downtime, highlights the importance of maintaining vigilance during off-peak hours, when many cyberattacks are launched to avoid immediate detection.

The heist also underscores the growing role of state-sponsored cybercrime in the global financial system. The Lazarus Group's ability to orchestrate such a complex and high-stakes attack demonstrates the increasing sophistication of APT groups, which often combine cyber espionage with financially motivated attacks. For cybersecurity professionals, this case serves as a reminder that protecting financial systems requires constant vigilance, regular updates to security protocols, and close collaboration between governments, financial institutions, and law enforcement agencies.

Case Study Summary

The Bangladesh Bank heist by the Lazarus Group in 2016 was one of modern history's most brazen and successful cyberattacks. The theft of 81 million dollars via fraudulent SWIFT transactions exposed critical vulnerabilities in the bank's internal systems and the global financial infrastructure. Key takeaways from this case include the importance of securing external network interfaces, implementing proactive monitoring and anomaly detection, and preparing for the increasing role of state-sponsored cybercrime. The lessons learned from this attack continue to shape cybersecurity practices in the financial sector as institutions work to prevent future incidents of this scale and complexity.

CHAPTER CONCLUSION

The case studies presented in this chapter highlight the evolving and persistent nature of APTs and their significant impact on global cybersecurity. From APT1's widespread cyber espionage to the Shadow Brokers' release of NSA tools, these attacks showcase the increasing sophistication of cyber adversaries, often backed by state sponsorship. The common thread throughout these incidents is the attackers' ability to remain undetected for extended periods, using a range of techniques such as spear-phishing, zero-day exploits, and custom malware. These APTs target critical sectors such as government, healthcare, technology, and infrastructure, underscoring the need for comprehensive cybersecurity strategies beyond traditional defense mechanisms.

One of the key lessons from these case studies is the importance of proactive detection and response. In many of these attacks, organizations were compromised long before the breach was discovered, allowing attackers to exfiltrate vast amounts of sensitive data. From the information available, I have extrapolated details about how detection and response efforts unfolded based on media reports and industry analyses. In some cases, organizations were unprepared to deal with the level of sophistication displayed by these attackers, leading to devastating consequences. This highlights the necessity for cybersecurity professionals to invest in advanced detection tools, threat intelligence sharing, and continuous monitoring to identify anomalies before attackers can fully exploit their access.

For today's cybersecurity professionals, these APTs serve as a stark reminder of the multifaceted nature of modern cyber threats. Defending against APTs requires technological solutions, strong cybersecurity governance, regular employee training to combat phishing, and robust incident response plans. Cybersecurity teams must also be prepared for the complexity of these threats, which often involve a combination of espionage, financial gain, and political motivations. By staying vigilant, continuously updating systems, and collaborating with both private and public sectors, cybersecurity professionals can better defend against these persistent threats.

In conclusion, the key takeaway from this chapter is that no organization, whether public or private, is immune to the risk posed by APTs. These attacks highlight the critical need for a layered defense strategy, which includes proactive monitoring, timely patching of vulnerabilities, and the adoption of advanced security measures. As APTs continue to evolve, the role of cybersecurity professionals becomes more critical than ever, requiring constant adaptation to emerging threats and an emphasis on securing the ever-expanding digital landscape.

7

POLITICAL AND GEOPOLITICAL HACKS

When it comes to politics, we're all used to mudslinging, backdoor deals, and debates that go on longer than a rebooted movie franchise. But throw in some hackers and a few well-placed phishing emails, and you've got a political thriller worthy of its own Netflix special. Cyberattacks on elections, government agencies, and political campaigns sound like something out of a spy novel, but they're more common than we would like to think. In the digital age, even the most secure government websites can become as vulnerable as when your parents clicked on an email promising them a free vacation to the Bahamas.

Joking aside, the stakes in these political cyberattacks are incredibly high. Elections can be influenced, public trust eroded, and national security compromised, all with a few well-targeted lines of code. This chapter delves into some of the most significant political cyberattacks over the past decade (see Figure 7.1). These cases reveal a new reality where cyber warfare and politics have become deeply intertwined. It is no longer just about nation-states flexing their military muscles or diplomats trading barbs; today, governments and political organizations must defend themselves against adversaries armed with malware, botnets, and disinformation campaigns.

Throughout this chapter, I have detailed several high-profile political hacks, from the infamous Democratic National Committee (DNC) breach to the Qatar News Agency hack that ignited a diplomatic crisis. While much of what we know comes from media reports and available data, I've had to extrapolate certain details about response and detection efforts when such information is sparse or nonexistent. In many cases, we can infer strategies based on the scale and nature of the attack. Still, these incidents also highlight the need for transparency and better information sharing in the cybersecurity world.

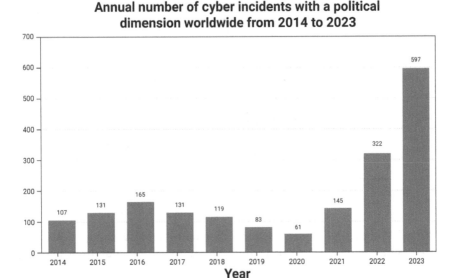

Figure 7.1   The number of politically motivated cyberattacks (*source*: Statista Search Department)

Understanding how these attacks unfolded is crucial for professionals defending against them.

This chapter aims to provide a comprehensive look at these attacks, analyze the tactics used by the perpetrators, and offer lessons that today's cybersecurity professionals can apply. By studying how these breaches occurred, how the victims responded (or failed to), and what the long-term consequences were, we can better prepare for the future. After all, in cybersecurity, being proactive is the name of the game, and learning from the past is our best tool for staying one step ahead of the next political hack.

WHAT IS A POLITICAL HACK?

A political hack refers to a cyberattack targeting individuals, organizations, or systems involved in political processes or government operations. These attacks are often designed to disrupt, influence, or undermine political activities, elections, or governmental functions. Unlike traditional cyberattacks aimed at financial gain or espionage, political hacks directly impact public discourse, democratic processes, and governance stability.

Political hacks frequently involve the theft or manipulation of sensitive information, such as emails, confidential government documents, or voter data, used to influence public opinion or destabilize political institutions. A well-known example is the 2016 DNC hack, where internal emails were stolen and leaked to the public, sparking political controversy, and impacting election outcomes. Such hacks are often employed by nation-states or politically motivated groups seeking to influence foreign or domestic politics, often destabilizing or manipulating public perception.

The rise of political hacks has been facilitated by the increasing reliance on digital systems in government operations and elections and the growing use of social media platforms for political discourse. These hacks often target vulnerabilities in government networks, campaign systems, or social media accounts to spread disinformation, manipulate narratives, or sway voters. In many cases, the true impact of a political hack is not just the immediate breach but the long-term effect it has on public trust in political institutions and electoral processes. Political hacks have become critical in modern geopolitical conflicts as cyber capabilities evolve.

The following chart illustrates the timeline associated with the attacks that will be explored in this chapter (see Figure 7.2).

GEORGIAN GOVERNMENT WEBSITES ATTACKS (2008)

The 2008 cyberattacks on Georgian government websites represent one of the first notable instances where cyber warfare was used with conventional military operations. These attacks occurred during the Russo-Georgian War, a five-day conflict between Russia and Georgia over the breakaway regions of South Ossetia and Abkhazia. As Russian troops advanced on the ground, a coordinated cyber campaign was launched, targeting key Georgian government websites and media outlets. The attacks aimed to disrupt communications, spread propaganda, and undermine public morale, marking a new era of cyber conflict that integrated kinetic and digital operations.

Georgia, a post-Soviet state, was emerging as a focal point in the geopolitical struggle between Russia and Western-aligned states. By 2008, the country had modernized its telecommunications infrastructure, but its cybersecurity defenses were still nascent. The attacks primarily focused on government websites, media outlets, and financial institutions, disrupting Georgia's ability to communicate both internally and with the international community. The technological landscape and geopolitical tensions made Georgia a prime

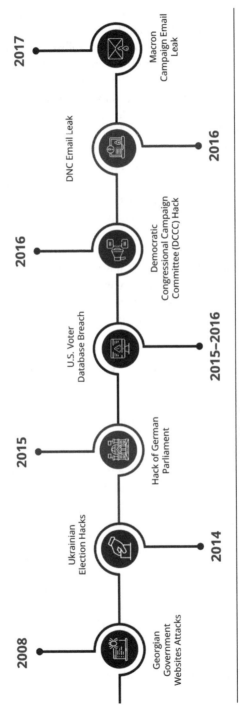

Figure 7.2 The timeline of attacks discussed in this chapter

target for a multifaceted attack that combined military, political, and cyber elements.

Key stakeholders included the Georgian government, its military forces, the Russian government, and global audiences monitoring the conflict. Additionally, international cybersecurity firms and NATO became involved in the aftermath as they sought to analyze the attacks and assist Georgia in rebuilding its digital infrastructure. The use of cyberattacks in this conflict signaled a shift in how nation-states could wield cyber capabilities to augment traditional warfare.

Unfolding the Attack

The cyberattacks against Georgia unfolded rapidly in the days leading up to and during the armed conflict. It is believed that the attackers used distributed denial-of-service (DDoS) attacks as their primary disruption method. By overwhelming servers with massive amounts of traffic, the attackers were able to render several key Georgian websites inaccessible, including those of the president, parliament, and foreign ministry. From the information available, it can be assumed that the attackers likely utilized botnets to amplify the scale of the DDoS attacks, a common method used by state-sponsored actors at the time.

The first phase of the attacks began in late July 2008 with their escalation on August 7, the day before the war officially started. Websites were defaced with images comparing Georgian President Mikheil Saakashvili to Adolf Hitler, signaling that the cyber campaign was aimed not just at disrupting communications but also at discrediting the Georgian leadership. The second phase, which began when Russian forces entered Georgian territory, intensified the disruption of government services, with hackers targeting media outlets and financial institutions. At this stage, the attackers focused on cutting off Georgian access to critical information sources, creating confusion and chaos among the population.

While the exact entry point for the attacks remains unclear, the attackers likely exploited known vulnerabilities in Georgia's information technology (IT) infrastructure, which was unprepared for large-scale cyber aggression. The use of relatively simple methods, such as DDoS attacks and website defacements, suggests that the attackers prioritized speed and disruption over stealth. However, the coordination between cyber and physical military operations indicates a level of planning and strategic alignment that points to the involvement of state actors.

Detection and Response Efforts

Detection of the cyberattacks came quickly, as the disruptions to government websites and communications were immediately apparent. However, Georgia could not mount an effective response in real time. Initial response efforts were chaotic, as Georgian IT teams worked to restore access to critical websites while under continuous assault. At the time, Georgia had limited cybersecurity capabilities, and the scale of the attacks overwhelmed its existing infrastructure. From this situation, we can infer that the attackers took advantage of Georgia's relatively weak cyber defenses, exploiting technical and procedural vulnerabilities.

Georgia sought external assistance from international cybersecurity firms and NATO's Cooperative Cyber Defence Centre of Excellence, which offered technical support and advice. One of the more creative responses involved Georgia hosting some of its critical websites on servers located in other countries, including Poland and Estonia, to maintain access to essential communication channels. This response strategy highlights the importance of international collaboration during cyber crises, particularly for smaller nations with limited resources.

Despite these efforts, the attacks continued throughout the conflict, and the Georgian government struggled to regain full control of its online infrastructure until after the physical hostilities had subsided. The attackers, having achieved their objectives of disruption and disinformation, gradually wound down the cyber campaign once the military operations came to a close. Law enforcement involvement was minimal, as attribution to specific attackers proved challenging, given the anonymity of cyber operations.

Assessing the Impact

The immediate impact of the cyberattacks on Georgia was significant, especially in disrupting government operations and public communications. The DDoS attacks crippled access to critical websites, leaving citizens and international observers in the dark about official government actions and updates during the conflict. This information blackout created confusion and uncertainty, amplifying the psychological effects of the physical military invasion. The attacks also succeeded in spreading disinformation, with the defacement of websites and dissemination of propaganda aimed at undermining the Georgian government's credibility.

In the long term, the cyberattacks damaged Georgia's digital infrastructure and highlighted the country's vulnerability to cyber aggression. The attack exposed several weaknesses in Georgia's cybersecurity posture, including the lack of redundancy in its IT systems, inadequate cybersecurity training for personnel, and limited collaboration with international cybersecurity experts before the conflict. The incident also served as a wake-up call for many other countries in the region, who realized that cyberattacks could be used as a prelude or complement to traditional warfare.

The broader geopolitical impact was also profound. The coordinated nature of the attacks suggested that cyber warfare would become a critical element of future conflicts between nation-states, particularly in regions of geopolitical tension. The Georgian cyberattack became a case study of how digital infrastructure could be targeted with military action, influencing how countries approached offensive and defensive cyber capabilities in the following years.

Lessons Learned and Takeaways

The attacks on the Georgian government website provided several key lessons for the global cybersecurity community. First, the attacks underscored the importance of preparing for cyberattacks in geopolitical conflict. For governments, particularly those in conflict-prone regions, building resilient cyber infrastructure is as crucial as maintaining traditional military defenses. The attacks demonstrated that the digital domain can be a critical battleground in modern warfare, requiring a holistic approach to national security that includes both physical and cyber elements.

Another important lesson is the value of international cooperation in responding to cyber incidents. Georgia's decision to relocate some of its critical websites to servers in other countries proved to be a highly effective way to mitigate the impact of the attacks. This approach highlights the need for international partnerships and the importance of working with allies to protect critical infrastructure in times of crisis.

Finally, the attacks revealed the necessity of investing in cybersecurity training and preparedness. Georgia's lack of readiness for a large-scale cyberattack left it vulnerable, and the chaotic response efforts underscored the need for more robust incident response plans. Moving forward, governments and organizations must prioritize cybersecurity training and ensure they have the resources and expertise to respond effectively to cyber incidents.

Case Study Summary

The 2008 Georgian government website attacks represent a milestone in the history of cyber warfare, illustrating how cyberattacks can be used with military operations to disrupt communications, spread propaganda, and

continued

undermine national morale. The coordinated nature of the attacks, which coincided with Russia's military invasion of Georgia, highlighted the growing importance of cybersecurity in modern conflicts.

Key takeaways from this case include the critical role of cyber preparedness in national security, the importance of international collaboration during cyber crises, and the necessity of investing in robust incident response plans. The attacks on Georgia served as an early warning for other nations, signaling that cyber warfare was no longer a hypothetical threat but a reality that would shape the future of geopolitical conflicts. As a case study, it provides valuable insights into how nation-states can defend against similar attacks in the future, emphasizing the need for vigilance, resilience, and proactive cybersecurity measures.

UKRAINIAN ELECTION HACKS (2014)

The Ukrainian election hacks of 2014 provide a stark example of how cyberattacks can be used to disrupt and manipulate democratic processes, particularly in a politically volatile environment. In the wake of Russia's annexation of Crimea and the ongoing conflict in Eastern Ukraine, the 2014 Ukrainian presidential election was seen as a critical test of the country's sovereignty and ability to conduct free and fair elections. The stakes were high as Ukraine sought to elect a new president following the ousting of Viktor Yanukovych. In this context, a series of cyberattacks targeted the Ukrainian election system, aiming to undermine the legitimacy of the election and spread confusion.

The technological landscape in Ukraine at the time was relatively vulnerable, with outdated cybersecurity measures in place and limited resources to defend against large-scale cyberattacks. Many government systems were not equipped to handle sophisticated threats, making them prime targets for disruption. The attacks highlighted the growing use of cyber warfare as a geopolitical tool, with nation-states exploiting the vulnerabilities of weaker nations to achieve their strategic objectives.

Key stakeholders in this case included the Ukrainian Central Election Commission (CEC), political candidates, international observers, and foreign governments. Russia, widely suspected of being behind the attacks, played a central role in the geopolitical tensions surrounding the election, though direct attribution of the attacks remains a topic of debate.

Unfolding the Attack

The Ukrainian election hacks unfolded over several stages, beginning with an initial compromise of the CEC's systems. From the information available, it can be assumed that the attackers used spear-phishing emails to access internal networks. These emails likely contained malicious links or attachments that, once opened, allowed the attackers to install malware on critical election infrastructure systems. The malware enabled them to manipulate voter data and disrupt the CEC's ability to report accurate results.

One of the most significant aspects of the attack occurred just days before the election. Hackers infiltrated the CEC's website and uploaded false results that showed a fringe nationalist candidate, Dmytro Yarosh, as the frontrunner. This false data was set to be broadcast on Ukrainian television stations as the official result of the election. Fortunately, cybersecurity experts and government officials detected and removed the fake results quickly, preventing their dissemination to the public.

The attack timeline reveals that, in addition to manipulating election results, the attackers also launched DDoS attacks against the CEC's systems. These attacks aimed to disrupt the reporting of real-time election data, creating further confusion and chaos. The attackers were able to cripple the CEC's infrastructure temporarily, delaying the reporting of official results and raising concerns about the election's integrity.

Detection and Response Efforts

The detection of the Ukrainian election hacks came as the CEC and its cybersecurity partners noticed anomalies in their systems, particularly the unauthorized access to voter data and the tampering of election results. Ukrainian officials swiftly addressed the issue, working with domestic and international cybersecurity experts to remove the malware and secure the CEC's infrastructure. Removing the false election results from the CEC's website was a critical moment in the response efforts since it prevented the spread of disinformation at a crucial time.

External cybersecurity firms, including those from the United States and Europe, were brought in to assist with the investigation and response efforts. These firms helped identify the malware in the attacks and provided technical support to restore the CEC's systems. The collaboration between Ukrainian authorities and international experts highlighted the importance of cross-border cooperation in responding to cyberattacks on democratic institutions.

Despite successfully removing the false results, the attack raised alarms about the vulnerability of Ukraine's election infrastructure. The response efforts were largely reactive, with many improvements to the CEC's cybersecurity posture only implemented after the attack. The attack also underscored the challenges of defending against state-sponsored cyber operations, particularly in countries with limited cybersecurity capabilities.

Assessing the Impact

The immediate impact of the Ukrainian election hacks was significant in terms of public trust in the election process. Although the CEC prevented the false results from being broadcast, the attack raised doubts about the integrity of the election and heightened political tensions in an already unstable environment. The fact that hackers could manipulate election data, even temporarily, cast a shadow over the election and fueled suspicions of foreign interference.

The long-term consequences of the attack extended beyond the 2014 election. It warned other countries about the potential for cyberattacks to disrupt democratic processes, particularly in politically sensitive regions. The attack caused Ukraine to reassess its cybersecurity strategies, with the government investing in stronger defenses to protect future elections. The incident also spurred international dialogue about the need for global standards and cooperation to safeguard electoral systems from cyber threats.

Geopolitically, the attack further strained relations between Ukraine and Russia. Although Russia denied involvement, many cybersecurity experts and intelligence agencies attributed the attack to Russian state-sponsored groups, citing the timing of the hack and its alignment with Russian strategic interests in Ukraine. The incident highlighted the growing use of cyber warfare as a tool of political influence and underscored the importance of securing critical national infrastructure in an era of digital conflict.

Lessons Learned and Takeaways

The Ukrainian election hacks offer several important lessons for the global cybersecurity community. First, the attack emphasized the need for robust cybersecurity measures in election infrastructure. Countries must invest in securing their electoral systems, including voter databases and reporting mechanisms, to prevent unauthorized access and data manipulation. Stronger access controls, continuous monitoring, and regular security audits can help reduce the risk of similar attacks in the future.

Second, the attack demonstrated the importance of rapid detection and response. Ukrainian officials prevented the broadcast of false election results by detecting the breach in time, but this incident highlighted how close they came to a major disinformation disaster. Governments must prioritize the development of incident response plans and train election officials to recognize and respond to cyber threats quickly.

Finally, the attack revealed the importance of international cooperation in defending against cyberattacks on democratic institutions. The collaboration between Ukrainian authorities and foreign cybersecurity firms was essential in mitigating the attack's impact. Moving forward, governments must foster stronger international partnerships to share intelligence, resources, and best practices for securing elections against cyber threats.

Case Study Summary

The 2014 Ukrainian election hacks serve as a clear example of how cyber-attacks can be weaponized to disrupt democratic processes and create political instability. The attacks that targeted Ukraine's CEC just before a critical presidential election involved manipulating election data and DDoS attacks that were designed to undermine the election's credibility. Although the CEC did detect and remove the false results before they were broadcast, the attack raised significant concerns about the security of Ukraine's election infrastructure.

Key takeaways from this case include the importance of securing election systems against cyber threats, the need for rapid detection and response, and the value of international cooperation in responding to state-sponsored cyberattacks. The Ukrainian election hacks underscore the growing use of cyber warfare as a tool of geopolitical influence and serve as a warning to countries around the world to strengthen their defenses against future attacks on democratic institutions.

HACK OF GERMAN PARLIAMENT (BUNDESTAG) (2015)

The 2015 hack of the German Parliament, known as the Bundestag hack, marked a significant event in the history of cyberattacks against democratic institutions. The attack was a sophisticated, large-scale cyber-espionage operation targeting the Bundestag's internal network, leading to the exfiltration of up to 16 gigabytes of sensitive data. The attack took place amidst rising tensions between Western countries and Russia, and there are strong indications that Russian state-sponsored hackers were behind the breach, specifically the group *APT28*, also known as *Fancy Bear*.

The Bundestag is one of Germany's most critical political institutions, housing lawmakers and staff responsible for shaping the nation's policies and international relations. The timing of the attack—during a period when Europe was grappling with a range of political challenges, including the ongoing conflict in Ukraine—raised even more suspicions about the geopolitical motivations behind the breach. At the time of the attack, cybersecurity defenses in political institutions like the Bundestag were not as robust as today, making it a relatively easy target for advanced persistent threat (APT) groups looking to gather intelligence.

Key stakeholders in this case included the German government, specifically its lawmakers and cybersecurity agencies, as well as international allies and intelligence services monitoring the breach. The attack also had broader implications for Germany's relations with Russia, as evidence of Russian involvement fueled diplomatic tensions between the two nations.

Unfolding the Attack

The attack on the Bundestag began in early May 2015 when members of parliament and staff received phishing emails designed to look like official correspondence. From the data I was able to obtain, it is assumed that the emails contained malicious links that, once clicked on, deployed malware into the Bundestag's network. This method of spear-phishing is a common tactic used by APT groups to gain initial access to targeted systems by exploiting human vulnerabilities. The malware, once installed, created a backdoor that allowed the attackers to maintain persistent access to the network and exfiltrate data without immediate detection.

The attackers remained undetected for several weeks, accessing sensitive documents, emails, and internal communications. It is believed that their objective was to gather intelligence on German foreign and domestic policy, particularly concerning relations with Russia and the European Union. Given the attackers' ability to move laterally within the network, they were able to compromise multiple systems, suggesting a level of sophistication consistent with state-sponsored cyber espionage operations.

The breach was discovered in early June 2015 when IT staff detected unusual network activity. At this point, the attack had already inflicted significant damage, with large amounts of data exfiltrated to servers controlled by the attackers. The timeline of the attack shows that the attackers could maintain a foothold within the network for at least several weeks, highlighting the challenges of detecting and responding to advanced cyber threats in real time.

Detection and Response Efforts

The Bundestag hack was detected when IT security personnel noticed abnormal traffic patterns on the network. By the time the breach was discovered, the attackers had already siphoned off a considerable amount of data. The German government's initial response focused on containing the attack and preventing further data exfiltration. However, the complexity of the malware and the extent of the network infiltration made it difficult to completely remove the attackers from the system.

In response, German cybersecurity agencies worked closely with private sector experts and international partners to analyze the malware and assess the full scope of the breach. It can be inferred that the attack required a comprehensive network shutdown and overhaul since the Bundestag's IT systems were considered compromised. Law enforcement agencies, including the German Federal Office for Information Security (BSI), investigated the attack's origins, eventually linking it to APT28, a group believed to be associated with Russian military intelligence (GRU).

The response efforts highlighted several vulnerabilities in the Bundestag's cybersecurity posture, including insufficient monitoring and detection capabilities. In the aftermath of the attack, the German government strengthened its cybersecurity defenses, including improving threat detection systems, increasing cybersecurity awareness among lawmakers and staff, and fostering closer collaboration with international intelligence services.

Assessing the Impact

The immediate effects of the Bundestag hack were severe regarding data loss and operational disruption. Sensitive political information was stolen, including internal communications between lawmakers, policy documents, and classified data. The full scope of the exfiltrated data remains unclear. Still, it is believed that the attackers gained access to highly sensitive materials that could be used to influence or undermine German political decision making.

Beyond the operational impact, the attack also caused significant reputational damage to the Bundestag and raised questions about Germany's cybersecurity readiness. The breach underscored the vulnerability of democratic institutions to cyber espionage, particularly at a time when nation-states are increasingly using cyberattacks as tools of political influence. The incident also strained Germany's relationship with Russia, as mounting evidence pointed to Russian involvement in the attack. Although the Russian government denied any role in the breach, the attack fueled suspicions of Russian interference in European politics.

The long-term consequences of the hack included heightened awareness of the need for stronger cybersecurity measures within political institutions, not only in Germany but across Europe. The incident served as a wake-up call for governments worldwide to reassess their cybersecurity strategies and prepare for the growing threat of state-sponsored cyberattacks targeting critical national infrastructure.

Lessons Learned and Takeaways

Several important lessons emerged from the Bundestag hack. First, the attack underscored the critical importance of cybersecurity training and awareness, particularly for high-level political figures often targeted by phishing campaigns. Spear-phishing remains one of the most effective methods attackers use to gain access to sensitive systems, and the Bundestag attack demonstrated how human error can be exploited to achieve significant breaches.

Second, the attack highlighted the need for more robust network monitoring and threat detection capabilities. The attackers were able to move laterally within the Bundestag's network for weeks before being detected, suggesting that more advanced detection systems and continuous monitoring could have limited the damage. The German government implemented stricter cybersecurity protocols in response to the attack, including enhanced monitoring tools and regular security audits.

Finally, the geopolitical context of the attack revealed the growing use of cyber espionage as a tool of statecraft. The Bundestag hack is one example of how nation-states use cyberattacks to gather intelligence, influence political outcomes, and destabilize rival governments. Political institutions worldwide must recognize the importance of integrating cybersecurity into their national security strategies to protect themselves from future threats.

Case Study Summary

The 2015 Bundestag hack is a stark reminder of the growing threat of cyber espionage against democratic institutions. The attack, attributed to the Russian-affiliated APT28 group, involved a sophisticated spear-phishing campaign that gave attackers access to sensitive political data and communications. The breach caused significant disruption to the German parliament's operations and raised broader concerns about the vulnerability of political institutions to state-sponsored cyberattacks.

Key takeaways from this case include the importance of cybersecurity awareness, the need for advanced threat detection capabilities, and the geopolitical implications of cyber espionage. The Bundestag hack illustrates the evolving nature of cyber threats in the political arena and provides valuable lessons for governments worldwide in strengthening their defenses against state-sponsored cyber operations. As cyberattacks continue to play a central role in global conflicts, political institutions must remain vigilant and proactive in securing their digital infrastructure.

U.S. VOTER DATABASE BREACH (2015-2016)

The U.S. voter database breach of 2015–2016 represents a critical moment in the evolution of political and geopolitical cyberattacks, particularly concerning democratic processes. During this period, cyberattacks targeted voter registration databases in several U.S. states, exposing the vulnerabilities in election systems and raising concerns about the integrity of democratic elections. The breaches were part of a broader wave of cyber operations that took place in the run-up to the 2016 U.S. presidential election, prompting fears of foreign interference in election infrastructure. Although there is no definitive evidence that the breaches altered voter data or influenced the election outcome, they exposed gaps in the cybersecurity of electoral systems. They highlighted the increasing threat of cyberattacks on democratic institutions.

At the time of the breaches, the technological landscape in the United States was one of rapid digitalization, including integrating more electronic systems into election processes. Managed by state and local governments, voter registration databases were increasingly stored digitally, making them attractive targets for cyberattacks. Often underfunded and outdated, these systems were not designed to withstand the sophisticated cyberattacks that would follow. The potential risks to the integrity of election systems created a sense of urgency among security experts and government officials.

Key stakeholders in this case included state election officials, the U.S. Department of Homeland Security (DHS), law enforcement agencies, and cybersecurity firms. Voters were also impacted, as the breaches raised concerns about privacy and the potential misuse of personal data. The operation added to the mounting evidence of foreign state actors, particularly Russia, aiming to disrupt or undermine confidence in the U.S. electoral process.

Unfolding the Attack

The U.S. voter database breach unfolded over several months in 2015 and 2016, as cybercriminals targeted voter registration systems across multiple states. After studying the existing information, it can be assumed that attackers used a combination of phishing emails and vulnerabilities in state-level systems to gain unauthorized access to voter databases. In at least two confirmed instances, the attackers successfully exfiltrated data, obtaining sensitive information such as names, addresses, dates of birth, and, in some cases, partial social security numbers.

The initial entry point for the attack appeared to be phishing emails sent to election officials in various states. These emails contained malicious links or attachments that, once clicked, installed malware on the targeted systems. This allowed the attackers to move laterally within the network and gain access to voter databases. It is possible that the attackers also exploited weak passwords or outdated software, further highlighting the vulnerabilities in election infrastructure at the time.

When breaking down the timeline of the attacks, the first breach occurred in mid-2015. However, many states were unaware of the intrusion until the summer of 2016, when federal authorities, including DHS, began warning state governments about potential breaches. From the information available, it can be inferred that the attackers had ample time to extract data and potentially manipulate records, although no evidence of such manipulation was ever confirmed.

Detection and Response Efforts

Detection of the breaches was slow, primarily because many state election offices lacked the resources or capabilities to monitor their systems for suspicious activity. It wasn't until federal agencies, including DHS and the FBI became involved, that the full scope of the attack became clear. DHS alerted state governments, warning them of potential vulnerabilities in their election infrastructure and encouraging them to strengthen their cybersecurity measures. The FBI also investigated the breaches, concluding that foreign actors, likely associated with Russian intelligence, were behind the attacks.

State election officials responded by working with federal agencies and private cybersecurity firms to secure voter registration systems. Immediate response actions included patching known vulnerabilities, improving access controls, and conducting forensic analyses of the affected systems. DHS also offered states the designation of election systems as critical infrastructure, which provided additional resources and support for securing these systems. However, some states resisted federal involvement, citing concerns over states' rights and autonomy in managing elections.

Despite these efforts, the response was largely reactive, with many states implementing even stronger cybersecurity measures after the breaches. The incident highlighted the fragmented nature of election security in the United States, where each state is responsible for securing its systems, leading to varying preparedness and response capabilities.

Assessing the Impact

The immediate impact of the U.S. voter database breach was significant, although the attackers did not appear to have altered voter data or disrupted the election itself. The theft of personal voter information raised concerns about identity theft, the potential for voter suppression, and the misuse of personal data for targeted disinformation campaigns. The fact that voter databases had been compromised also eroded public trust in the security of election systems, contributing to a broader sense of unease surrounding the integrity of the 2016 U.S. presidential election.

In the long term, the breach had far-reaching consequences for election security in the United States. It spurred federal and state governments to reassess the security of their election infrastructure and prompted the development of new cybersecurity protocols to protect against similar attacks in the future. The designation of election systems as critical infrastructure in 2017 directly resulted from these concerns, allowing for greater federal involvement in protecting these systems. Additionally, the breach fueled ongoing debates about the role of foreign interference in democratic elections and the need for stronger international norms to prevent cyberattacks on election systems.

The breach also prompted increased collaboration between state and federal governments and private sector cybersecurity firms to detect and prevent future attacks. However, the fragmented nature of U.S. election security, with states retaining primary control over their systems, continues to present challenges for ensuring a coordinated and consistent response to cyber threats.

Lessons Learned and Takeaways

The U.S. voter database breach provided several critical lessons for election security and the broader field of cybersecurity. First, the attack underscored the importance of securing election infrastructure at both the state and federal levels. Many state election systems were underfunded and lacked the cybersecurity measures to defend against sophisticated cyberattacks. Moving forward, state governments must prioritize cybersecurity in their election budgets, while the federal government must continue providing resources and support.

Second, the attack highlighted the role of phishing and social engineering in gaining access to critical systems. The use of phishing emails to trick election officials into compromising their systems demonstrated how human error can be exploited to devastating effect. Strengthening cybersecurity awareness training for election officials and implementing stronger authentication measures became key takeaways for improving election security.

Finally, the breach revealed the geopolitical dimensions of cyberattacks on democratic institutions. The suspected involvement of foreign actors, particularly Russia, raised concerns about the potential for cyberattacks to undermine democratic processes and disrupt elections worldwide. The U.S. voter database breach is a cautionary tale for other nations, highlighting the need for robust election security measures and international cooperation to prevent foreign interference.

Case Study Summary

The U.S. voter database breach of 2015–2016 is a significant example of how cyberattacks can target democratic processes and election infrastructure. The attack, which involved the theft of sensitive voter information from several state databases, raised serious concerns about the security of U.S. elections and the potential for foreign interference in the democratic process. Although no data manipulation was found, the breach exposed significant vulnerabilities in the U.S. election system and prompted a nationwide reassessment of election security practices.

Key takeaways from this case include the need for stronger cybersecurity measures at both the state and federal levels, the importance of defending against phishing and social engineering attacks, and the geopolitical risks associated with cyberattacks on democratic institutions. The U.S. voter database breach is a stark reminder of the evolving nature of cyber threats and the critical importance of protecting election infrastructure in an increasingly digital world.

DEMOCRATIC CONGRESSIONAL CAMPAIGN COMMITTEE HACK (2016)

The Democratic Congressional Campaign Committee (DCCC) hack in 2016 represents one of the most notable cyber incidents in modern political history, primarily because it unfolded during a crucial election cycle in the United States. The DCCC, the official campaign arm for Democratic members of the House of Representatives, found itself the target of a sophisticated cyberattack that, upon investigation, appeared to be aimed at influencing the 2016 U.S. elections. This hack is significant not only because of its immediate political implications but also because it highlights the increasing use of cyber warfare in political and geopolitical arenas.

The DCCC, founded in 1866, raises funds and provides strategic advice to Democratic congressional candidates. In 2016, with the U.S. political landscape already deeply polarized, the committee played a pivotal role in managing congressional races that would determine the balance of power in Congress.

The attack on this key political organization came when cybersecurity became an ever-present concern, particularly following the revelations about the 2016 hack of the DNC, a closely related political entity.

In the broader technological landscape, 2016 was marked by an increasing awareness of cyberattacks aimed at undermining democratic institutions. Cybersecurity experts had already flagged the potential for politically motivated attacks, especially with heightened tensions between the United States and Russia, which many assumed to be involved in such operations. The DCCC hack involved various stakeholders, from political operatives to cybersecurity professionals, law enforcement, and even international intelligence agencies. Its far-reaching consequences would eventually be felt across the political spectrum.

Unfolding the Attack

The attack on the DCCC began with a targeted phishing campaign, a common yet highly effective method employed by cyber adversaries. It can be assumed that the attackers crafted highly convincing emails that lured recipients into unknowingly providing their login credentials. This allowed the attackers to access the DCCC's internal network, much like the techniques used in the simultaneous hack of the DNC. The phishing campaign succeeded due to a mix of well-researched social engineering tactics and the human vulnerabilities that such attacks often exploit.

Once inside the DCCC's network, the attackers navigated sensitive areas of the organization's IT infrastructure. It is reasonable to assume that the attackers exfiltrated significant amounts of data, including campaign strategies, internal communications, and donor information. The attackers then utilized sophisticated malware to maintain access, allowing them to observe and collect data over a prolonged period without detection. One hallmark of this attack was its subtlety; the hackers ensured their presence remained hidden for as long as possible, likely gathering intelligence in preparation for a strategically timed release.

The breach is believed to have occurred in April 2016, though it wasn't publicly revealed until later. During this time, the attackers may have been probing for weaknesses and collecting information they deemed valuable for release. The leak of this information, alongside the DNC emails, was disseminated via platforms like WikiLeaks and was timed to have maximum political impact. The attackers exploited not just the technological vulnerabilities of the DCCC but also the hyper-partisan political climate of 2016, which amplified the effects of the breach.

Detection and Response Efforts

The detection of the DCCC hack came relatively late in the process, as is common with APTs of this nature. Initial signs of the breach were discovered in June 2016, but it wasn't until cybersecurity experts were called in to investigate that the full scale of the attack became evident. The cybersecurity firm CrowdStrike, which had already been working with the DNC, played a significant role in identifying the methods used by the attackers and attributed the hack to the same group responsible for the DNC attack, likely the Russian-affiliated group Fancy Bear (APT28). This finding was based on the tools and techniques employed by the hackers, which bore striking similarities to previous Russian state-sponsored attacks.

Upon discovery, the DCCC moved quickly to mitigate the damage, though much of the stolen information had already been exfiltrated. The DCCC's response included severing affected network connections, removing the malware, and enhancing security protocols across the organization. However, the public dissemination of stolen documents severely limited cybersecurity measures' impact in mitigating the overall damage. The attackers had achieved their goal: leaking sensitive information at a politically advantageous time, thus stirring public distrust and disrupting the campaign process.

External entities, including U.S. law enforcement agencies and intelligence organizations, were brought in to assess the scope of the attack and trace its origins. Although cybersecurity firms were quick to point to Russian involvement, definitive attribution remains difficult in cyberattacks due to the complexities of tracing online activities. Nevertheless, the broader investigation by U.S. authorities and intelligence agencies continued long after the election, seeking to uncover the full extent of foreign interference in the 2016 U.S. elections.

Assessing the Impact

The immediate impact of the DCCC hack was significant, both in terms of the political fallout and the damage to the organization itself. The release of sensitive documents, including internal communications and strategic campaign data, caused considerable disruption to Democratic candidates nationwide. Donor information, financial strategies, and internal discussions about vulnerable districts were now public, putting Democratic congressional campaigns at a strategic disadvantage. Quantifying the exact financial impact is difficult, but the reputational damage and operational disruptions were undoubtedly severe.

In the long term, the hack raised serious questions about political organizations' security and preparedness to defend against cyber threats. The hack, alongside the DNC breach, cast a shadow over the 2016 election, fueling debates about foreign interference, election integrity, and cybersecurity in politics. The implications for U.S./Russia relations were also profound, as the DCCC hack became a central point of discussion in the broader investigation into Russia's attempts to influence the U.S. election.

The political ramifications extended far beyond the DCCC itself. Public trust in the electoral process was eroded, and questions about the role of cyberattacks in shaping democratic outcomes became a central issue for policymakers and cybersecurity professionals alike. The hack also set a dangerous precedent for future elections, with the 2016 breach serving as a template for similar cyber operations in other countries, highlighting the need for stronger international agreements on cybersecurity.

Lessons Learned and Takeaways

Several important lessons emerged from the DCCC hack. First and foremost, the attack underscores the importance of phishing awareness and prevention. The use of targeted phishing emails demonstrates how even the most technologically advanced organizations are still vulnerable to social engineering attacks. Moving forward, political organizations must invest in continuous cybersecurity training for their staff, focusing on recognizing phishing attempts and using technologies such as multifactor authentication to reduce the risk of compromise.

Another lesson from the DCCC breach is the critical need for advanced monitoring and detection systems. The attackers could dwell inside the DCCC network for months, gathering sensitive data without detection. Continuous monitoring, threat hunting, and advanced threat intelligence could have helped identify anomalous activity sooner, limiting the scope of the damage. For political campaigns with limited cybersecurity budgets, partnerships with cybersecurity firms and government agencies can play a pivotal role in providing protection.

Finally, the broader geopolitical context of the attack points to the growing use of cyber operations as tools of statecraft. This attack clearly shows that nation-states may use cyberattacks to achieve strategic objectives, such as influencing elections. Political organizations must view cybersecurity as an IT issue and a critical part of safeguarding democracy. The DCCC hack is a powerful reminder of how interconnected cybersecurity and politics have become in the modern age.

Case Study Summary

The 2016 DCCC hack was a defining moment in cybersecurity and politics. The targeted phishing campaign that compromised the DCCC's network revealed technological and human vulnerabilities in political organizations. The attack's sophisticated execution, lengthy undetected presence, and timely release of sensitive information had far-reaching consequences for the DCCC and the broader political landscape in the United States.

Key takeaways from this case include the importance of phishing prevention, the necessity of advanced detection systems, and the realization that cyberattacks are now an integral part of geopolitical strategy. The DCCC hack's impact, while difficult to quantify in exact terms, played a role in shaping the narrative of foreign interference in elections and underscored the need for enhanced cybersecurity measures in political campaigns. The hack's long-term consequences will likely influence how political organizations prepare for and respond to cyber threats in future elections.

DNC EMAIL LEAK (2016)

In 2016, the DNC was the target of a cyberattack that would have far-reaching consequences for the DNC and the entire U.S. political landscape. The attack resulted in the unauthorized access and subsequent leak of thousands of internal emails and documents, many of which contained sensitive political information. The DNC email leak, which occurred during the heat of the U.S. presidential election, raised serious concerns about the role of nation-state actors in manipulating democratic processes through cyber espionage.

The technological landscape at the time of the attack was characterized by political organizations' increasing use of digital communication platforms, including email and cloud-based services. While the DNC had implemented standard cybersecurity measures, these proved insufficient to prevent a highly sophisticated attack from a well-resourced adversary. The attack is widely believed to have been orchestrated by Russian state-sponsored hackers, particularly the groups known as Fancy Bear (APT28) and *Cozy Bear (APT29)*. However, the Russian government has consistently denied involvement.

Given the implications for global election security, the key stakeholders involved in this case included the DNC, its staff and affiliates, the American public, and the broader international community. In particular, U.S. intelligence agencies and cybersecurity experts were called to investigate the attack and mitigate its impact. At the same time, the public was left to grapple with the consequences of leaked private communications that had been strategically released to influence public opinion.

Unfolding the Attack

The DNC email leak began as a highly targeted cyber espionage campaign, with the initial breach likely occurring in the summer of 2015. From the available information, I assume that the attackers first gained access through spear-phishing emails sent to key individuals within the DNC. These emails contained malicious links or attachments that, once clicked, allowed the attackers to access user credentials. The attackers used these credentials to infiltrate the DNC's network and, over time, escalated their privileges to access sensitive data.

Once inside the network, the attackers were methodical in their approach. They carefully exfiltrated emails, documents, and other sensitive information from the DNC's servers over several months, ensuring their presence remained undetected for as long as possible. The attackers utilized malware and other tools to maintain persistence within the network, allowing them to siphon information continuously. The precise timeline suggests that the attackers waited until the critical months leading up to the 2016 presidential election before releasing the stolen data.

The data was first leaked publicly in June 2016 when WikiLeaks published a trove of DNC emails. These emails revealed internal discussions and strategies within the Democratic Party, some of which led to controversy and outrage, particularly regarding the treatment of Bernie Sanders during the primary campaign. From the information available, it appears that the attackers released the information in a calculated manner to maximize its political impact, suggesting a clear intent to influence the outcome of the election.

Detection and Response Efforts

Unfortunately, the DNC's detection and response efforts were delayed, with the organization initially unaware that its network had been compromised. The first signs of a breach came in April 2016, when the cybersecurity firm CrowdStrike was called to investigate unusual activity within the DNC's network. CrowdStrike quickly identified the presence of sophisticated malware and attributed the attack to the Russian state-sponsored groups Fancy Bear and Cozy Bear based on the techniques and tools used.

The initial response actions included isolating the affected systems and working to remove the malware from the network. However, the attackers had already exfiltrated a substantial amount of data by the time the breach was discovered. From the information, I assume the DNC's internal cybersecurity measures were insufficient to detect the attackers' presence earlier, and the organization struggled to regain control of its narrative once the emails were leaked to the public.

External parties played a significant role in the response efforts. In addition to CrowdStrike, U.S. intelligence agencies and law enforcement became involved in the investigation. The FBI launched an inquiry into the attack, and U.S. government officials publicly attributed the breach to Russian state actors. The response also included public messaging from the DNC and political figures, though much of the damage had already been done by the time the leaks became public knowledge.

Assessing the Impact

The immediate impact of the DNC email leak was felt during the 2016 U.S. presidential election, as the leaked emails led to a scandal within the Democratic Party. The contents of the emails revealed internal favoritism toward Hillary Clinton over Bernie Sanders during the primaries, which caused outrage among Sanders supporters and led to the resignation of key DNC officials, including Chairwoman Debbie Wasserman Schultz. The political fallout damaged the party's image and created divisions within the Democratic base during a critical election period.

From a financial and operational perspective, the attack forced the DNC to overhaul its cybersecurity infrastructure and invest heavily in new security measures to prevent future breaches. The organization also faced reputational damage since the breach raised questions about its ability to protect sensitive data. This loss of trust extended beyond the DNC itself, as the attack cast doubt on the security of political campaigns and election processes across the United States.

Long-term consequences of the DNC email leak include ongoing concerns about foreign interference in democratic elections, not only in the U.S. but globally. The attack raised awareness of the vulnerabilities in digital election infrastructure and led to greater scrutiny of the role of nation-state actors in cyber warfare. Additionally, the attack contributed to a broader narrative of Russian interference in the 2016 U.S. election, which has had lasting geopolitical implications.

Lessons Learned and Takeaways

The DNC email leak taught political organizations and the cybersecurity industry critical lessons. One of the most important takeaways is the need for stronger cybersecurity protocols within political organizations, which often lack the resources or expertise to defend against nation-state actors. From the information available, it is clear that the DNC's network was insufficiently protected against a sophisticated adversary, underscoring the need for more advanced security measures, such as multifactor authentication, network segmentation, and real-time monitoring.

Another key lesson is the value of rapid detection and response. The DNC was slow to detect the breach, allowing the attackers to exfiltrate sensitive data over several months. This delay in detection highlights the importance of continuous monitoring and threat detection capabilities, which could have limited the extent of the damage if implemented effectively. Additionally, this case underscored the importance of public relations management after a cyberattack, as the DNC struggled to control the narrative once the emails were released.

The broader implications of the attack extend beyond the DNC and the 2016 election. The attack demonstrated the growing use of cyber espionage as a tool of geopolitical influence, where nation-state actors use cyberattacks to manipulate public opinion and destabilize political systems. As a result, governments and organizations worldwide have become more focused on securing their digital assets against similar attacks, particularly during election periods.

Case Study Summary

The 2016 DNC email leak is a prime example of how cyberattacks can have far-reaching political, operational, and reputational consequences. The key takeaways from this case study include the importance of advanced cybersecurity protocols, rapid detection and response, and the growing threat of nation-state actors using cyberattacks as tools of influence in democratic processes.

While the DNC was able to recover from the immediate aftermath of the attack, the incident left lasting scars on both the organization and the broader political system. The DNC email leak serves as a reminder of political and election infrastructure vulnerabilities. It highlights the need for continuous vigilance and proactive cybersecurity measures in an era where cyber threats have become integral to geopolitical strategy.

MACRON CAMPAIGN EMAIL LEAK (2017)

The Macron campaign email leak in 2017 is a significant example of how political and geopolitical motivations intersected with cybersecurity in the digital age. Emmanuel Macron, the centrist candidate for the French presidency, was thrust into the international spotlight for his political ascent and the cyberattack that targeted his campaign. This incident occurred just days before the crucial second round of the French presidential elections, threatening to undermine the democratic process and cast doubts on the legitimacy of Macron's campaign. The leak involved the unauthorized release of tens of thousands of internal campaign documents, including emails, contracts, and financial information, reminiscent of earlier politically motivated hacks.

At the time of the attack, the global technological landscape was shaped by heightened concerns over cybersecurity breaches in politics following the highly publicized DNC email hack during the 2016 U.S. presidential elections. Cybersecurity experts and analysts quickly compared the two incidents regarding their scale and potential impact on public trust in the electoral process. The Macron campaign leak promptly became a focal point for discussions around foreign interference in national elections, with speculation about the potential involvement of state-sponsored actors, particularly from Russia.

Key stakeholders involved in this case were Emmanuel Macron and his campaign team, the French media, French citizens preparing to vote in the upcoming election, and cybersecurity experts. Additionally, law enforcement agencies, political observers, and international stakeholders closely monitored the situation as the attack unfolded. The Macron campaign, aware of the risks posed by digital espionage, had already taken some precautions against cyber threats. However, the scale and timing of the attack indicated that even these efforts could not prevent the breach.

Unfolding the Attack

The attack on the Macron campaign began with a well-coordinated phishing scheme designed to trick members of Macron's team into providing their login credentials. Attackers sent emails that appeared to be from legitimate sources, targeting specific individuals in the campaign with carefully crafted messages. This technique, known as spear-phishing, exploits human vulnerabilities rather than technical flaws, often an effective entry point for cyber adversaries. From the information available, it can be assumed that the attackers gradually gained access to a wider array of accounts over time, patiently gathering information in the months leading up to the leak.

Once inside the campaign's email system, the attackers exfiltrated large volumes of data, including emails, financial documents, and internal communications. The exact timeline of the attack remains unclear, but it is widely believed that the initial compromise occurred several months before the leak in May 2017. The attackers could quietly monitor and gather valuable intelligence from the campaign's internal workings by remaining undetected for such a long period.

The final phase of the attack occurred just 48 hours before the election when a massive data dump containing more than 20,000 emails and other sensitive documents was published online. The attackers strategically timed the release of the information, making it nearly impossible for the Macron campaign to effectively respond or counter the narrative in the days leading up to the vote. This move, designed to cause maximum disruption, mimicked the playbook used in other high-profile geopolitical cyberattacks and further suggested the involvement of highly organized, possibly state-backed actors.

Detection and Response Efforts

The Macron campaign, aware of the potential for cyberattacks, had implemented measures to protect against such threats. However, the sophisticated phishing campaign managed to bypass these defenses. Detection of the attack came only after the massive data dump was made public, meaning that the campaign had little opportunity to respond in real time. The attackers' ability to remain undetected for months highlights organizations' challenges in defending against well-executed spear-phishing attacks.

The immediate response from the Macron campaign was to downplay the significance of the leak, with officials stating that much of the information was either irrelevant or had been doctored. This strategic response aimed to mitigate the potential damage by casting doubt on the authenticity of the leaked documents. In parallel, French law enforcement and cybersecurity experts began investigating the breach. However, the proximity of the leak to the election meant that any detailed findings would come only after the vote.

International cybersecurity firms were also brought in to analyze the attack. Preliminary reports suggested that the tactics, techniques, and procedures used bore striking similarities to those employed in the DNC hack, with some experts pointing to the involvement of the Russian group Fancy Bear (APT28). However, concrete attribution was never definitively established. From the information available, one can assume that this was likely an example of the same methods used to influence the outcomes of other foreign elections.

Assessing the Impact

Regarding immediate consequences, the Macron campaign was fortunate that the leak did not significantly alter the election outcome. Macron won a decisive victory over far-right candidate Marine Le Pen despite the extensive data dump. However, the attack did spark concerns about the integrity of democratic elections and the potential for future cyberattacks on political campaigns, not just in France but globally. It also reignited the debate about the role of foreign powers in influencing elections through cyber means.

The long-term consequences for Macron and his administration were somewhat mitigated because his victory was decisive. However, the attack served as a stark reminder of the vulnerability of political campaigns to cyberattacks. It also demonstrated how cyberattacks are increasingly being used as tools of geopolitical strategy, with nation-states leveraging hacking capabilities to achieve their objectives on the world stage.

For the broader political and cybersecurity landscape, the Macron campaign leak underscored the importance of robust cybersecurity practices for political organizations, which are often less prepared for sophisticated cyberattacks than their corporate counterparts. This incident helped accelerate the push for improved cybersecurity measures in future elections, both in France and worldwide, including implementing stricter regulations and more stringent security protocols for political parties and election infrastructure.

Lessons Learned and Takeaways

Several critical lessons can be drawn from the Macron campaign email leak. First, the incident reinforced the importance of training individuals to recognize phishing attempts. Spear-phishing remains one of the most effective methods for attackers to gain access to sensitive systems, and the Macron case demonstrated how even a tech-savvy campaign could fall victim to such an attack. Security awareness training and technological defenses like multifactor authentication could have made it more difficult for the attackers to succeed.

Second, the timing of the attack demonstrated the value of preemptive cybersecurity strategies. While the Macron campaign had taken steps to protect against cyber threats, the attackers could still execute their plan. Proactive measures, such as continuous monitoring and regular security audits, may have helped detect the breach earlier, potentially preventing the large-scale data dump that occurred just before the election.

Finally, the geopolitical implications of the attack highlighted the growing role of cyber warfare in global politics. From this case, it is clear that political organizations must be aware of the broader geopolitical context in which they operate. Foreign actors may have strategic interests in influencing the outcome of elections, and cybersecurity must be seen not just as a technical issue but as a political one. This realization has pushed governments worldwide to consider cybersecurity a critical element of national security.

Case Study Summary

The Macron campaign email leak of 2017 is a key example of how political campaigns are vulnerable to cyberattacks, particularly in the high-stakes arena of national elections. From the sophisticated spear-phishing techniques used to compromise the campaign to the timed release of sensitive documents just before the election, this case highlights the risks and the broader geopolitical implications of cyber espionage.

Key takeaways include the importance of phishing awareness and prevention, the value of proactive cybersecurity measures, and the realization that cyberattacks are becoming increasingly integrated into geopolitical strategy. While Macron's victory suggests that the leak did not decisively alter the election outcome, the case serves as a sobering reminder of the potential for cyberattacks to undermine democratic processes and the need for vigilance in protecting political campaigns from such threats.

CHAPTER CONCLUSION

In reviewing the political cyberattacks we have explored throughout this chapter, several key themes emerge that are vital for today's cybersecurity professionals. First and foremost, many of these attacks reveal the increasing intersection between cyber capabilities and geopolitical goals. Whether the target is an election, a government institution, or critical infrastructure, these cyberattacks aim to undermine public trust, manipulate public opinion, or destabilize political systems. The broadening scope of these attacks, moving from financial motivations to political manipulation, illustrates how deeply integrated cyber warfare has become in statecraft. As a result, cybersecurity professionals must remain vigilant against conventional threats and increasingly sophisticated political and nation-state-driven attacks.

A critical takeaway for cybersecurity professionals today is the importance of resilience and preparedness. Many of the case studies in this chapter highlighted the unpreparedness of organizations, especially political institutions, to defend against coordinated and persistent threats. The attacks on Georgia and Ukraine, along with the U.S. voter database breaches all share a commonality. These targets were ill-equipped to handle the scale and complexity of the cyber operations against them. Strengthening cybersecurity infrastructure, particularly for government and election-related systems, is no longer an option but an urgent necessity. The capacity to detect, respond to, and recover from such attacks requires technical upgrades, organizational agility, and international collaboration.

Moreover, a key point is the need for robust detection and response mechanisms, even when response information is often inferred from available media sources, as in many of the cases we examined. While full forensic details may not always be publicly available, timely detection—such as in the DCCC or Macron campaign hacks—demonstrates that proactive measures can mitigate the impact of a breach. Integrating threat intelligence, advanced monitoring, and incident response plans should be central to any cybersecurity strategy. This chapter underscores the critical role that cybersecurity professionals play in defending systems and shaping organizational policy, enhancing public awareness, and contributing to international cooperation to combat politically motivated cyberattacks.

Finally, there is a growing need for cybersecurity professionals to view these incidents as a call to action to implement long-term strategies that go beyond patching vulnerabilities. Recommendations include fostering international partnerships, improving training against social engineering and phishing attacks, and developing more comprehensive frameworks for securing critical political and governmental infrastructure. Many of the breaches analyzed in this book could have been prevented or mitigated with better controls, training, and collaboration across sectors. Today's cybersecurity professionals are responsible for not only defending against these immediate threats but also building systems resilient enough to withstand the next evolution of cyber warfare.

8

THE ERA OF RANSOMWARE AND DESTRUCTIVE ATTACKS

Imagine a world where the phrase "my computer has a virus" doesn't mean a few weird pop-ups or sluggish performances but rather a complete lockdown, a demand for Bitcoin, and your entire business grinding to a halt. Ransomware might sound like the digital equivalent of getting a parking ticket—annoying but manageable. However, as this chapter will explain, ransomware attacks are far more like being held hostage by a master criminal with a PhD in cybersecurity. Welcome to the world where one wrong click can send an entire hospital offline, halt global shipping, or take down your favorite video game for weeks. Don't worry, though—you won't need to pay a ransom to read this chapter (unless your device has other plans).

But behind the slightly dark humor of *ransom demands* lies a serious issue. Ransomware and its more destructive siblings, such as wipers and data extortion schemes, have become some of the most significant cybersecurity threats of the modern age (see Figure 8.1). The attacks we will examine in this chapter—from WannaCry and NotPetya to the Conti assault on Ireland's health service—are not just stories of malicious code but cautionary tales about the vulnerabilities inherent in our interconnected world. These attacks have crippled companies, disrupted critical infrastructure, and, in some cases, risked human lives. The purpose of this chapter is not only to understand how these attacks happened but also to glean critical lessons on how we, as cybersecurity professionals, can prevent similar disasters in the future.

Definite details about how organizations detected and responded to these attacks are often scarce. Information on the exact response procedures is often extrapolated from media reports and cybersecurity analysis and pieced together from information released in the aftermath. This lack of transparency leaves a gap in understanding the best practices for incident detection

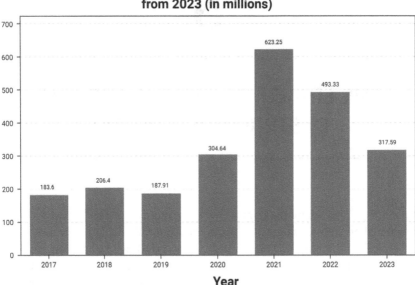

Figure 8.1   Worldwide ransomware attacks (*source*: Statista Search Department)

and response, but it also provides an opportunity for reflection. Cybersecurity professionals must recognize that each organization's response—or lack thereof—offers valuable lessons, even when the full story has not been told.

Ultimately, this chapter serves as a historical review and a practical guide. By examining some of the most notorious ransomware and cyberattacks of the last decade, we aim to uncover what went wrong, how the damage was contained (or worsened), and what steps should be taken to protect against future threats. While it is easy to be alarmed by the sheer scale of some of these incidents, the key takeaway is that preparation, transparency, and global cooperation are crucial to defending against the next major attack.

WHAT IS RANSOMWARE?

Ransomware is malicious software (malware) designed to encrypt a victim's data or lock them out of their systems, holding those assets hostage until a ransom is paid. Typically, cybercriminals behind ransomware attacks demand payments in cryptocurrency, such as Bitcoin, after which they will provide the decryption key or restore access to the affected systems. Ransomware attacks can target individuals, businesses, or even large organizations, causing significant disruption to operations and financial losses.

The mechanics of a ransomware attack often involve phishing emails, malicious attachments, or exploiting vulnerabilities in unpatched systems to gain access to a network. Once inside, the ransomware spreads across the network, encrypting files and locking out users. In more recent ransomware attacks, cybercriminals have adopted a *double-extortion* tactic, where not only is the data encrypted, but sensitive information is stolen and threatened to be leaked if the ransom is not paid. This tactic pressures the victim to pay, as they face operational downtime and reputational damage if their data is exposed.

Ransomware has evolved into a lucrative criminal enterprise, often supported by organized groups that operate ransomware-as-a-service models. In these setups, ransomware developers lease their tools to affiliates for a share of the ransom profits. The scale and sophistication of ransomware attacks have escalated in recent years, with critical sectors such as healthcare, government, and energy increasingly being targeted. The impact of ransomware extends beyond financial losses, as attacks can disrupt essential services, endanger lives, and undermine trust in cybersecurity defenses.

The following chart illustrates the timeline associated with the attacks that will be explored in this chapter (see Figure 8.2).

WANNACRY RANSOMWARE (2017)

The WannaCry ransomware attack in May 2017 was one of history's most devastating and far-reaching cyberattacks. It affected hundreds of thousands of computers in over 150 countries, targeting various sectors, including healthcare, transportation, government, and telecommunications. The attack, which leveraged a vulnerability in the Windows operating system, caused significant operational disruptions and financial losses across the globe. At its core, WannaCry was a ransomware that encrypted files on infected computers, demanding payment in Bitcoin to decrypt the data.

The technological landscape at the time was characterized by the widespread use of legacy systems, particularly in industries such as healthcare, where updating critical systems can be slow. The attack exposed the dangers of relying on outdated software and the global consequences of unpatched vulnerabilities. The vulnerability exploited by WannaCry, known as EternalBlue, had been discovered by the U.S. National Security Agency and was

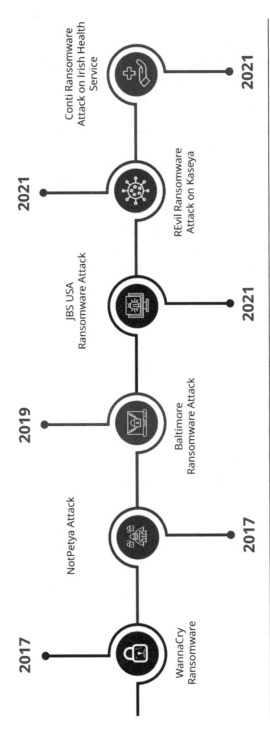

Figure 8.2   The timeline of attacks discussed in this chapter

leaked online by the hacker group Shadow Brokers just a few months before the attack.

Key stakeholders in this case included organizations across various industries, cybersecurity firms, government agencies, and law enforcement. The most notable victim was the UK's National Health Service (NHS), which experienced severe disruptions, with many hospitals and clinics forced to cancel appointments and delay surgeries due to the attack.

Unfolding the Attack

The WannaCry ransomware attack began on May 12, 2017, when cybercriminals launched a global campaign that spread the ransomware through vulnerable Windows systems. The attackers exploited the EternalBlue vulnerability, which allowed them to spread the malware across networks without requiring user interaction. Once installed, the ransomware would encrypt files on the infected machines, displaying a message that demanded $300 in Bitcoin to restore access to the files. If the ransom was not paid within three days, the amount doubled. After seven days, the files were reportedly deleted.

From the information available, it is assumed that the initial entry point for the attack was likely a phishing email or other form of social engineering. However, once inside a network, WannaCry's self-propagating capabilities allowed it to spread rapidly, infecting individual systems and entire networks. The attack timeline shows that within just a few hours, WannaCry had spread to tens of thousands of systems worldwide, including critical infrastructure such as hospitals, government agencies, and transportation companies.

The ransomware spread so quickly due to the worm-like nature of EternalBlue, which allowed WannaCry to move laterally within networks and affect unpatched systems. Many organizations had not yet applied the security patch that Microsoft released in March 2017 to address the vulnerability, exposing them to the attack. The rapid spread of WannaCry highlighted the global scale of the risk posed by unpatched vulnerabilities and inadequate cybersecurity practices.

Detection and Response Efforts

The WannaCry ransomware attack was detected almost immediately after its spread began, with organizations worldwide reporting disruptions to their operations. Security researchers and cybersecurity firms quickly identified that the attack was leveraging the EternalBlue vulnerability and started working on ways to contain the spread of the malware. Microsoft also released emergency updates for unsupported versions of Windows to help prevent further infections.

One of the key turning points in the response to WannaCry came when a security researcher known as *MalwareTech* discovered a kill switch within the code. The kill switch was a domain that the ransomware attempted to contact, and if the domain was live, the ransomware would stop spreading. MalwareTech quickly registered the domain, effectively halting the spread of the malware. This action significantly mitigated the attack's impact, though it did not help those whose systems had already been infected.

Government agencies, including the U.S. Department of Homeland Security and the UK's National Cyber Security Centre, issued alerts and guided affected organizations. Law enforcement agencies, including Europol, investigated the attack's origins, eventually linking it to North Korean state-sponsored hackers. While the discovery of the kill switch was a major success, the response efforts were largely reactive, with many organizations struggling to recover from the attack and restore their systems.

Assessing the Impact

The immediate impact of the WannaCry ransomware attack was severe, causing widespread operational disruptions and financial losses across multiple industries. The UK's NHS was one of the hardest-hit organizations, with over 80 hospitals affected, leading to the cancellation of thousands of appointments, delayed surgeries, and patients being turned away from emergency rooms. The total cost of the attack on the NHS was estimated to be over 92 million UK pounds, though the broader global financial impact of WannaCry reached billions of U.S. dollars.

In addition to the financial losses, the attack exposed the vulnerabilities in critical infrastructure systems that rely on outdated technology. Many of the affected organizations were using unsupported or unpatched versions of Windows, making them prime targets for the attack. The disruption caused by WannaCry also highlighted the interconnected nature of modern systems since the ransomware spread across networks and affected organizations far beyond its initial targets.

The long-term consequences of the attack included increased scrutiny of cybersecurity practices and a renewed focus on promptly applying security patches. WannaCry served as a wake-up call for organizations worldwide, demonstrating the need for better cybersecurity hygiene and more proactive measures to protect against ransomware attacks. The attack also led to increased collaboration between governments and private sector cybersecurity firms, as they worked together to identify vulnerabilities and prevent future incidents.

Lessons Learned and Takeaways

Several key lessons can be drawn from the WannaCry ransomware attack. First, the attack underscored the importance of patch management and keeping systems current. Many organizations affected by WannaCry had not applied the security patches to address the EternalBlue vulnerability, leaving them exposed to the attack. Moving forward, organizations must prioritize the timely application of security updates to prevent similar attacks in the future.

Second, the attack demonstrated the need for comprehensive backup strategies. Organizations with secure, up-to-date backups of their data could recover more quickly from the attack, while those without adequate backups were forced to either pay the ransom or lose their data. A robust backup and recovery plan is essential to mitigating the impact of ransomware attacks.

Finally, WannaCry highlighted the importance of international cooperation in responding to cyberattacks. The attack affected organizations in over 150 countries, and the response required coordination between governments, cybersecurity firms, and law enforcement agencies. The discovery of the kill switch and the subsequent investigation into the attack's origins showed the value of collaboration in mitigating the impact of large-scale cyber incidents.

Case Study Summary

The WannaCry ransomware attack in 2017 was a landmark event in the history of cyberattacks, affecting hundreds of thousands of systems in over 150 countries and causing billions of dollars in financial losses. The attack exploited the EternalBlue vulnerability in Windows systems, spreading rapidly across networks and encrypting files on infected computers. A security researcher's discovery of a kill switch helped to halt the ransomware spread, but the damage had already been done.

Key takeaways from this case include the critical importance of applying security patches, the need for robust backup strategies, and the value of international cooperation in responding to cyberattacks. The WannaCry attack serves as a reminder of the growing threat posed by ransomware and the need for organizations to remain vigilant in protecting their systems and data from cyber threats. As ransomware evolves, the lessons learned from WannaCry remain relevant for organizations looking to strengthen their cybersecurity posture.

NOTPETYA ATTACK (2017)

The NotPetya attack of 2017 is widely regarded as one of the most destructive cyberattacks in history, causing unprecedented global financial and operational damage. What initially appeared to be a ransomware attack targeting Ukrainian organizations quickly spread across the globe, affecting major multinational companies and critical infrastructure. NotPetya exploited vulnerabilities in Windows systems, similar to the WannaCry attack earlier that year. Still, its destructive nature soon became apparent—it was not designed to recover data but to disrupt systems permanently. The attack is believed to have been politically motivated, with strong indications that Russian state-sponsored actors launched it as part of the ongoing geopolitical tensions between Russia and Ukraine.

At the time of the attack, the global cybersecurity landscape still grappled with the implications of large-scale ransomware attacks. Many organizations were unprepared for the speed and scale of NotPetya's impact. Unlike typical ransomware, where victims have the potential to recover data by paying the ransom, NotPetya was a *wiper* in disguise. Once it infected a system, it encrypted the Master Boot Record, making recovery nearly impossible. Key stakeholders affected by the attack included government agencies, global corporations, and infrastructure organizations such as Maersk, FedEx, and Merck, all of which suffered significant financial and operational losses.

Unfolding the Attack

The NotPetya attack began on June 27, 2017, with the initial target being Ukraine's financial, government, and critical infrastructure systems. From the available information, it can be assumed that the attackers used a compromised update to a popular Ukrainian tax accounting software called MeDoc to deliver the malware. MeDoc, widely used by Ukrainian businesses for tax reporting, was an ideal vector for distributing the malware to many organizations within the country. Once inside a network, NotPetya spread rapidly, leveraging the same EternalBlue vulnerability exploited in the WannaCry attack.

The attack timeline shows that within hours, NotPetya had spread beyond Ukraine, affecting organizations worldwide. It used a combination of the EternalBlue exploit and credential theft tools like Mimikatz to propagate across networks. The malware was designed to lock users out of their systems by encrypting critical files and displaying a ransom demanding $300 in Bitcoin to decrypt the data. However, investigators later discovered that NotPetya was not true ransomware; even if the ransom was paid, the encryption was irreversible, and the data could not be recovered. The primary aim appeared to be destroying systems rather than financial gain.

Exploited vulnerabilities included unpatched Windows systems and weak password protections, which allowed NotPetya to move laterally across networks with relative ease. The attack affected organizations globally, from shipping giants like Maersk to pharmaceutical companies like Merck. Even though the initial attack vector was through Ukrainian systems, the interconnected nature of modern businesses meant that the malware spread rapidly to subsidiaries, partners, and global networks.

Detection and Response Efforts

The detection of NotPetya occurred almost immediately after the attack began, with organizations worldwide reporting system failures and ransom demands. However, many organizations struggled to respond effectively due to the unprecedented scale and nature of the attack. Unlike traditional ransomware, which typically provides an opportunity for recovery through ransom payments, NotPetya's destructive payload made recovery impossible in most cases. The immediate response from cybersecurity firms and law enforcement agencies involved analyzing the malware to determine how it spread and finding ways to prevent further infections.

Many organizations resorted to isolating affected systems from their networks to prevent the malware from spreading further. Government agencies and cybersecurity firms worked together to issue warnings and provide patches for the EternalBlue vulnerability, though this came too late for many organizations. As the attack unfolded, it became clear that the ransom demand was a diversion and that the true intent of NotPetya was system destruction.

Law enforcement agencies, including the Federal Bureau of Investigation (FBI) and European authorities, investigated the attack's origins. The consensus among cybersecurity experts was that NotPetya was a state-sponsored attack, with Russia being the most likely culprit due to the malware's initial focus on Ukraine. This hypothesis was further supported by the geopolitical context of the time, with tensions between Russia and Ukraine running high following the annexation of Crimea in 2014 and the ongoing conflict in eastern Ukraine.

Assessing the Impact

The immediate impact of the NotPetya attack was catastrophic, both financially and operationally. Major global companies experienced significant disruptions to their operations, with some reporting hundreds of millions of dollars in losses. For example, shipping giant Maersk had to temporarily halt operations, losing an estimated 300 million dollars, while pharmaceutical company Merck reported over 870 million dollars in losses due to production and research disruptions. The attack also caused significant damage to Ukraine's infrastructure, particularly in the banking and energy sectors.

The long-term consequences of the attack went beyond the financial impact. It exposed the vulnerabilities in global supply chains and the interconnected nature of digital infrastructures. Many organizations, even those with robust cybersecurity measures, were caught off guard by the speed and scale of the attack. The destructive nature of NotPetya also raised concerns about using cyberattacks as tools of geopolitical warfare since the attack appeared to be less about financial gain and more about causing widespread chaos and disruption.

Reputational damage was another key consequence, with affected organizations facing criticism for not having stronger cybersecurity defenses. The attack also prompted governments and industries to reassess their cybersecurity strategies, particularly when protecting critical infrastructure and supply chains from state-sponsored attacks.

Lessons Learned and Takeaways

Several key lessons emerged from the NotPetya attack. First, the incident highlighted the importance of patch management and maintaining up-to-date systems. Many organizations affected by NotPetya had failed to apply the security patches for the EternalBlue vulnerability, exposing them to the attack. Moving forward, organizations must prioritize the timely application of patches and updates to prevent similar vulnerabilities from being exploited.

Second, the attack underscored the importance of network segmentation and isolation in limiting the spread of malware. NotPetya's ability to move laterally across networks and infect multiple systems simultaneously was a major factor in its rapid spread. Organizations can reduce the risk of malware spreading uncontrollably across their systems by segmenting networks and implementing stronger access controls.

Finally, the attack demonstrated the growing role of state-sponsored cyberattacks in geopolitical conflicts. NotPetya was not a typical ransomware attack; its purpose was destruction, not financial gain. The attack served as a wake-up call for organizations and governments alike to take state-sponsored cyber threats seriously and to develop more robust defenses against such attacks. International cooperation, threat intelligence sharing, and stronger deterrence measures will be crucial in addressing the rise of destructive cyberattacks.

Case Study Summary

The NotPetya attack in 2017 was one of the most devastating cyberattacks in history, affecting hundreds of organizations worldwide and causing billions of dollars in financial losses. The attack, which originated in Ukraine and quickly spread globally, exploited the EternalBlue vulnerability in Windows systems to spread across networks. Unlike traditional ransomware, NotPetya was designed to destroy data, not extort money, making recovery impossible for most victims.

Key takeaways from this case include the importance of patch management, network segmentation, and recognizing the role of state-sponsored cyberattacks in modern geopolitical conflicts. The NotPetya attack serves as a stark reminder of the destructive potential of cyberattacks and the need for organizations to remain vigilant in protecting their systems and infrastructure from similar threats in the future.

BALTIMORE RANSOMWARE ATTACK (2019)

The Baltimore ransomware attack of 2019 was a devastating cyber incident that paralyzed the city's digital infrastructure for nearly a month, crippling vital services such as real estate transactions, water billing, and email communications. On May 7, 2019, Baltimore was hit by a ransomware attack that used a strain known as *RobbinHood*. The attackers encrypted the city's data and demanded 13 Bitcoin (about 76 thousand dollars) to release the files. Baltimore's refusal to pay the ransom set off a protracted recovery process that would cost the city more than 18 million dollars.

At the time, municipal governments across the United States were increasingly targeted by ransomware attacks, but many lacked the resources and cybersecurity infrastructure to respond effectively. Baltimore's digital landscape was especially vulnerable, with outdated systems and insufficient defenses to mitigate cyberattacks of this magnitude. The incident highlighted the growing threat of ransomware against local governments, who are seen as attractive targets due to their dependence on critical services and often insufficient cybersecurity measures.

Key stakeholders in the attack included city officials, the residents of Baltimore, third-party contractors, and external cybersecurity firms that were called in to assist in the aftermath. The attack also drew national attention, underscoring the potential for ransomware to disrupt entire cities, bringing public services to a standstill.

Unfolding the Attack

The Baltimore ransomware attack began with the introduction of the Robbin-Hood malware into the city's network, though the exact entry point remains unclear. From the data made available, it is assumed that the attackers may have used phishing or other social engineering techniques to compromise an internal system. Once inside the network, the ransomware spread quickly, encrypting files across the city's infrastructure. The attackers left a ransom note demanding payment in Bitcoin, warning that the decryption keys would be destroyed if the ransom was not paid within a specific time frame.

The attack was detected when city employees reported that they could not access critical systems, including email and payment processing services. The ransomware disabled many services—from water billing and property taxes to essential communications channels—halting city operations. The timeline of the attack reveals that the initial infection and encryption occurred rapidly, leaving little time for city officials to respond before significant damage was done.

Baltimore's mayor, Bernard C. "Jack" Young decided early on to refuse the ransom demand, stating that the city would not negotiate with cybercriminals. This decision, while principled, came at a steep cost, as the city faced weeks of recovery efforts and millions in financial losses. The ransomware's strong encryption and the lack of decryption keys meant that much of the city's data remained inaccessible throughout the recovery period.

Detection and Response Efforts

Baltimore's response to the ransomware attack was immediate but hampered by the scale of the attack and the city's limited cybersecurity resources. Once the attack was detected, city officials worked with cybersecurity firms to assess the damage and begin recovery efforts. The city's information technology (IT) systems were taken offline to prevent further spread of the malware, though, by this point, most critical services had already been encrypted. The city's water billing, property tax payments, and real estate transactions were among the hardest-hit areas, causing significant disruptions for residents and businesses.

External cybersecurity firms and federal agencies, including the FBI, were brought in to assist with the investigation and response efforts. However, Baltimore's decision not to pay the ransom complicated the recovery process because the city had to rely on backup systems and manually rebuild its network infrastructure. The city also faced a shortage of technical expertise, which delayed the restoration of services.

Recovery efforts were slow and expensive, with some systems remaining offline for weeks. For example, the city's email system was not fully restored until several weeks after the attack. In total, it took nearly two months for most services to return to normal, and even then, the city faced ongoing data recovery and security challenges.

Assessing the Impact

The immediate impact of the Baltimore ransomware attack was severe, both financially and operationally. The city's inability to process real estate transactions and issue property titles resulted in a sales backlog, affecting businesses and individuals. Water billing and other essential city services were disrupted for weeks, causing frustration among residents who could not make payments or access city resources. In total, the cost of the attack exceeded 18 million dollars, including 10 million dollars in recovery efforts and an estimated eight million dollars in lost revenue.

While the financial costs were significant, the attack also had reputational consequences for Baltimore's leadership. The city's vulnerability to such an attack exposed gaps in its cybersecurity defenses and raised questions about why more had not been done to protect critical systems. The fact that the attackers used relatively simple techniques to infiltrate the city's network further underscored the need for improved security measures.

The long-term consequences of the attack included heightened awareness of the risks posed by ransomware and a renewed focus on improving cybersecurity in local governments. Baltimore's experience served as a cautionary tale for other municipalities, many of which began investing in stronger defenses and backup systems to mitigate the risk of similar attacks in the future.

Lessons Learned and Takeaways

Several important lessons emerged from the Baltimore ransomware attack. First, the attack highlighted the importance of strong cybersecurity practices, particularly for municipal governments and other public institutions. The city's reliance on outdated systems and insufficient cybersecurity defenses made it an easy target for attackers. Moving forward, cities and local governments must invest in modern cybersecurity solutions, including regular security updates, employee training, and robust backup strategies.

Second, the attack underscored the need for comprehensive backup and recovery plans. One of the key challenges Baltimore faced was the lack of readily available backups, which prolonged the recovery process. Organizations, particularly those responsible for critical public services, must ensure they have secure, up-to-date backups that are regularly tested to facilitate recovery in a ransomware attack.

Finally, the attack demonstrated ransomware's growing threat to public institutions. As ransomware attacks become more sophisticated, local governments and public services are increasingly targeted. Collaboration between federal agencies, local governments, and cybersecurity firms is essential to promptly detecting and responding to these threats.

Case Study Summary

The Baltimore ransomware attack of 2019 was a devastating incident that crippled the city's digital infrastructure for nearly two months, causing significant financial losses and operational disruptions. The attack, which used the RobbinHood ransomware, encrypted critical city services and demanded a ransom payment in Bitcoin. Baltimore's decision not to pay the ransom led to a prolonged recovery process, costing the city over 18 million dollars.

Key takeaways from this case include the importance of investing in modern cybersecurity practices, maintaining secure backups, and improving collaboration between local governments and cybersecurity experts. The Baltimore attack is a stark reminder of the growing threat posed by ransomware and the need for municipalities to strengthen their defenses against future attacks.

JBS USA RANSOMWARE ATTACK (2021)

The JBS USA ransomware attack in May 2021 was a significant and high-profile cyber incident that targeted one of the largest meat processing companies in the world. JBS, a Brazilian company with major operations in the United States, is responsible for producing about one-fifth of the country's beef supply. The attack forced the company to shut down its beef, pork, and poultry production plants across North America and Australia, causing widespread disruption in the food supply chain. The attack was part of a larger wave of ransomware attacks targeting critical infrastructure, including the Colonial Pipeline attack, which had occurred just weeks earlier.

At the time of the attack, the cybersecurity landscape was marked by an alarming rise in ransomware attacks, particularly against industries considered critical to national infrastructure. JBS, being a key player in the global food supply chain, became an attractive target for cybercriminals seeking large payouts. The attackers, a notorious ransomware group known as *REvil* (also known as *Sodinokibi*), demanded 11 million dollars in Bitcoin to release the company's encrypted data and allow operations to resume.

Key stakeholders included JBS management, the U.S. and Australian governments, cybersecurity firms, and the public, particularly those dependent on the food supply chain. The attack underscored the growing risks critical industries face and the potential for ransomware to disrupt essential services.

Unfolding the Attack

The JBS ransomware attack began on Memorial Day weekend in late May 2021. After studying the existing information, I can assume that the initial compromise may have occurred through phishing emails or other social engineering techniques, though specific details about the entry point remain unclear. Once inside the JBS network, the attackers deployed the REvil ransomware, which encrypted critical systems and data, halting operations across the company's processing plants in the United States, Australia, and Canada.

The attack timeline shows that within hours of detecting the ransomware, JBS decided to shut down its IT systems to contain the spread of the malware. The shutdown led to widespread disruption in meat production, as the company's facilities rely heavily on digital systems for managing processing operations, supply chains, and logistics. Beef processing plants in the United States, particularly in states such as Colorado, Texas, and Nebraska, were significantly affected, with production grinding to a halt.

JBS quickly notified federal authorities, including the U.S. Department of Agriculture (USDA) and the FBI, to assist in the response and investigation. The company also engaged external cybersecurity firms to help assess the situation and develop a strategy for restoring operations. Meanwhile, news of the attack spread rapidly, raising concerns about potential food shortages and price increases.

Detection and Response Efforts

JBS detected the ransomware attack early in the infection process, allowing them to respond swiftly. By taking their systems offline, JBS prevented the ransomware from spreading further and compromising more critical data. The company worked with cybersecurity firms to investigate the breach, assess the damage, and begin recovery efforts. However, despite these efforts, the disruption to production lasted several days, leading to significant operational challenges.

The FBI and other law enforcement agencies in the United States and Australia were involved in the response and investigation. These agencies collaborated with JBS to identify the perpetrators and explore possible avenues for mitigating the attack's impact. The REvil ransomware group, a well-known cybercriminal organization with a history of targeting large companies, was quickly identified as the responsible party.

Despite efforts to recover encrypted data, JBS ultimately paid the ransom demand of 11 million dollars in Bitcoin. The company's CEO later stated that the payment was made to protect its plants, employees, and customers from further disruption. This decision was controversial, as paying ransoms can encourage further attacks, but JBS prioritized restoring operations to avoid more severe consequences for the food supply chain.

Assessing the Impact

The immediate impact of the JBS ransomware attack was significant, with widespread disruptions to meat production in the United States, Australia, and Canada. The shutdown of processing plants caused a temporary halt in meat deliveries, leading to concerns about shortages and potential price increases. In the United States, the shutdown affected roughly 20–25 percent of the country's beef production, and while the disruption lasted only a few days, the ripple effects were felt across the supply chain.

Financially, the attack cost JBS millions in lost revenue along with the 11-million-dollar ransom payment. The company also faced reputational damage as questions arose about its cybersecurity practices and preparedness. For the food industry, the attack underscored the vulnerabilities in the supply chain and the need for stronger cybersecurity defenses.

The attack prompted increased scrutiny of the food and agriculture sector's cybersecurity practices in the long term. Governments in the United States and Australia began discussions about improving the resilience of critical infrastructure, focusing on industries like food production, energy, and healthcare. The attack also increased companies' awareness of the importance of robust incident response plans and regularly updated security measures to defend against ransomware.

Lessons Learned and Takeaways

The JBS ransomware attack highlighted several important lessons for the food industry and the broader cybersecurity community. First, the attack demonstrated the importance of having a comprehensive incident response plan. JBS's quick shutting down of its systems prevented the ransomware from spreading further, but the company's reliance on paying the ransom revealed gaps in its preparedness for such an attack. Moving forward, companies must develop robust recovery strategies that minimize the need to engage with cybercriminals.

Second, the attack underscored the vulnerability of critical infrastructure industries to ransomware. Like many other essential services, food production relies heavily on digital systems that, if compromised, can have wide-reaching consequences. The JBS attack highlighted the need for stronger defenses in sectors vital to national and global supply chains.

Finally, the attack demonstrated the importance of government and industry collaboration in responding to ransomware. The involvement of federal agencies like the FBI and USDA played a key role in mitigating the attack and assisting with recovery efforts. Public-private partnerships will strengthen defenses against future cyberattacks on critical infrastructure.

Case Study Summary

The JBS ransomware attack in 2021 was a significant cyber incident that disrupted one of the largest food production companies in the world. The attack, carried out by the REvil ransomware group, halted meat production in the United States, Australia, and Canada, causing temporary disruptions to the global food supply chain. JBS's decision to pay an 11-million-dollar ransom to restore its operations highlighted the challenges companies have when dealing with ransomware attacks.

Key takeaways from this case include the importance of having a comprehensive incident response plan, the vulnerabilities of critical infrastructure industries to cyberattacks, and the need for greater collaboration between the public and private sectors in responding to and preventing future ransomware incidents. The JBS attack serves as a reminder that even industries not traditionally seen as targets of cyberattacks must remain vigilant and proactive in their cybersecurity efforts.

REVIL RANSOMWARE ATTACK ON KASEYA (2021)

The REvil ransomware attack on Kaseya in July 2021 was a sophisticated and large-scale supply chain attack that demonstrated how cybercriminals could exploit IT management software vulnerabilities to amplify an attack's scope. Kaseya, a U.S.-based IT and network management solutions provider, was targeted by the notorious REvil ransomware group, which compromised its VSA (virtual system administrator) software to deploy ransomware to hundreds of organizations worldwide. The attack was especially devastating because Kaseya's clients included managed service providers (MSPs), whose own customers—thousands of small and medium-sized businesses—were indirectly affected.

At the time, the global cybersecurity environment was facing increasing threats from ransomware, with the Kaseya attack coming just weeks after the high-profile ransomware incidents involving Colonial Pipeline and JBS Foods. This attack, however, stood out due to the attackers' method of leveraging a single software provider to compromise numerous downstream customers. The attackers demanded a 70-million-dollar ransom in exchange for a universal decryption key, making it one of the largest ransomware demands in history.

Key stakeholders in the attack included Kaseya, its MSP clients, the affected downstream businesses, government agencies, and cybersecurity firms. The attack raised serious concerns about the security of supply chains and the vulnerability of IT service providers to sophisticated cyberattacks.

Unfolding the Attack

The REvil ransomware attack began over the July 4th holiday weekend in the United States, when many businesses had reduced staffing and were, therefore, less likely to notice or respond quickly to the breach. The available information assumes that the attackers exploited a zero-day vulnerability in Kaseya's VSA software to gain unauthorized access. This allowed them to deploy ransomware to Kaseya's clients—primarily MSPs—who unknowingly pushed the malicious software to their customers.

The timeline of the attack indicates that Kaseya first detected suspicious activity on July 2, 2021. Upon realizing the extent of the breach, the company took immediate steps to shut down its VSA servers, thereby preventing the ransomware from spreading further. However, the damage had already been done—thousands of businesses worldwide found their data encrypted, with operations grinding to a halt. The REvil ransomware group left ransom notes demanding payment in Bitcoin to decrypt the files, and the attackers sought a massive 70-million-dollar payment for a universal decryption key that would unlock all affected systems.

The entry point for the attack was Kaseya's on-premises VSA servers, which had not been updated with a patch for the zero-day vulnerability that REvil exploited. This vulnerability allowed the attackers to execute arbitrary code, leading to widespread compromise. The sophistication of the attack, including its rapid propagation through the IT supply chain, made it difficult for businesses to contain the threat in the early stages.

Detection and Response Efforts

Kaseya responded swiftly once the attack was detected, issuing a public advisory within hours of discovering the ransomware and instructing all VSA customers to shut down their VSA servers immediately. The company worked closely with cybersecurity experts, including the FBI and the Cybersecurity and Infrastructure Security Agency, to assess the extent of the damage and devise a recovery strategy. Kaseya also coordinated with external cybersecurity firms to investigate how the attackers gained access and provided guidance to affected customers.

Despite Kaseya's efforts to mitigate the attack, many businesses faced significant operational disruptions. MSPs and their customers struggled to restore their systems, and the decentralized nature of the attack complicated recovery efforts, as each organization had to manage its own response. Some organizations opted to pay the ransom in an attempt to recover their data, while others relied on backups to restore operations. On July 13, 2021, Kaseya announced that it had obtained a universal decryption key, though it did not disclose whether the ransom had been paid or how the key had been acquired.

Law enforcement agencies, including Europol, launched investigations to track the REvil group. Just days after the attack, REvil's online infrastructure vanished, leading some to speculate that law enforcement had taken down the group's servers. However, the extent to which law enforcement actions directly contributed to REvil's disappearance remains unclear.

Assessing the Impact

The immediate impact of the REvil ransomware attack on Kaseya was widespread and devastating, affecting over 1,500 businesses in more than 17 countries. Small and medium-sized businesses that relied on MSPs for IT services were particularly hard hit, with many facing significant downtime and financial losses as they attempted to recover from the attack. The attack disrupted retail and healthcare industries, forcing some businesses to temporarily close or severely curtail their operations.

Financially, the attack resulted in millions of dollars in damages in terms of lost revenue and the costs associated with recovery efforts. Businesses affected by the attack faced prolonged disruptions. For some, the financial strain was compounded by the ransom demands, which ranged from 45,000 dollars to several million dollars, depending on the organization's size. The broader impact on supply chains and business continuity further highlighted the dangers posed by ransomware attacks that target critical service providers.

The long-term consequences of the attack included increased scrutiny of IT service providers and the security of supply chains. The incident prompted many businesses to reassess their reliance on third-party vendors for IT services, and it underscored the need for stronger cybersecurity practices across the supply chain. Governments worldwide also called for greater collaboration between public and private sectors to combat the growing ransomware threat, and the attack accelerated discussions on ransomware regulations and international cooperation.

Lessons Learned and Takeaways

Several key lessons emerged from the REvil ransomware attack on Kaseya. First, the attack highlighted the importance of securing supply chains, particularly when it comes to IT service providers that manage critical infrastructure for multiple businesses. Using Kaseya's VSA software as an attack vector demonstrated how a single vulnerability in a widely used service could lead to widespread disruption. Moving forward, organizations must prioritize supply chain security and ensure that their vendors implement rigorous security measures.

Second, the attack underscored the importance of timely patch management and vulnerability disclosure. Kaseya's on-premises VSA servers had not been updated with a patch for the zero-day vulnerability exploited in the attack. Organizations must maintain strong patch management practices, regularly updating their systems and applying security patches as soon as they become available.

Finally, the attack emphasized the growing need for international collaboration in addressing ransomware. The global nature of the attack, which affected businesses in multiple countries, highlighted the importance of coordinated efforts between governments, law enforcement agencies, and cybersecurity firms. The involvement of law enforcement in the aftermath of the Kaseya attack also raised questions about how ransomware groups could be effectively dismantled through international cooperation.

Case Study Summary

The REvil ransomware attack on Kaseya in 2021 was a large-scale supply chain attack that affected over 1,500 businesses worldwide. By exploiting a zero-day vulnerability in Kaseya's VSA software, the REvil group could deploy ransomware to thousands of organizations through MSPs. The attackers demanded a 70-million-dollar ransom, marking one of the largest ransom demands in history.

Key takeaways from this case include the critical importance of securing supply chains, the need for timely patch management, and the role of international cooperation in combating ransomware. The Kaseya attack is a stark reminder of the growing sophistication of ransomware operations and the need for businesses and governments to remain vigilant in defending against such threats.

CONTI RANSOMWARE ATTACK ON IRISH HEALTH SERVICE (2021)

In May 2021, the *Conti* ransomware group launched a highly disruptive attack on the Health Service Executive (HSE) of Ireland, crippling the nation's healthcare infrastructure. The HSE manages public health services in Ireland, making it a critical part of its healthcare delivery system. The attack forced the shutdown of IT systems across multiple hospitals, delaying surgeries, appointments, and treatments, and it severely impacted healthcare delivery at a time when the world was still grappling with the COVID-19 pandemic.

At the time, ransomware attacks were becoming increasingly sophisticated, with the Conti group employing advanced techniques to penetrate networks and exfiltrate sensitive data before deploying encryption malware. The attack on the Irish Health Service stood out due to the critical nature of the target and the extent of the disruption caused. Unlike previous ransomware attacks that primarily sought financial gain, the impact on human life and health made this incident particularly severe.

Key stakeholders involved in the attack included the Irish government, HSE leadership, healthcare providers, patients, and cybersecurity firms brought in to assist with the recovery. The attack served as a stark reminder of the vulnerability of healthcare systems to ransomware and the need for stronger cybersecurity measures in critical infrastructure sectors.

Unfolding the Attack

The Conti ransomware attack on the HSE began with a phishing email that led to the initial compromise of the health service's IT network. From the information available, it is assumed that once the attackers gained access to the network, they moved laterally across systems, harvesting credentials and gaining control over key infrastructure segments. This process likely occurred over several days or weeks, during which the attackers could exfiltrate data before executing the ransomware.

The timeline of the attack indicates that the ransomware was deployed in mid-May 2021, triggering widespread encryption of the HSE's systems. This resulted in the near-total shutdown of IT services across Ireland's public hospitals, affecting everything from medical records to diagnostic tools. The attackers issued a ransom demand of 20 million dollars, threatening to leak sensitive patient data if their demands were not met.

The entry point for the attack was likely through an unpatched vulnerability or an unwitting employee falling victim to a phishing attack. Conti's method of operation, which involves double extortion tactics, meant that even if the HSE chose not to pay the ransom, it still faced the threat of data being leaked publicly. The scale of the attack was unprecedented in Ireland, impacting thousands of patients and healthcare workers and drawing widespread international attention.

Detection and Response Efforts

The attack was detected when hospital staff nationwide began reporting that they could no longer access critical systems, including patient records, scheduling systems, and diagnostic tools. The Irish Health Service responded by shutting down its IT systems to contain the spread of ransomware, but the damage was already extensive by this point. The HSE declared a major emergency, and hospitals were forced to revert to manual systems to continue providing care.

External cybersecurity firms and government agencies, including the Irish National Cyber Security Centre, were brought in to assist with the investigation and recovery efforts. The FBI and Europol were also involved due to the cross-border nature of the attack. Despite the severity of the situation, the Irish government decided not to pay the ransom, instead focusing on restoring systems from backups and working with cybersecurity experts to rebuild the affected infrastructure.

The recovery process was slow and complicated, given the complexity of the HSE's IT network and the sensitivity of the data involved. Hospitals operated under extreme pressure, with doctors and nurses relying on paper records and alternative care delivery methods. The situation was exacerbated by the ongoing COVID-19 pandemic, which placed an additional strain on Ireland's healthcare system.

Assessing the Impact

The immediate impact of the Conti ransomware attack on the HSE was devastating. Hospitals across Ireland were forced to cancel appointments, delay surgeries, and operate without access to digital records. Diagnostic services, including X-rays and MRIs, were delayed, and patients faced significant disruptions in their care. For weeks, healthcare providers struggled to deliver basic services while IT teams worked to restore systems and recover from the attack.

Financially, the attack is estimated to have cost the Irish government tens of millions of euros in recovery efforts, lost productivity, and the implementation of stronger cybersecurity measures. The disruption to healthcare services also had a long-term impact on patient outcomes, with some individuals experiencing delays in critical treatments. The reputational damage to the HSE was significant, raising concerns about the ability of public institutions to protect sensitive data and continue operations in the face of cyberattacks.

The long-term consequences of the attack included a renewed focus on healthcare cybersecurity, not only in Ireland but worldwide. The incident prompted discussions about the vulnerabilities in healthcare IT systems and the need for better resilience and incident response strategies in critical infrastructure sectors. It also led to the development of new cybersecurity policies and guidelines to protect healthcare institutions from future ransomware attacks.

Lessons Learned and Takeaways

The Conti ransomware attack on the Irish Health Service highlighted several key lessons for healthcare organizations and critical infrastructure providers. First, the attack underscored the importance of proactive cybersecurity measures, such as employee training on phishing, regular vulnerability assessments, and the implementation of multifactor authentication. The initial compromise through phishing demonstrated that human error remains a major vulnerability for organizations.

Second, the attack emphasized the need for robust incident response plans and backup strategies. While the HSE had backups in place, the complexity of restoring systems in a healthcare environment delayed the recovery process.

Organizations must ensure that their backup systems are tested regularly and can be repaired quickly during an attack.

Finally, the attack demonstrated the critical need for international cooperation in addressing ransomware threats. The involvement of Europol and the FBI in the investigation underscored the global nature of ransomware operations and the importance of cross-border collaboration in tracking down and prosecuting cybercriminals. Moving forward, healthcare institutions must work closely with government agencies and cybersecurity firms to bolster their defenses and share threat intelligence.

Case Study Summary

The Conti ransomware attack on the Irish Health Service in 2021 was one of the most severe cyberattacks on a healthcare system in recent history. The attack, which crippled Ireland's healthcare infrastructure and disrupted patient care, highlighted the vulnerability of critical sectors to ransomware. The decision by the Irish government not to pay the ransom set a precedent for handling such attacks, though the recovery process was slow and costly.

Key takeaways from this case include the importance of employee training, the need for robust incident response plans, and the value of international cooperation in combatting ransomware. The Conti attack serves as a stark reminder of the devastating impact that ransomware can have on critical services, particularly in sectors where human lives are directly affected.

CHAPTER CONCLUSION

The major themes emerging from the ransomware and cyberattacks discussed in this chapter paint a clear picture of the evolving threat landscape cybersecurity professionals face today. From WannaCry and NotPetya to more targeted attacks, these incidents illustrate how a combination of unpatched vulnerabilities, social engineering, and increasingly sophisticated malware can disrupt entire industries, governments, and critical infrastructure. One consistent theme is the importance of patch management—many of the most significant breaches were made possible by outdated systems and software vulnerabilities, as seen in the EternalBlue exploit used by multiple attackers. These cases underscore that a proactive approach to patching and system updates is essential to prevent similar exploits in the future.

For today's cybersecurity professionals, the lessons learned from these attacks extend far beyond just patching systems. The complexity and scale of modern cyberattacks, particularly ransomware, highlight the need for multilayered defenses and comprehensive incident response plans. The rise of double extortion schemes, where attackers encrypt data and threaten to leak sensitive information, forces organizations to rethink their data protection and backup strategies. Cyber professionals must ensure that their networks are segmented, backups are secure and regularly tested, and employees are trained to recognize phishing attempts and other social engineering tactics that often serve as the initial entry point.

A key challenge throughout this chapter has been the limited availability of detailed information regarding how organizations detected and responded to these attacks. In many cases, I have had to extrapolate response strategies from media reports and third-party analyses. This lack of transparency points to a broader issue within the cybersecurity community: the need for more open sharing of lessons learned. Without clear data on how incidents were handled, it becomes harder for other professionals to learn from past mistakes and successes. Transparency and collaboration within organizations and across industries will be crucial in addressing future threats.

Ultimately, the recommendations for cybersecurity professionals are clear: prioritize patch management, invest in robust incident response capabilities, and embrace a culture of vigilance. The attacks in this chapter are stark reminders that cybersecurity is not just about responding to incidents but preventing them through technology, training, and preparedness. As cyber threats continue to evolve, so must the strategies and tools used to defend against them. By learning from these high-profile attacks, cybersecurity professionals can better prepare for tomorrow's digital battleground challenges.

9

SUPPLY CHAIN ATTACKS AND CLOUD SECURITY

If there's one thing we have learned from recent cyberattacks, you can never be too sure where the next threat is coming from. Hackers have moved from breaking into your digital *front door* to sneaking in with trusted software updates, like a burglar dressed as the pizza delivery guy. And when it comes to cloud security, let's say that storing data in *the cloud* is not as serene as it sounds—especially when you realize that storm clouds can also bring cyber-criminals. Jokes aside, the reality is that supply chain and cloud-based attacks have become some of the most insidious threats facing organizations today, capable of undermining even the best security strategies.

This chapter dives deep into some of the most recent notorious supply chain and cloud security breaches. We explore how sophisticated attackers could infiltrate trusted software providers and cloud platforms, exposing vulnerabilities in systems that many organizations depend on for critical operations. While it is easy to point fingers at third-party vendors, the truth is that these incidents highlight a much broader issue: the interconnectedness of modern technology makes it certain that no organization is an island. Attackers have found creative ways to exploit this interdependence, whether through a compromised software update or a breach in a cloud service (see Figure 9.1).

This chapter aims to analyze these attacks in detail, extracting valuable lessons for cybersecurity professionals. In many cases, I have had to extrapolate details about how organizations detected and responded to these breaches based on available media reports and other informational sources. It is important to note that not all incidents are documented in full, and there are gaps in publicly available information about response efforts. However, by piecing together what we know, we can still identify patterns and strategies that can help protect against future attacks.

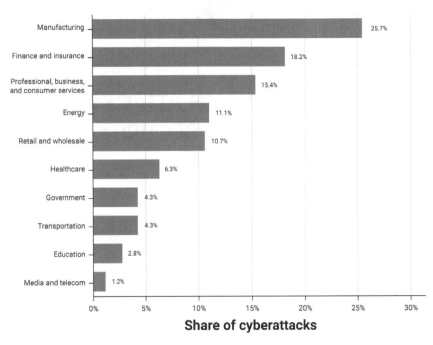

Figure 9.1   Cyberattacks worldwide across industries (*source*: Statista Search Department)

Ultimately, this chapter serves as both a wake-up call and a guide. The growing threat of supply chain and cloud security breaches requires a shift in how we think about cybersecurity. It is no longer enough to secure only what is inside your organization—you need to keep a close eye on who you are letting in through your vendors and what is happening in your cloud environments. Cybersecurity professionals can better defend against the evolving challenges of today's interconnected digital landscape by understanding the risks and learning from past attacks.

WHAT IS A SUPPLY CHAIN ATTACK?

A supply chain attack is a cyberattack that targets the weaker links in an organization's supply chain rather than directly attacking the organization itself. In a typical supply chain attack, cybercriminals compromise third-party vendors, service providers, or software that an organization relies on, using these as a backdoor to infiltrate the primary target. Since companies often trust their suppliers and partners, attackers exploit this trust, embedding malicious code into legitimate software updates, manipulating hardware, or gaining unauthorized access to sensitive systems through vendor credentials. This makes supply chain attacks particularly dangerous since they can bypass many traditional security defenses.

One of the most concerning aspects of supply chain attacks is their potential to affect many victims simultaneously. A single compromised vendor can lead to widespread damage, involving hundreds or even thousands of organizations that use the vendor's software or services. This was seen in high-profile incidents like the SolarWinds attack, where a malicious software update infected numerous U.S. government agencies and private companies. Attackers leverage the scale of modern supply chains, recognizing that they can gain access to a wide range of networks, systems, and data by attacking one trusted supplier.

Supply chain attacks also highlight the challenge of visibility and control in today's interconnected digital landscape. Organizations often rely on multiple vendors, contractors, and cloud service providers, creating a complex ecosystem where not every element is directly under their control. This complexity makes it harder to monitor and secure all potential entry points. Defending against supply chain attacks requires a multilayered security approach that includes vetting and monitoring vendors, implementing strict access controls, and ensuring that third-party software and systems adhere to the same security standards as internal systems.

The following chart illustrates the timeline associated with the attacks that will be explored in this chapter (see Figure 9.2).

Figure 9.2   The timeline of attacks discussed in this chapter

CCLEANER SUPPLY CHAIN ATTACK (2017)

The CCleaner supply chain attack in 2017 is one of the most significant examples of a cybercriminal group targeting trusted software to infiltrate thousands of devices. CCleaner, a popular utility program designed to clean unwanted files from computers and enhance performance, was owned by Piriform, a subsidiary of Avast. With over two billion downloads globally, CCleaner was widely trusted by individuals and businesses, making it a prime target for a supply chain attack to compromise many users.

At the time of the attack, the technological landscape witnessed an increased reliance on trusted software vendors, making supply chain attacks a potent threat vector. Cybercriminals recognized that targeting widely used software could gain access to an enormous number of endpoints, amplifying the scale of potential damage. CCleaner was particularly vulnerable because its updates reached millions of users daily, making any compromise of its code a high-impact event.

The key stakeholders involved in this case were Piriform (the developers of CCleaner), Avast (its parent company), and the millions of users who unknowingly downloaded the compromised version of the software. The attack raised significant concerns about the security of supply chains and the role of trusted software vendors in protecting their customers from sophisticated threats.

Unfolding the Attack

The CCleaner supply chain attack began in August 2017, when attackers inserted malicious code into a legitimate software update for CCleaner version 5.33. From the information available, I assume the attackers gained access to Piriform's development environment through compromised credentials or a vulnerability in their build system. Once inside, the attackers injected malware directly into the software update that would later be distributed to millions of users.

The malicious update contained a multistage payload. The first stage collected basic system information from infected devices, such as Internet Protocol addresses, installed software, and system configurations. This data was then sent to the attackers' command-and-control servers, where they could evaluate which systems were worth targeting for further exploitation. The second stage involved a more selective attack on high-value targets, allowing the attackers to deploy additional malware on devices belonging to major technology and telecommunications companies.

The attack timeline reveals that the compromised version of CCleaner was distributed between August and September 2017, during which time over 2.27 million users downloaded the infected software. The attackers' methods were highly sophisticated and precisely operated to infiltrate the development environment and the end-user systems. Their ability to remain undetected during the attack underscores organizations' challenges in securing their software supply chains.

Detection and Response Efforts

The CCleaner supply chain attack was detected in mid-September 2017 when Cisco Talos and Avast security researchers identified unusual network activity and communications originating from CCleaner installations. Once the breach was identified, Piriform, Avast, and other cybersecurity firms worked quickly to analyze the scope of the attack, determine how the malware had been inserted into the software, and develop a remediation plan to protect affected users.

Piriform immediately responded by pulling the compromised version of CCleaner from its distribution channels and releasing a clean update (version 5.34) for users. From what I have reviewed, Avast and other cybersecurity experts conducted forensic analyses to understand the full extent of the attack and assess whether any additional malware had been deployed on high-value targets. The quick response likely prevented the attackers from fully exploiting their access to sensitive systems.

The response timeline highlights the importance of collaboration between security researchers, software vendors, and law enforcement agencies. Although the attack was detected within a month of onset, the damage could have been far more severe if it had gone unnoticed for longer. Piriform and Avast's transparency in acknowledging the breach and releasing updates to mitigate the threat helped reassure users and limit further damage.

Assessing the Impact

The immediate impact of the CCleaner attack was significant, affecting millions of users who had downloaded the compromised version of the software. While the initial stage of the malware primarily collected system information, the second-stage payload aimed to infiltrate high-value targets, including major technology companies such as Google, Microsoft, and Intel. Fortunately, the attack was detected before widespread exploitation occurred, but it still raised concerns about the security of widely trusted software vendors.

Financially, Piriform and Avast faced costs associated with incident response, remediation, and potential legal liabilities. The breach also led to reputational damage for Avast, as users questioned how a cybersecurity company could allow such an attack to infiltrate its products. However, the long-term financial impact appears to have been mitigated by the company's swift response and transparency in addressing the breach.

The broader industry impact of the CCleaner attack was significant since it underscored the vulnerabilities present in supply chain security and the importance of securing software development environments. The attack highlighted the dangers of targeting widely used utility software, where a single compromised update could potentially impact millions of devices globally. For users and businesses alike, the incident prompted a reevaluation of the trust in software vendors and their ability to safeguard their supply chains.

Lessons Learned and Takeaways

The CCleaner supply chain attack offers several important lessons for improving cybersecurity practices and supply chain security. One of the key takeaways is the importance of securing the software development environment. It appears that the attackers gained access to Piriform's build systems, allowing them to insert malicious code directly into the software update. To prevent such compromises, organizations must implement stringent security controls in their development environments, including code-signing practices, continuous monitoring, and vulnerability management.

Another critical lesson is the need for proactive threat detection and monitoring. The attack went undetected for several weeks, allowing the compromised version of CCleaner to spread to millions of users. Organizations must invest in advanced threat detection tools to identify unusual network activity and potential supply chain compromises in real time, thereby reducing attackers' dwell time.

Finally, the attack underscores the growing threat of supply chain attacks and the importance of transparency in incident response. Piriform and Avast's quick public acknowledgment of the breach and efforts to mitigate the threat helped prevent further damage. This case highlights the need for software vendors to be transparent with their users, work closely with cybersecurity researchers, and ensure timely updates to mitigate the risks posed by supply chain attacks.

Case Study Summary

The CCleaner supply chain attack of 2017 serves as a stark reminder of the vulnerabilities inherent in trusted software supply chains. The attackers' ability to compromise a widely used utility program like CCleaner, combined with the sophistication of the malware, demonstrates the growing risks posed by supply chain attacks. Key takeaways from the case include securing software development environments, investing in proactive threat detection, and maintaining transparency in incident response. The broader impact of the attack extends beyond the immediate victims, prompting the cybersecurity community to reconsider how trusted software vendors can better protect their products and users from similar threats in the future.

ASUS LIVE UPDATE UTILITY SUPPLY CHAIN ATTACK (2018)

The ASUS Live Update Utility supply chain attack in 2018 was one of the most impactful and sophisticated cyber incidents targeting a trusted software distribution channel. ASUS, a leading computer hardware manufacturer, had its Live Update utility compromised, allowing attackers to distribute malicious updates to hundreds of thousands of users. The Live Update utility, preinstalled on ASUS devices, delivers firmware and software updates to maintain device security and performance. However, it became a vector for malicious code insertion in this case.

At the time, ASUS was considered one of the most reputable hardware vendors globally, which made this attack particularly alarming. The technological landscape of 2018 was one where supply chain security was becoming an increasingly critical focus due to the rise of sophisticated attacks that directly targeted trusted vendors rather than end users. The ASUS attack exemplified the growing threat of compromised supply chains, highlighting vulnerabilities even within the most trusted software ecosystems.

The key stakeholders involved in this case were ASUS, its customer base, cybersecurity firms such as Kaspersky and Symantec, and government agencies that later became involved in addressing the broader security concerns surrounding this incident. The attack exposed the weaknesses in ASUS's development environment, spotlighting the security of automatic software update mechanisms across the tech industry.

Unfolding the Attack

The ASUS Live Update Utility attack unfolded in 2018 when a group of attackers, believed to be state-sponsored, gained access to ASUS's software development environment. From the available information, I assume the attackers inserted a malicious backdoor into the Live Update utility by compromising the software's build pipeline. They signed the malicious updates with ASUS's legitimate digital certificates, allowing the tainted software to bypass security checks and appear as legitimate updates to users.

The malicious updates were delivered to nearly 500,000 ASUS users, but the attackers targeted a smaller group of high-value individuals using a predefined list of MAC addresses. These MAC addresses allowed the malware to activate selectively, ensuring that only specific devices were compromised while most infected systems remained inactive. This targeted approach indicated that the attackers knew their intended victims well.

From what I understand, the attackers used advanced techniques such as code signing and sophisticated malware payloads to remain undetected for an extended period. The attack timeline suggests that the initial compromise occurred months before the malware was discovered. The attackers were able to infiltrate ASUS's systems, insert the backdoor, and distribute the compromised updates while avoiding detection from security systems and antivirus software.

Detection and Response Efforts

The ASUS attack was first detected in early 2019 by Kaspersky Lab, a cybersecurity firm monitoring suspicious activity within its user base. Kaspersky researchers identified anomalous behavior linked to the ASUS Live Update utility and discovered compromised software. Their investigation revealed that malicious updates had been distributed for several months before the breach was uncovered.

Upon discovering the attack, Kaspersky contacted ASUS and other cybersecurity firms, including Symantec, to assist in the investigation and contain the damage. ASUS initially denied the breach but later acknowledged the issue after further evidence came to light. The company issued a clean update to replace the compromised version of Live Update. It provided a diagnostic tool to help users determine if their devices had been affected by the malware.

The response timeline shows that while ASUS's initial reaction was slow, the involvement of third-party cybersecurity researchers played a crucial role in detecting the breach and mitigating the attack. ASUS's collaboration with cybersecurity firms helped contain the spread of the malware and provided users with tools to check for infection. However, the delay in acknowledging the breach and the initial lack of transparency from ASUS raised concerns about the company's incident response capabilities.

Assessing the Impact

The immediate impact of the ASUS Live Update Utility attack was significant, as nearly half a million users unknowingly received malicious software updates. However, the number of compromised systems was far lower since the attackers used a targeted approach, focusing on high-value individuals. The attack did not appear to cause widespread operational disruption, but it raised serious concerns about the potential for future exploitation, data theft, and espionage.

Financially, ASUS faced considerable costs related to incident response, security investigations, and reputational damage. The company's delay in addressing the breach and lack of initial transparency likely contributed to the loss of trust among customers and industry partners. While no large-scale financial losses were reported, the reputational damage was perhaps the most significant consequence because ASUS's ability to secure its software development environment was questioned.

The broader industry implications of the ASUS attack were profound. The incident highlighted the vulnerabilities in automatic update mechanisms, even for well-established hardware manufacturers. It prompted other organizations to reevaluate their software supply chains and the security of their development environments. The attack served as a reminder for ASUS's customers that even trusted vendors could be targeted by sophisticated attackers, emphasizing the need for constant vigilance.

Lessons Learned and Takeaways

The ASUS Live Update Utility attack offers several critical lessons for improving cybersecurity practices and supply chain security. One of the most important takeaways is the need for organizations to secure their software development environments. It appears that the attackers were able to infiltrate ASUS's build systems, allowing them to insert a backdoor into a trusted software update. Companies must ensure that their build environments are secure and that access is tightly controlled to prevent unauthorized modifications to software.

Another key lesson is the importance of code-signing and verifying software updates. While the attackers used legitimate digital certificates to sign the malicious updates, organizations can implement additional verification mechanisms to ensure the integrity of their software before it is distributed to users. Proactive monitoring of software distribution channels can help detect and prevent such compromises in the future.

Finally, the ASUS attack underscores the importance of transparency and prompt incident response. ASUS's initial reluctance to acknowledge the breach delayed the response and caused customer frustration. Moving forward, organizations must be transparent with their users and partners when a breach occurs, providing timely updates and clear guidance on mitigating the risks.

Case Study Summary

The ASUS Live Update Utility supply chain attack of 2018 demonstrates the growing sophistication of cyberattacks targeting trusted software distribution channels. The attackers' ability to infiltrate ASUS's development environment and distribute malicious updates to nearly half a million users underscores the need for stronger security controls in the software development process. Key takeaways from this case include the importance of securing build environments, verifying software integrity, and maintaining transparency in incident response. The broader implications of the attack highlight the critical need for vigilance in securing supply chains and ensuring that trusted vendors can safeguard their products against sophisticated cyber threats.

SOLARWINDS HACK (2020)

The SolarWinds hack of 2020, also known as the SUNBURST attack, was one of the most sophisticated and far-reaching cyberattacks in recent history. It targeted the Orion software platform, developed by SolarWinds, which provides information technology (IT) management tools to various organizations, including government agencies and private enterprises. The attackers, allegedly associated with a Russian state-sponsored group, infiltrated SolarWinds' software supply chain, compromising over 18,000 clients by embedding malicious code into legitimate software updates.

At the time, SolarWinds was a major player in IT infrastructure monitoring, with customers spanning industries such as government, finance, healthcare, and technology. In 2020, the technological landscape saw an increasing reliance on third-party vendors and cloud services, creating opportunities for attackers to exploit weaknesses in supply chain security. In this case, SolarWinds' critical role in managing IT systems across many sectors made it a prime target for a supply chain attack with widespread consequences.

The key stakeholders in this breach included SolarWinds, its customers (ranging from Fortune 500 companies to government agencies like the U.S. Department of Homeland Security), and global cybersecurity firms involved in responding to the breach. The hack raised serious concerns about supply chain vulnerabilities and prompted a reevaluation of third-party security practices across industries.

Unfolding the Attack

The SolarWinds hack began in March 2020 when attackers inserted malicious code, later dubbed SUNBURST, into a legitimate SolarWinds Orion software update. From the available information, I assume the attackers exploited weaknesses in SolarWinds' build environment, gaining unauthorized access and inserting malware during development. The tainted updates were then distributed to SolarWinds' customers through the company's normal update channels, allowing the attackers to access the networks of affected organizations.

The attack timeline suggests the compromised software update was distributed between March and June of 2020. Once installed, the malware created a backdoor that allowed attackers to move laterally within the targeted networks, exfiltrating sensitive data and maintaining persistent access for months. The attackers used sophisticated techniques to evade detection, including using legitimate software certificates and domain names to disguise their activities.

From what I have reviewed, the scale of the attack was immense, affecting numerous high-profile organizations, including U.S. government agencies like the Department of Defense, the Treasury Department, and private companies like Microsoft and FireEye. The attackers exploited multiple vulnerabilities, including weaknesses in network segmentation and security monitoring, allowing them to collect valuable intelligence and compromise sensitive systems stealthily.

Detection and Response Efforts

The SolarWinds hack went undetected for several months until December 2020 when the cybersecurity firm FireEye identified the breach after noticing unusual activity in its network. FireEye's detection of the breach led to the discovery of the SUNBURST malware embedded in SolarWinds Orion updates. This prompted a rapid response from both SolarWinds and affected organizations along with a broader investigation by U.S. government agencies and cybersecurity firms worldwide.

Once the breach was discovered, SolarWinds quickly worked with law enforcement and cybersecurity experts to remove the compromised software updates and mitigate the damage. The company issued emergency patches and advised its customers to disconnect compromised versions of Orion software. From the information I have seen, SolarWinds also initiated a comprehensive review of its internal security practices to identify how the attackers had gained access to its development environment.

The timeline of the response reveals the complexity of dealing with a supply chain attack of this magnitude. Thousands of organizations were forced to conduct forensic investigations to determine whether they had been compromised and to what extent. The U.S. government launched a multiagency response, including the Federal Bureau of Investigation, the Cybersecurity and Infrastructure Security Agency, and the National Security Agency, to assess the damage and coordinate a unified response. The breach underscored the importance of collaboration between the public and private sectors in responding to large-scale cyberattacks.

Assessing the Impact

The immediate impact of the SolarWinds hack was profound. Many affected organizations were critical to national security, financial stability, and global commerce, creating widespread concern about the potential damage. Financial losses were substantial, with costs associated with remediation efforts, legal fees, and the disruption of normal business operations. The U.S. government and private companies alike faced significant challenges in restoring trust in their IT infrastructure and securing sensitive data that may have been compromised.

In the long term, the reputational damage to SolarWinds was severe since the company was seen as a weak link in the supply chain. Customers and partners began to question third-party vendors' security, leading to increased scrutiny of supply chain security practices across industries. Additionally, the attack exposed vulnerabilities in how organizations manage software updates and highlighted the need for more robust security measures in the software development life cycle.

The broader implications of the SolarWinds hack extended beyond the affected organizations. The breach prompted widespread discussions about the risks associated with supply chain attacks, particularly as companies increasingly rely on third-party vendors for critical IT services. The incident also reinforced the importance of zero-trust security models, which assume that attackers may already be inside the network and, therefore, emphasize continuous monitoring and verification of users and device before granting permission to any system or data.

Lessons Learned and Takeaways

The SolarWinds hack offers several critical lessons for improving cybersecurity practices and protecting against future supply chain attacks. One of the most important takeaways is the need for greater visibility into the software development process. The available information shows that SolarWinds lacked adequate security controls in its build environment, allowing attackers to inject malicious code into legitimate updates. Organizations must implement rigorous security measures throughout the development life cycle, including code signing, vulnerability scanning, and continuous monitoring of software builds.

Another key lesson is the importance of adopting a zero-trust security model. The SolarWinds attack demonstrated how attackers could bypass traditional perimeter defenses by exploiting trusted software updates. Organizations must assume that attackers could be inside the network and take steps to limit lateral movement, such as implementing strong identity and access management controls, network segmentation, and real-time monitoring for suspicious activity.

Finally, the breach underscored the need for a coordinated incident response plan that includes internal and external stakeholders. FireEye's rapid detection of the breach and the subsequent collaboration between private companies and government agencies helped mitigate some of the damage. This case highlights the importance of building strong relationships with cybersecurity firms, law enforcement, and industry partners to effectively respond to and recover from large-scale cyberattacks.

Case Study Summary

The SolarWinds hack of 2020 exposed vulnerabilities in the software development process, led to widespread disruptions in government and private sectors, and raised critical concerns about third-party vendors' security. Key takeaways from this case include securing the software supply chain, adopting a zero-trust security model, and fostering collaboration between public and private sectors in responding to cyber threats. The SolarWinds breach is a cautionary tale about the growing risks of supply chain attacks and the need for constant vigilance in an increasingly interconnected world.

MICROSOFT EXCHANGE SERVER HACK (2021)

The Microsoft Exchange Server Hack of 2021 was one of the most significant cyberattacks of the year, impacting thousands of organizations globally. This supply chain attack exploited vulnerabilities in Microsoft Exchange Server, a widely used email and calendaring server. The attack allowed unauthorized access to email accounts, data exfiltration, and further exploitation of compromised systems. It involved a sophisticated cyber espionage campaign that affected businesses, government entities, and critical infrastructure organizations across various sectors.

At the time, the Microsoft Exchange Server was a critical component of corporate infrastructure, relied upon by organizations for internal communication and business operations. As one of the largest software vendors globally, Microsoft was seen as a leader in secure infrastructure solutions, making this breach all the more alarming. As the technological landscape shifted toward cloud services and hybrid infrastructures, vulnerabilities in on-premise server software like Exchange became major targets for attackers seeking to exploit less secure environments.

The key stakeholders in this breach included Microsoft, the organizations running on-premise Exchange Servers, their customers, and multiple government agencies impacted by or involved in the response. The attack also highlighted how major software providers manage vulnerabilities and how quickly they can respond to exploits.

Unfolding the Attack

The Microsoft Exchange Server hack began when a group of attackers allegedly affiliated with a Chinese state-sponsored threat actor, *Hafnium*, exploited four zero-day vulnerabilities in Microsoft's on-premise Exchange Servers. The attack started in early January 2021 but came to light publicly in March when Microsoft disclosed the vulnerabilities. From the information available, I assume the attackers leveraged these vulnerabilities to gain initial access to the servers, enabling them to take control of email accounts and install web shells to maintain persistent access to the compromised networks.

The attack's entry point involved exploiting a combination of vulnerabilities. CVE-2021-26855, a server-side request forgery vulnerability, allowed the attackers to authenticate as an Exchange server. Once inside, they chained other vulnerabilities to execute arbitrary code and elevate privileges, eventually gaining full control of the system. The attackers installed web shells that acted as backdoors, enabling them to continue accessing and exfiltrating data long after the initial compromise.

From what I have analyzed, the attack's timeline shows that while it began in early January 2021, it rapidly escalated in February, and thousands of organizations worldwide were affected by March. Microsoft quickly released security patches in early March 2021, but the damage had been done by then. Many organizations had not applied the patches, leaving them vulnerable to further attacks even after the breach was disclosed. The methods used by the attackers—primarily exploiting software vulnerabilities—underscore the importance of timely patching and the challenges organizations face in securing on-premise servers.

Detection and Response Efforts

The detection of the Microsoft Exchange Server hack came after Microsoft was alerted by cybersecurity researchers who had been investigating unusual activity on Exchange Servers. By the time Microsoft publicly disclosed the vulnerabilities and released patches on March 2, 2021, attackers had already compromised thousands of systems. Microsoft's response was swift in terms of releasing security updates. However, the scale of the attack meant that many organizations were still exposed, particularly those without the capability to respond rapidly to the patches.

Once the breach was disclosed, affected organizations scrambled to secure their systems. Microsoft provided detailed instructions for mitigation, but the initial response was chaotic due to the sheer number of organizations impacted. Security firms, law enforcement, and government agencies quickly became involved, offering guidance and assisting organizations in applying the patches and remediating compromised systems. For many businesses, the response involved patching the Exchange Servers, removing the installed web shells, and securing any sensitive data that had been exfiltrated.

Despite these efforts, the response timeline revealed significant delays in detection and patching. Many organizations struggled with identifying the attack and dealing with the aftermath due to the complex nature of the vulnerabilities. Additionally, the reliance on external cybersecurity firms and government resources highlighted the importance of having strong incident response plans and cybersecurity expertise in-house.

Assessing the Impact

The immediate impact of the Microsoft Exchange Server hack was felt across industries and sectors. With tens of thousands of servers affected, the breach had global ramifications, disrupting business operations, exposing sensitive data, and leading to widespread security concerns. Financial losses were significant in terms of direct costs, such as hiring incident response teams, and indirect costs, such as operational downtime and lost customer trust. Many small and medium-sized businesses were particularly vulnerable, lacking the resources to mitigate the attack effectively.

Long-term consequences of the hack included reputational damage for Microsoft because the vulnerabilities in its widely used server software exposed thousands of organizations to significant risk. The attack also led to regulatory scrutiny, with governments and cybersecurity agencies warning organizations to enhance their security practices, particularly concerning the use of on-premise servers. In response, Microsoft accelerated its push for customers to move to its cloud-based services, arguing that cloud solutions offered greater security and easier management than on-premise systems.

The stakeholders impacted by the breach included the compromised organizations and their customers and partners, whose data may have been exposed. For government entities, the attack raised concerns about national security, as the compromised systems could have been used for cyber espionage. The breach also led to a broader reevaluation of the security of supply chain infrastructures, as it demonstrated how a single point of vulnerability in widely used software could have devastating consequences across industries.

Lessons Learned and Takeaways

Several important lessons emerged from the Microsoft Exchange Server hack. One critical takeaway is the importance of timely patching and vulnerability management. The breach exploited zero-day vulnerabilities that, once disclosed, spread quickly across thousands of organizations that had not yet patched their systems. This incident underscored the need for organizations to prioritize security updates and have processes in place to respond rapidly to critical vulnerabilities.

Another lesson is the complexity of securing on-premise infrastructure in a world increasingly moving toward cloud-based solutions. From what I have gathered, many organizations struggled to maintain the security expertise to manage their on-premise Exchange Servers effectively. This hack highlighted the risks associated with outdated or inadequately managed infrastructure, prompting organizations to consider cloud migration a more secure alternative.

The attack also reinforced the importance of strong detection and incident response capabilities. The breach went undetected for weeks, giving the attackers ample time to establish persistent access to compromised systems. A robust security monitoring system and the ability to respond quickly to signs of compromise are essential in mitigating the damage caused by such attacks.

In the wake of the breach, many organizations have improved their cybersecurity posture by investing in better detection tools, incident response plans, and employee training.

Case Study Summary

The Microsoft Exchange Server hack of 2021 serves as a stark reminder of the vulnerabilities inherent in widely used infrastructure software. The attack demonstrated how unpatched vulnerabilities could be exploited on a massive scale, impacting organizations worldwide. Key takeaways include the importance of timely patching, the risks associated with on-premise infrastructure, and the need for robust detection and incident response mechanisms. The broader impact of the attack led to a rethinking of supply chain security practices and reinforced the importance of cybersecurity in an increasingly interconnected world.

CHAPTER CONCLUSION

The supply chain attacks detailed in this chapter illustrate modern cyber threats' growing complexity and sophistication. These incidents underscore the significant vulnerabilities when organizations rely on third-party vendors and cloud services. Attackers have increasingly shifted their focus from direct attacks on organizations to targeting trusted software providers and cloud platforms, enabling them to compromise multiple victims with a single, well-placed intrusion. This shift highlights the critical importance of securing the entire digital supply chain because any weakness in third-party services can become a gateway for attackers to infiltrate otherwise well-defended organizations.

For cybersecurity professionals today, these attacks serve as a reminder of the evolving threat landscape. Defenders must not only focus on securing their internal systems but also scrutinize the security practices of their vendors and partners. This chapter's case studies reveal that many large and small organizations are vulnerable to sophisticated adversaries exploiting supply chain weaknesses. In some cases, attackers were able to bypass traditional security measures by leveraging compromised software updates that were signed with legitimate certificates. This emphasizes the need for organizations to implement more rigorous security controls across their development and supply chain environments.

Throughout the chapter, I have relied on available information and, where necessary, extrapolated details about detection and response efforts from media reports and other credible sources. In many instances, public information on how organizations initially detected and responded to these breaches is incomplete or unavailable, leaving room for interpretation. Cybersecurity professionals must recognize that media reports may not always provide the full picture of an incident. However, by analyzing these incidents with the available data, valuable lessons can still be drawn to inform future security practices and strategies.

To improve defenses against supply chain and cloud-based threats, cybersecurity professionals should prioritize a proactive approach. This includes conducting regular security assessments of third-party vendors, implementing robust access controls, and monitoring for unusual activity internally and within vendor systems. Professionals should also advocate for transparency in incident reporting and work to build resilience by assuming that no vendor or system is immune to compromise. By applying the lessons learned from these high-profile incidents, organizations can better position themselves to defend against the growing threat of supply chain and cloud security attacks in today's interconnected digital world.

This book has free material available for download from the
Web Added Value™ resource center at *www.jrosspub.com*

10

CRITICAL INFRASTRUCTURE AND INDUSTRIAL CONTROL SYSTEMS CHALLENGES

Imagine waking up one morning, sipping your coffee, and suddenly realizing that the electricity is out, the water is contaminated, and the trains aren't running—sounds like a dystopian nightmare, right? Or just a Monday after a cyberattack on critical infrastructure. While Hollywood often paints a dramatic picture of hackers shutting down entire cities with the tap of a keyboard, the reality is far more complex—and, unfortunately, not far from the truth. The attacks on critical infrastructure systems discussed in this chapter might not come with Hollywood's flair for explosions. Still, they represent some of the most sophisticated and potentially dangerous threats in modern cybersecurity.

But let's drop the jokes because we're talking about the potential for real-world harm from cyberattacks targeting essential services such as power, water, and transportation systems. The case studies in this chapter cover significant incidents such as the Trisis/Triton attack, which aimed to disable safety systems in a petrochemical plant. These incidents highlight a disturbing trend: cyberattacks are no longer just about stealing data or causing temporary digital headaches—they're about targeting the systems that keep our society running. As we analyze each of these attacks, we'll explore how they occurred and what they mean for the future of cybersecurity and public safety.

Throughout this chapter, it's important to note that, in many cases, I have extrapolated certain details about detection and response efforts from available information. Often, these attacks are shrouded in secrecy or incomplete reporting, meaning I've had to piece together insights from media, industry reports, and expert analysis. This mirrors a challenge that cybersecurity

professionals face daily operating in an environment where perfect information is rarely available, and decisions must be made quickly based on the best
data. The ability to interpret incomplete data and anticipate future threats is
critical for anyone defending critical infrastructure.

This chapter aims to take a deep dive into the most significant cyberattacks
on critical infrastructure and industrial control systems (ICS) and to draw
valuable lessons from each incident. From understanding how these attacks
unfolded to recognizing the recurring vulnerabilities that make ICS environments attractive to adversaries, this chapter will equip you with insights that
can help shape future defensive strategies. Whether you're a seasoned cybersecurity professional or new to the field, these case studies remind you of
the high stakes involved in protecting the systems that modern life depends
on—and the evolving nature of the threats we all face.

WHAT ARE INDUSTRIAL CONTROL SYSTEMS AND THEIR CYBER RISKS?

Critical infrastructure encompasses the essential systems and services that
support the functioning of modern society, from energy grids and water
treatment plants to transportation networks and healthcare systems. These
systems are the backbone of daily life, and any disruption can have far-reaching consequences, impacting millions of people. ICS play a crucial role in
managing the physical processes of critical infrastructure, enabling operators
to monitor, control, and automate essential functions. However, as these systems have become more connected and integrated with information technology (IT) networks, they have become more vulnerable to cyberattacks.

The unique challenge of securing ICS lies in their legacy design, which
often prioritizes functionality and reliability over security. Many ICS were
developed long before the modern cyber threat landscape existed, and as a
result, they lack the built-in protections necessary to defend against today's
sophisticated attacks. This is especially problematic as critical infrastructure
systems are increasingly exposed to the Internet for remote access and monitoring, making them an attractive target for malicious actors. The convergence of IT and operational technology (OT) has expanded the attack surface,
allowing cybercriminals to exploit weaknesses in IT systems to gain access to
OT environments, where they can manipulate physical processes.

Cyber risks to critical infrastructure include a range of threats, from ransomware and data theft to nation-state attacks designed to cause large-scale

disruption. The potential consequences of a successful cyberattack on critical infrastructure are severe: physical damage, economic loss, public safety hazards, and even threats to national security. These incidents underscore the need for robust cybersecurity measures to protect IT and OT systems from increasingly sophisticated threats.

To mitigate these risks, cybersecurity professionals must adopt a multilayered approach that includes network segmentation, advanced threat detection, incident response plans, and continuous monitoring of both IT and ICS environments. Additionally, securing the supply chain—ensuring that third-party vendors and software providers follow strict security protocols—has become essential in preventing attacks like the Havex Remote Access Trojan. The stakes are high, and the consequences of failing to secure critical infrastructure can be catastrophic, making it imperative for organizations to stay ahead of emerging cyber threats and implement best practices across their systems.

The following chart illustrates the timeline associated with the attacks that will be explored in this chapter and online (see Figure 10.1).

HAVEX REMOTE ACCESS TROJAN (2013–2014)

The Havex Remote Access Trojan (RAT) was part of a broader campaign targeting ICS between 2013 and 2014, marking one of the early and sophisticated attacks on critical infrastructure through advanced malware. Havex was attributed to a group often called "Dragonfly" or "Energetic Bear," believed to be state-sponsored actors. The campaign primarily targeted the energy sector and pharmaceutical and defense companies, aiming to compromise ICS environments in Europe and North America.

At the time, the convergence of IT and OT systems was becoming more common, making ICS environments more efficient but simultaneously exposing them to cyber risks. Havex was especially dangerous because it targeted industrial control systems through compromised software vendors—posing a significant supply chain threat. The key stakeholders affected by this attack included ICS vendors, energy companies, the industrial sector at large, and government agencies tasked with responding to cybersecurity incidents.

The Havex attack was part of a broader wave of advanced persistent threats (APTs) targeting critical infrastructure, illustrating the evolving risk landscape for industries increasingly dependent on interconnected and often poorly secured systems.

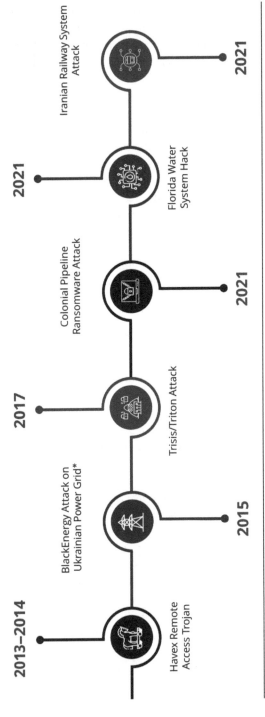

Figure 10.1   The timeline of attacks discussed in this chapter. *This case study can be found online in the WAV section of the publisher's website at www.jrosspub.com/wav.

Unfolding the Attack

The Havex malware was primarily spread through a supply chain attack, where attackers compromised legitimate software vendors and infected the ICS software used by energy companies and other critical infrastructure operators. From the information available, it is assumed that attackers inserted malicious code into legitimate software updates. When these updates were installed, the malware provided remote access to the attackers, allowing them to monitor, control, and gather information from ICS environments.

The timeline of the attack began in early 2013 when the attackers breached the networks of ICS software vendors. They distributed Havex via infected updates, targeting industrial organizations that relied on these vendors for their ICS software. In addition to the supply chain compromise, the attackers used other methods, such as phishing emails and watering hole attacks, to spread the malware. Watering hole attacks involved compromising websites frequently visited by ICS operators, further increasing the attack's reach.

Havex was designed to collect intelligence on the targeted ICS environments, providing the attackers insight into how these systems operated. The malware used a custom-built OPC (OLE for Process Control) scanner to map out ICS networks and gather information about devices connected to these environments. The level of detail gathered suggested that the attackers were conducting reconnaissance for potential future attacks rather than immediately disrupting operations.

Detection and Response Efforts

Havex remained undetected for a significant period due to its stealthy approach and the use of legitimate software vendors to spread the malware. The initial compromise went unnoticed because the updates came from trusted sources, making it difficult for ICS operators to recognize the threat. Detection only occurred later, as cybersecurity firms began analyzing anomalous activity in the energy and industrial sectors, eventually tracing the source to the compromised software updates.

When the attack was discovered, ICS operators and software vendors launched response efforts to mitigate the damage. Initial response actions included isolating infected systems and removing compromised software updates. ICS operators worked with cybersecurity firms and government agencies to investigate the extent of the breach and prevent further exploitation. The involvement of external cybersecurity firms like F-Secure and Symantec played a critical role in identifying the malware's behavior and scope, leading to its classification as an APT.

The timeline of response efforts highlights the complexity of dealing with a supply chain attack. Since the malware was distributed through legitimate channels, the recovery process required close collaboration between affected companies and their software vendors. Government agencies, including the U.S. Department of Homeland Security (DHS), issued alerts to industries that could have been affected by the Havex malware.

Assessing the Impact

The immediate impact of the Havex campaign was more related to espionage than direct disruption. The attackers used the malware to gather intelligence on ICS environments rather than causing operational downtime or damage. However, the long-term risks were significant. The attackers' ability to gain visibility into critical infrastructure systems suggested that they were positioning themselves for future, more destructive attacks.

Financially, the attack led to costs associated with investigating the breach, removing the malware, and restoring compromised systems. While no major operational disruptions were reported, the reputational damage to affected companies and software vendors was substantial. The incident raised awareness of the vulnerability of ICS environments, particularly regarding the supply chain risks that had not been widely recognized before this attack.

For stakeholders, including energy companies and ICS vendors, the Havex attack highlighted the need for stronger cybersecurity measures in the supply chain. It also demonstrated the risks posed by APT groups targeting critical infrastructure. The attack prompted greater collaboration between governments, private companies, and cybersecurity experts to bolster defenses against similar threats in the future.

Lessons Learned and Takeaways

The Havex Remote Access Trojan attack offers several key lessons for improving the cybersecurity posture of critical infrastructure. One of the most significant lessons is securing the supply chain. The attackers exploited ICS operators' trust in their software vendors, using this relationship to infiltrate critical infrastructure environments. This incident underscores the need for thorough vetting of third-party vendors and the implementation of stronger authentication and verification measures for software updates.

Another critical takeaway is the need for enhanced monitoring and detection capabilities in ICS environments. The attackers were able to remain undetected for months, highlighting the difficulty in identifying advanced threats in industrial networks. ICS operators must adopt more sophisticated intrusion detection systems and employ continuous monitoring to detect abnormal activity that could indicate the presence of malware like Havex.

Following the attack, affected organizations and vendors implemented stronger security controls, including better monitoring of software updates and improved threat intelligence sharing with the wider industry. The incident also led to increased efforts by governments and regulatory bodies to develop guidelines for securing ICS environments and addressing supply chain risks.

Case Study Summary

The Havex Remote Access Trojan attack of 2013–2014 is a critical example of the growing risks to ICS, particularly through supply chain compromises. The attackers' use of compromised software updates to infiltrate critical infrastructure highlighted the vulnerability of ICS environments to sophisticated cyber threats. Key takeaways from this case include securing the supply chain, enhancing detection capabilities, and improving collaboration between industries and government agencies to defend against APTs.

The broader implications of the Havex attack emphasize the evolving nature of cyber threats to critical infrastructure. The need for stronger cybersecurity practices, especially in supply chain security, will only grow as industrial environments become increasingly connected. This attack serves as a reminder that even trusted systems and vendors can be exploited by determined adversaries, making vigilance and proactive defense essential in the fight against cyber threats.

TRISIS/TRITON ATTACK (2017)

The Trisis (also known as Triton) attack in 2017 represents a critical moment in the evolution of cyber threats targeting ICS. This event involved a sophisticated attack against a petrochemical facility in Saudi Arabia, specifically targeting its safety instrumented systems (SIS). Safety instrumented systems are designed to monitor industrial processes and automatically shut down operations if unsafe conditions are detected. The deliberate targeting of these systems marked a dangerous escalation in the realm of cyberattacks, as the consequences of a successful compromise could have led to catastrophic physical damage or even loss of life.

At the time of the attack, ICS were increasingly interconnected with broader IT networks, making them more vulnerable to cyber intrusions.

However, the direct targeting of safety mechanisms was unprecedented, raising alarms about the potential for future attacks on critical infrastructure. The key stakeholders in this incident included the affected petrochemical company, the manufacturer of the targeted SIS, and cybersecurity firms that were later brought in to investigate and mitigate the attack.

The technological landscape in 2017 saw widespread adoption of digital systems to monitor and control critical infrastructure, but security was not always a top priority in many industrial sectors. This case underscored the growing risks to national security and public safety posed by cyber threats aimed at industrial environments.

Unfolding the Attack

The attack unfolded in stages, with the adversaries managing to breach the facility's network and implant malware into its SIS controllers. From the information gathered, the attackers likely gained access by exploiting known vulnerabilities in the facility's IT infrastructure, possibly through phishing or spear-phishing campaigns, which allowed them to bypass perimeter defenses and establish a foothold within the network. Once inside, they moved laterally to the OT environment, where they began probing the SIS systems.

The attack timeline indicates that the adversaries were patient and conducted extensive reconnaissance before deploying the Trisis malware. The attackers manipulated the Triconex SIS controllers, a specific type of safety system designed by Schneider Electric, intending to cause the system to fail in an unsafe manner. However, a critical error in the malware's configuration triggered an automatic shutdown of the plant's operations, inadvertently alerting the company to the intrusion.

The methods used by the attackers were highly sophisticated, and the malware was purpose-built to compromise industrial safety mechanisms—a level of specialization rarely seen in typical cyberattacks. The use of APTs and their ability to navigate between IT and OT environments without immediate detection highlights the attackers' technical expertise and deep understanding of industrial systems.

Detection and Response Efforts

The attack was detected when the SIS controllers unexpectedly triggered a shutdown of the facility's operations, which appeared to be a system malfunction. However, further investigation revealed that the SIS had been deliberately targeted. The facility's internal IT and security teams responded swiftly by initiating a more thorough investigation. Still, they quickly realized the sophistication of the malware was beyond their internal capabilities.

External cybersecurity firms were called to aid the response efforts, including the cybersecurity company Dragos and the Department of Homeland Security's ICS cyber emergency response team. These teams identified the Trisis malware and confirmed that it had been designed to disrupt the SIS controllers. The response involved isolating the compromised systems, preventing further malicious activity, and analyzing the full extent of the attacker's infiltration.

The timeline of the response reveals that, despite the sophistication of the attack, the swift detection of the SIS shutdown allowed the company to avoid catastrophic damage. However, the complexity of the malware meant that response efforts took considerable time, with cybersecurity experts working closely with the SIS manufacturer to ensure that the systems were properly restored and secured.

Assessing the Impact

The immediate effects of the Trisis attack were operational disruption and financial loss for the petrochemical facility. The plant's shutdown led to significant downtime, and while the attackers did not cause physical harm, the potential consequences of the attack were severe. Had the malware succeeded in disabling the safety systems without detection, it could have resulted in explosions, fires, or toxic gas releases, endangering both workers and nearby communities.

Long-term consequences included reputational damage to the affected company and heightened scrutiny of cybersecurity measures across the industrial sector. The attack raised awareness about the vulnerabilities in critical infrastructure and prompted other organizations to reevaluate the security of their ICS environments. Additionally, the incident led to increased collaboration between government agencies, cybersecurity firms, and industrial companies to strengthen defenses against future threats.

The attack had far-reaching implications for stakeholders, including the petrochemical industry, national governments concerned with protecting critical infrastructure, and vendors of industrial control systems. It also led to regulatory discussions about enhanced security standards for ICS and SIS.

Lessons Learned and Takeaways

The Trisis attack exposed several critical security weaknesses in the ICS environment. Chief among these was the insufficient segmentation between

IT and OT networks, allowing attackers to move from the corporate network into the operational domain. Additionally, the reliance on outdated or improperly configured systems contributed to the vulnerability of the SIS controllers, emphasizing the need for regular updates and security patches in industrial environments.

One of the key lessons from this case is the importance of early detection and response. While the attackers could infiltrate the network and deploy malware, the timely shutdown of the SIS controllers prevented a potentially devastating outcome. Organizations operating critical infrastructure must prioritize monitoring and detection capabilities to respond rapidly to abnormal activity.

In the aftermath of the attack, the affected company implemented stricter security controls, including better network segmentation, enhanced monitoring of OT environments, and closer collaboration with cybersecurity experts. The incident also spurred broader changes in the industrial sector, with more companies adopting proactive cybersecurity measures and engaging in threat intelligence sharing to protect against similar attacks.

Case Study Summary

The Trisis/Triton attack was a landmark event in the history of cyber threats against critical infrastructure. The attack demonstrated adversaries' increasing sophistication and willingness to target systems designed to ensure physical safety. It also underscored the importance of strong cybersecurity defenses in industrial environments, particularly those involving critical safety systems.

Key takeaways from this case include the need for better segmentation between IT and OT networks, the value of early detection systems, and the importance of collaboration between industry and cybersecurity experts. The lessons learned from the Trisis attack continue to influence cybersecurity strategies for critical infrastructure, highlighting cyber threats' dynamic and evolving nature.

COLONIAL PIPELINE RANSOMWARE ATTACK (2021)

The Colonial Pipeline ransomware attack of 2021 marked a pivotal moment in cybersecurity, drawing global attention to the vulnerabilities in critical infrastructure. Colonial Pipeline is one of the largest pipeline operators in the United States, responsible for supplying around 45 percent of the East Coast's fuel. When the ransomware group *DarkSide* compromised its systems, the company was forced to shut down operations, leading to fuel shortages, price spikes, and some panic along the eastern seaboard. This attack highlighted the profound risks ransomware poses to essential services and critical infrastructure, making it one of the most significant cyber incidents in history.

At the time of the attack, ransomware was a rising threat globally, with attackers increasingly targeting large organizations and critical infrastructure to demand massive ransom payments. The technological landscape was also evolving, with cybercriminals leveraging sophisticated malware, exploiting weak security practices, and targeting interconnected systems. The stakeholders involved in this case included Colonial Pipeline's leadership, the U.S. government, cybersecurity firms, law enforcement agencies, and millions of consumers affected by the fuel shortages resulting from the attack.

Unfolding the Attack

The Colonial Pipeline attack began in early May 2021, when cybercriminals from the DarkSide group accessed the company's IT network. From the information available, it is assumed that the initial entry point may have been through compromised credentials, possibly via a phishing attack or a weak password on a virtual private network account. Once inside, the attackers deployed ransomware, which encrypted key systems in the company's IT environment. While the pipeline's OT systems remained unaffected, Colonial Pipeline proactively shut down its operations to prevent the ransomware from spreading and to contain the damage.

The timeline of the attack unfolded rapidly. On May 7, 2021, Colonial Pipeline announced the shutdown, and shortly after that, it became clear that a ransomware attack was the cause. The DarkSide ransomware group quickly took responsibility, offering to sell Colonial Pipeline a decryption tool in exchange for a ransom payment. Faced with operational paralysis and the potential for prolonged disruption, Colonial Pipeline opted to pay the ransom—approximately 4.4 million dollars in Bitcoin. The payment was made to restore access to the encrypted systems, although the decryption process proved slower than expected, delaying the company's ability to resume operations fully.

DarkSide employed typical ransomware tactics, leveraging weaknesses in Colonial Pipeline's cybersecurity posture to deploy their malware and encrypt critical systems. While the attack did not directly compromise the OT systems that controlled the pipeline's physical operations, the interdependence between IT and OT systems forced the company to halt all operations as a precautionary measure.

Detection and Response Efforts

Colonial Pipeline detected the ransomware attack relatively quickly, but the immediate challenge was containing the damage and restoring operations. Once the breach was identified, Colonial Pipeline swiftly shut down the pipeline to prevent further risk. The company notified federal authorities, including the Cybersecurity and Infrastructure Security Agency (CISA) and the Federal Bureau of Investigation (FBI), which assisted in the investigation. Colonial Pipeline's leadership decided to pay the ransom, citing the urgency of restoring fuel supplies and mitigating the broader impact on the U.S. economy.

The initial response focused on securing the network, isolating the affected systems, and working with cybersecurity experts to assess the full extent of the breach. Although Colonial Pipeline paid the ransom and received the decryption tool, reports suggest that the tool was not entirely effective, leading to additional delays in restoring systems. In the days following the attack, the U.S. government played a critical role in coordinating the response, with the FBI managing to recover a portion of the ransom payment through a seizure of cryptocurrency wallets used by the attackers.

The response timeline illustrates the complexity of recovering from a ransomware attack and the challenges organizations face in balancing business continuity with cybersecurity considerations. While the attack was detected early, the decryption and recovery took time, leading to prolonged operational disruptions.

Assessing the Impact

The immediate impact of the Colonial Pipeline ransomware attack was severe, causing a temporary shutdown of fuel supplies along the East Coast and leading to widespread fuel shortages. The disruption in fuel distribution caused panic buying, price spikes, and long lines at gas stations, thus affecting millions of consumers and businesses. The attack exposed the fragility of critical infrastructure and highlighted how interconnected systems can be vulnerable to cyber threats, even if the attack targets only part of the network.

Financially, the attack resulted in a significant loss for Colonial Pipeline from the ransom payment and the cost of recovery, investigation, and operational shutdown. While the company restored operations within a week, the reputational damage was substantial since the attack revealed weaknesses in its cybersecurity posture. The attack served as a wake-up call for the U.S. government and regulatory bodies about the need for stronger protections around critical infrastructure.

The broader implications of the attack extended far beyond Colonial Pipeline. It raised awareness of the increasing threat of ransomware to critical services, prompted new government initiatives to strengthen cybersecurity for critical infrastructure, and led to debates about the ethics of paying ransomware to cybercriminals. It also spurred discussions on the role of public-private partnerships in defending against ransomware and the importance of timely incident reporting.

Lessons Learned and Takeaways

The Colonial Pipeline ransomware attack offers critical lessons for organizations and cybersecurity professionals. One of the most important lessons is securing interdependencies between IT and OT systems. From what I have analyzed, it appears that while the OT systems were not directly affected, the shutdown of IT systems had a cascading effect on operations. Organizations with critical infrastructure must ensure that their IT and OT systems are properly segmented, with strong security controls in place to prevent cross-contamination in the event of an attack.

Another key takeaway is the importance of a robust incident response plan for ransomware attacks. Colonial Pipeline's decision to pay the ransom was driven by the urgent need to restore fuel supplies. Still, the effectiveness of the decryption tool was limited, highlighting the importance of having backup plans and alternative recovery methods. Organizations should invest in ransomware detection, response technologies, and offline backups to reduce reliance on paying ransoms.

Finally, this attack underscores the need for collaboration between the public and private sectors in responding to ransomware threats. The involvement of federal authorities in recovering part of the ransom payment was a significant development, showing the potential for government agencies to assist in mitigating the damage from cyberattacks. Going forward, cybersecurity professionals must focus on building stronger defenses around critical infrastructure, implementing zero-trust architectures, and preparing for the evolving threat landscape posed by ransomware and other cyber threats.

Case Study Summary

The Colonial Pipeline ransomware attack of 2021 is a powerful example of the vulnerabilities in critical infrastructure and the devastating impact of ransomware on essential services. The attack disrupted fuel supplies, caused widespread panic, and exposed significant gaps in the cybersecurity defenses of key infrastructure providers. The main takeaways from this case include the importance of securing IT-OT interdependencies, having a robust ransomware response plan, and fostering greater collaboration between private companies and government agencies in the fight against ransomware. As ransomware threats evolve, this case highlights the urgent need for stronger defenses and proactive measures to protect critical infrastructure from future attacks.

FLORIDA WATER SYSTEM HACK (2021)

The Florida Water System Hack in 2021 was a striking example of how cyber-attacks on critical infrastructure can endanger public safety. The incident occurred at a water treatment plant in Oldsmar, Florida, a small city responsible for supplying water to approximately 15,000 residents. In this case, an unknown actor gained unauthorized access to the plant's control systems and attempted to alter sodium hydroxide (lye) levels in the water supply to dangerous levels. Sodium hydroxide is used in water treatment to control acidity but can cause severe health risks in high concentrations.

At the time of the attack, many ICS, especially in small municipal utilities, were connected to the Internet for remote access and management. These connections, while convenient, were often inadequately secured, leaving them vulnerable to cyberattacks. The key stakeholders involved in this incident included the water treatment plant operators, local government officials, cybersecurity experts, and law enforcement agencies, including the FBI, which became involved in the investigation.

The technological landscape during the attack included growing concerns over the security of OT in critical infrastructure sectors. This was particularly true for small utilities, which often lacked the resources and expertise to implement robust cybersecurity measures, relying instead on basic or outdated defenses.

Unfolding the Attack

The attack began when an unknown actor accessed the water treatment plant's control systems via a remote access software tool called TeamViewer, which the plant operators commonly used for monitoring and adjusting operations. It can be assumed that the attacker may have gained access through weak or reused passwords or potentially by exploiting unpatched vulnerabilities in the system. The exact entry point remains unclear since public details about the investigation are limited.

Once inside the system, the attacker manipulated the chemical controls, increasing the amount of sodium hydroxide from 100 parts per million (ppm) to 11,100 ppm—a level that would have been harmful to anyone consuming the water. Fortunately, the attack was thwarted when an alert plant operator noticed the unusual changes on the control screen and immediately reversed the adjustment before the water supply was affected.

The timeline of events suggests that the attackers were opportunistic rather than highly sophisticated. The fact that the attacker manually altered the chemical levels in full view of the plant operator indicates a lack of stealth, suggesting that the goal may have been to cause immediate harm or panic. The vulnerabilities exploited in this attack were relatively simple but demonstrated the severe consequences of inadequate cybersecurity in critical infrastructure.

Detection and Response Efforts

A vigilant plant operator detected the attack in real time and noticed the unauthorized changes to the chemical levels on his screen. This rapid detection resulted from human intervention rather than automated security systems, underscoring the importance of operator awareness in managing ICS environments. The operator acted quickly, reversing the changes within minutes and reporting the breach to local authorities.

Initial response actions focused on securing the plant's systems and preventing further unauthorized access. The plant immediately disabled remote access capabilities to the affected systems and launched an internal investigation to understand how the breach occurred. Local law enforcement and federal agencies, including the FBI and the CISA, were called in to assist with the investigation.

The response timeline reveals that while the immediate threat was neutralized, the investigation and remediation efforts took time. Cybersecurity firms were brought in to evaluate the systems, identify vulnerabilities, and implement enhanced security measures to prevent future attacks. The plant also worked closely with external parties to assess the broader risks to the water supply system and ensure that no lasting damage had been done.

Assessing the Impact

The attack's immediate impact was the operational disruption and the risk posed to public health. Had the operator not detected and reversed the changes in time, the water supply could have been poisoned, leading to severe illness or even death for those consuming the water. The information shows that the plant avoided financial loss or significant operational downtime, but the psychological and reputational impact was significant.

In the long term, the attack raised serious questions about critical infrastructure security, particularly in small municipalities. The incident highlighted the vulnerabilities in aging or inadequately secured water systems, where basic cybersecurity measures were not always in place. The public outcry following the attack pressured local governments and utilities to invest in better cybersecurity practices, although many smaller utilities faced resource constraints.

The attack also had broader implications for stakeholders beyond Oldsmar, particularly for water utilities nationwide. Many water systems began re-evaluating their cybersecurity defenses, and national-level discussions ensued regarding the need for stronger federal regulations and funding to protect critical infrastructure from similar attacks.

Lessons Learned and Takeaways

One of the most critical lessons from the Florida Water System Hack is securing remote access tools. The attackers exploited a weakness in the TeamViewer software, likely due to a lack of strong authentication protocols or poor password management. This incident underscores the need for utilities to implement strong authentication measures such as multifactor authentication and to regularly update and patch their software systems to prevent similar attacks.

Additionally, the attack revealed the limitations of relying solely on technology to detect and mitigate threats. In this case, human vigilance was the key to preventing a potentially catastrophic outcome. This highlights the ongoing need for employee training and awareness programs, particularly in sectors like water utilities, where cybersecurity expertise may be limited.

Following the attack, the affected plant implemented several changes, including enhanced cybersecurity training for staff, improved monitoring tools, and elimination of unsecured remote access systems. These changes were intended to reduce the likelihood of a future breach and to ensure that any attempted attacks would be detected more quickly. The incident also prompted industry-wide efforts to improve collaboration between water utilities and cybersecurity experts, emphasizing the need for a proactive approach to securing critical infrastructure.

Case Study Summary

The Florida Water System Hack in 2021 is a stark reminder of the vulnerabilities present in critical infrastructure and the potential for cyberattacks to have life-threatening consequences. The incident demonstrated how a relatively simple breach, likely caused by weak passwords or outdated software, could have led to disastrous outcomes if not for the quick response of a vigilant operator.

   Key takeaways from this case include the importance of securing remote access tools, the value of human oversight in critical systems, and the need for ongoing investment in cybersecurity defenses for essential services like water treatment. This attack highlights the growing importance of protecting industrial control systems and raises awareness of the need for stronger regulations and resources to defend critical infrastructure from evolving cyber threats.

IRANIAN RAILWAY SYSTEM ATTACK (2021)

The Iranian Railway System attack in 2021 was a significant cyber incident that demonstrated the vulnerability of transportation infrastructure to cyberattacks. The attack, which occurred in July, disrupted the operation of trains across Iran, causing widespread delays and confusion. The attackers targeted the railway's IT infrastructure, paralyzing its digital systems, including scheduling and ticketing operations. This attack is notable because it appeared politically motivated, leveraging cyber means to create chaos and disruption in a critical transportation network.

At the time of the attack, Iran's infrastructure, like many other nations, increasingly relied on digital systems to manage complex operations. The convergence of OT with IT systems made these infrastructures more efficient but introduced significant cybersecurity risks. The key stakeholders in this incident included the Iranian government, the national railway system, passengers and customers affected by the disruptions, and external cybersecurity researchers who began analyzing the event.

The technological landscape of the time saw Iran's critical infrastructure becoming a focal point for cyberattacks, especially given the geopolitical tensions between Iran and other nations. This attack was part of a broader trend of state-sponsored and politically motivated cyberattacks, though the perpetrators of this incident remained unidentified at the time of writing.

Unfolding the Attack

The attack unfolded on July 9, 2021, when Iranian railway officials discovered their system had been compromised. Hackers had infiltrated the railway's IT infrastructure, leading to significant disruptions in the scheduling and operation of trains across the country. From the information available, it is assumed that the attackers gained access to the railway systems through malware, though the exact entry point remains unclear. Phishing emails or vulnerabilities in the railway's software systems could have been potential vectors for the initial compromise.

The attackers also took the unusual step of defacing message boards at train stations with mocking messages, directing passengers to call a nonexistent number for information about delays. This created confusion and frustration among passengers, exacerbating the operational disruptions caused by the attack. The timeline of events indicates that the hackers were able to cause widespread disruption for several hours before railway officials managed to regain control of the systems.

The methods used by the attackers included both disruption and psychological manipulation, as the messages displayed on public boards seemed designed to cause panic and frustration. This blend of cyber and psychological warfare indicated that the attackers were not solely interested in financial gain but likely had a political or ideological motive behind the operation. The vulnerabilities exploited in the railway's systems appeared to stem from poor cybersecurity practices, particularly protecting critical IT infrastructure.

Detection and Response Efforts

The attack was detected when the railway system's scheduling operations were thrown into disarray, and the public message boards began displaying the taunting messages. It quickly became clear that this was not a system malfunction but a coordinated cyberattack. The initial response involved shutting down the affected IT systems to prevent further disruptions, which unfortunately compounded passenger delays. The Iranian government, alongside railway officials, launched an investigation into the attack. Initial response actions included isolating the compromised systems and attempting to restore functionality through backup systems. However, due to the nature of the attack and the extent of the disruption, response efforts were slow and train schedules remained disrupted for several hours.

External cybersecurity experts analyzed the malware and determined how the attackers gained access to the system. According to the information available, it is assumed that Iranian officials struggled to fully understand the scope of the attack in real time, which led to delayed mitigation efforts. Despite the involvement of cybersecurity firms and government agencies, no group took official responsibility for the attack, and no suspects were publicly named.

Assessing the Impact

The immediate effects of the attack were widespread delays and confusion across Iran's railway network. Thousands of passengers were stranded at stations, with trains delayed or canceled. While no physical damage was reported, the disruption caused significant operational challenges, financial losses, and reputational damage to the Iranian railway system. The mocking messages displayed on public boards also caused panic among some passengers, which led to further dissatisfaction and criticism of the railway's management.

From a financial standpoint, the Iranian government and the railway system incurred costs due to operational downtime, loss of productivity, and the need for additional resources to restore the affected systems. While the attack did not appear to cause long-term operational damage, the reputational damage was significant, raising concerns about the security of critical infrastructure in Iran.

In the long term, the attack highlighted the vulnerabilities in Iran's transportation infrastructure and, more broadly, in its critical infrastructure. The attack's psychological impact on passengers and officials alike demonstrated the potential for cyberattacks to create chaos without necessarily causing physical harm. This increased calls for improved cybersecurity measures in Iran and other nations facing similar threats.

Lessons Learned and Takeaways

The Iranian Railway System attack provided several critical lessons for securing transportation infrastructure. First and foremost, the attack revealed significant weaknesses in the railway's IT systems, particularly the lack of robust cybersecurity defenses to prevent unauthorized access. The attackers exploited vulnerabilities in the system to cause widespread disruption, indicating that the railway's cybersecurity posture was insufficient to handle sophisticated threats.

One of the most important takeaways is the need for strong incident detection and response capabilities. The Iranian railway system's delayed response showed that organizations are vulnerable to prolonged attacks without real-time monitoring and robust incident response plans. Cybersecurity training for employees and better network segmentation could have reduced the attack's impact.

Following the attack, it is assumed that the Iranian government and railway authorities implemented stronger security measures, including better monitoring tools, stronger password policies, and the elimination of vulnerabilities in their IT systems. This attack also underscored the broader need for transportation systems worldwide to prioritize cybersecurity as part of their overall risk management strategies.

Case Study Summary

The Iranian Railway System attack in 2021 is a powerful example of how cyberattacks can disrupt critical infrastructure and create widespread chaos without causing physical harm. The attackers leveraged cyber techniques and psychological tactics to confuse and frustrate passengers, highlighting the potential for cyberattacks to have far-reaching impacts on society.

Key takeaways from this case include the importance of strong cybersecurity measures, the need for rapid incident detection and response, and the role of psychological manipulation in modern cyberattacks. This attack reminds transportation and critical infrastructure operators worldwide to be vigilant and proactive in securing their systems against evolving cyber threats.

CHAPTER CONCLUSION

Critical infrastructure cyberattacks such as Trisis/Triton, the Florida Water System Hack, and Havex reveal several recurring themes that highlight the evolving threat landscape. One major takeaway is the increasing sophistication of attacks targeting ICS and OT environments. These attacks demonstrate that adversaries are capable of causing widespread disruption and are willing to target systems that directly affect public safety and national security. This analysis reveals that critical infrastructure is now a primary battleground for cyber warfare, and these incidents serve as a stark reminder that cybersecurity professionals must adapt and evolve their defense strategies accordingly.

In many cases, the precise details of the response efforts, detection mechanisms, and even the methods used by attackers are not always publicly available. As an author, I have extrapolated certain details from available media reports and expert analysis, especially when official information is scarce or incomplete. This reflects cybersecurity professionals' broader challenge in dealing with complex, multifaceted threats where clear and complete data is often inaccessible. In a field where information is rapidly evolving, cybersecurity experts must often rely on intelligence from various sources to piece together the full picture, emphasizing the importance of collaboration and open communication across industries and governments.

One of the most critical lessons from these case studies is securing both IT and OT systems, particularly in ICS environments. The attacks highlight how vulnerabilities in IT systems can be exploited to gain access to OT systems, creating a pathway for adversaries to disrupt critical infrastructure. Cybersecurity professionals must prioritize robust network segmentation, continuous monitoring, and incident detection to defend against increasingly sophisticated threats. Equally important is ensuring that supply chains are secure, as seen in the Havex attack, where attackers used trusted vendors to distribute malware. Strengthening supply chain security and third-party risk management should be a top priority for professionals working in critical sectors.

Finally, today's cybersecurity professionals must focus on proactive rather than reactive strategies. This includes implementing advanced detection tools, conducting regular threat assessments, and fostering a culture of cybersecurity awareness within organizations. The future of cybersecurity will increasingly depend on collaborative efforts between industry, government, and cybersecurity firms to share intelligence, develop standards, and bolster defenses. As these case studies show, the stakes are high, and the cost of inaction can have far-reaching consequences for public safety and national security.

11

MILITARY HACKS

When we think of military hacks, it is tempting to imagine someone in a hoodie, hunched over a keyboard, furiously typing to bring down an entire nation's defenses in seconds. The reality is far less cinematic—there is no dramatic music, and the hackers probably are not wearing hoodies. But in a world where cyber warfare is real, the consequences of a well-executed attack on military infrastructure can be just as disruptive as any blockbuster movie. Forget battleships and tanks—sometimes, all it takes is a spear-phishing email to throw a military operation into chaos.

In this chapter, we dive into a series of cyberattacks that targeted military systems. While these attacks may not involve the Hollywood hacking we often envision, they are no less impactful. They illustrate how cyber threats have become a critical element of modern warfare, capable of disabling critical infrastructure and compromising national security without a single shot fired. Military forces now defend themselves against attacks from invisible battlefields where the enemy might be halfway across the world (see Figure 11.1).

This chapter examines the tactics used in these cyberattacks, how they unfolded, and the impact they had on their targets. Sometimes, the information available on detection and response efforts is limited, forcing me to extrapolate from media reports and other available sources. Based on the patterns of previous incidents and standard practices in cybersecurity, I have made reasonable assumptions about how the affected organizations may have responded. These assumptions help fill the gaps where official details are scarce, allowing us to draw valuable lessons about the importance of proactive defenses and rapid response capabilities.

Ultimately, this chapter serves as a reminder that the battlefield has evolved. Cyberattacks are now as much a part of military strategy as traditional

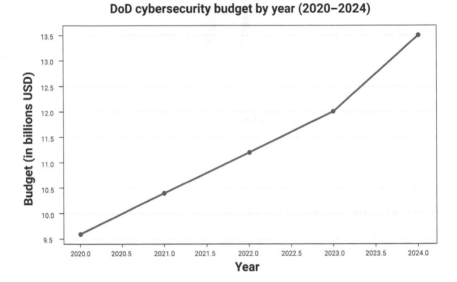

Figure 11.1   U.S. Department of Defense cybersecurity budget by year
(*source*: Statista Search Department)

weapons, and their impact can be just as devastating. For cybersecurity professionals, understanding how these attacks were carried out—and, in some
cases, how they could have been prevented—is crucial when preparing for
future threats. As we explore these incidents, the goal is to provide insights
that can help strengthen cybersecurity practices, especially in environments
with the highest stakes.

WHAT ARE THE RISKS OF MILITARY CYBERATTACKS?

Military cyberattacks represent a new frontier in warfare, where battles are
fought not just with weapons but with code and malware. In today's interconnected world, military operations rely heavily on digital infrastructure

for communications, command and control, logistics, and even weapons systems. This increased reliance on technology introduces significant cyber risks as adversaries seek to exploit vulnerabilities in these systems. A successful cyberattack on military infrastructure can disable critical systems, disrupt operations, and even compromise national security by exposing classified data or strategic plans.

The cyber risks faced by militaries today are numerous and complex. One of the primary risks is the threat of espionage, where attackers infiltrate military networks to steal sensitive information such as intelligence reports, operational plans, or weapon designs. State-sponsored actors often carry out these attacks using advanced techniques, including spear-phishing, malware, and zero-day exploits. In addition to espionage, militaries also face the risk of disruption attacks, where cyberattacks target communication systems, logistics networks, or even battlefield technologies to hinder military readiness and response capabilities.

One of the most concerning risks is the potential for cyberattacks on critical infrastructure like radar systems, satellites, or nuclear command-and-control systems. These systems are often targeted because they are essential to a nation's defense capabilities. A cyberattack that disables or manipulates these systems could give adversaries a significant strategic advantage, potentially leading to devastating consequences without direct military confrontation. As the threat landscape evolves, militaries must focus on defending physical borders and securing their digital perimeters from sophisticated cyber adversaries.

To mitigate these risks, militaries worldwide invest in advanced cybersecurity measures, including real-time threat detection, incident response teams, and stronger encryption protocols. However, the dynamic and evolving nature of cyber threats means that no defense is foolproof. Continuous vigilance, training, and collaboration with private cybersecurity firms are essential to adapting to the new realities of cyber warfare. In this landscape, quickly detecting and responding to a cyberattack can be the difference between maintaining military readiness and facing a serious national security breach.

The following chart illustrates the timeline associated with the attacks that will be explored in this chapter (see Figure 11.2).

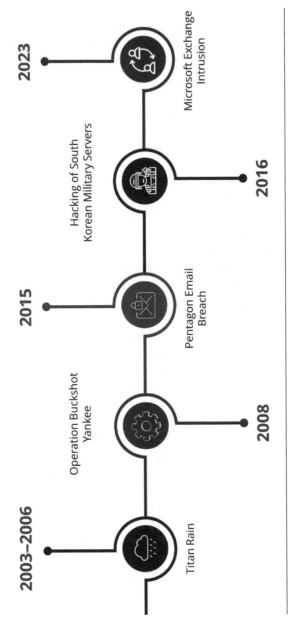

Figure 11.2   The timeline of attacks discussed in this chapter

TITAN RAIN (2003-2006)

In the early 2000s, sophisticated cyber espionage campaigns began to surface, with U.S. defense contractors and military organizations among the primary targets. One of the most notable operations—code-named Titan Rain—involved persistent cyber-attacks that originated from Chinese networks, targeting sensitive information related to U.S. military and defense systems. At that time, cyber espionage was becoming a growing concern, with nation-state actors increasingly using the internet to infiltrate adversaries' systems and steal valuable data. Titan Rain is often considered one of the earliest large-scale operations that highlighted the vulnerabilities in the digital infrastructure of military and government organizations.

The technological landscape during the Titan Rain attacks differed notably from today's highly interconnected systems. Firewalls and basic intrusion detection systems were prevalent, but more advanced cybersecurity measures, such as modern threat intelligence platforms and artificial intelligence (AI)-driven defenses, were still in their infancy. The attackers took advantage of this relative lack of sophistication in defense mechanisms, exploiting outdated security protocols and system misconfigurations to access networks. Key stakeholders in this case included U.S. government agencies, defense contractors, and private cybersecurity firms that later assisted in detecting and responding to the breach.

From the information available, it is reasonable to assume that many systems targeted during Titan Rain were unprepared for sustained, coordinated attacks. Cybersecurity practices were still developing, and organizations often lacked comprehensive incident response plans. Moreover, there was limited coordination between government agencies, leaving many entry points for sophisticated adversaries to exploit.

Unfolding the Attack

The Titan Rain operation, believed to have started around 2003, involved highly skilled attackers who launched systematic efforts to infiltrate U.S. military and government networks. Using techniques such as exploiting known software vulnerabilities, the attackers gained access to sensitive systems over several years. The operation was characterized by its stealthy and persistent nature, with attackers focusing on long-term espionage rather than immediate disruption.

The timeline of the attacks is difficult to reconstruct fully. Still, reports indicate that by 2005, U.S. defense contractors such as Lockheed Martin, Sandia National Laboratories, and Redstone Arsenal had suffered numerous intrusions. Entry points often involved targeted phishing emails that lured unsuspecting employees into providing credentials or clicking malicious links. Once inside the system, attackers used sophisticated malware to maintain access, moving laterally across networks to gather information on weapons systems and military operations.

I assume the attackers took advantage of relatively weak network segmentation and outdated software to escalate privileges and avoid detection for extended periods. The methods employed reflected early cyber espionage techniques but revealed how vulnerable critical infrastructure was to sustained cyberattacks. The fact that attackers could maintain their presence in these systems for so long points to a broader issue of inadequate monitoring and detection capabilities at the time.

Detection and Response Efforts

The detection of Titan Rain came after several years of persistent breaches. In 2004, Shawn Carpenter, a security analyst at Sandia National Laboratories, was among the first to discover evidence of the attacks. He noticed a series of data exfiltration activities from U.S. military and contractor networks, eventually linking them to Chinese servers. Despite his warnings, Carpenter faced internal resistance, and it took time for broader awareness of the issue to develop within the U.S. government.

Once the attacks were confirmed, various cybersecurity firms and government agencies were brought in to analyze the intrusions and help contain the breaches. The timeline of the response was slow, partly due to the stealthy nature of the attacks and the limited resources available to detect sophisticated threats. The attackers used advanced techniques to avoid detection, including encrypted communication channels and hidden malware, making it difficult for security teams to trace their activities. The U.S. government also faced challenges attributing the attacks because the attackers used Chinese Internet Protocol addresses but could have been masking their true location.

From the available information, I assume the slow response could be attributed to a lack of collaboration between affected organizations and the government, leading to delays in mitigating the attack. External cybersecurity firms played a crucial role in identifying the vulnerabilities exploited during the breach, but their involvement came later in the incident timeline. The absence of clear protocols for responding to cyber espionage, especially at a national level, exacerbated the situation, leaving military systems exposed for extended periods.

Assessing the Impact

The immediate impact of Titan Rain was the large-scale theft of military and defense-related information. Although the exact extent of the data compromised is still unknown, reports suggest that classified documents related to military aircraft, space command operations, and weapons systems were among the materials exfiltrated. For U.S. defense contractors, the operational disruptions were significant, as systems had to be audited and fortified following the discovery of the breaches.

Long-term consequences included heightened tensions between the U.S. and China because officials began to suspect that the Chinese government was either directly or indirectly involved in the attacks. Titan Rain also started a new era in cyber warfare, where espionage became a key tool for nation-states seeking an advantage in military and industrial development. The reputational damage to U.S. military cybersecurity capabilities was notable, as the breach exposed vulnerabilities in even the most sensitive systems.

From the information available, I assume that the broader implications of Titan Rain extended beyond the immediate organizations targeted. It set a precedent for cyber espionage campaigns, prompting governments and private sector entities to reevaluate their cybersecurity strategies. The attack also changed how sensitive information was stored and accessed, focusing more on network segmentation and encryption to mitigate future risks.

Lessons Learned and Takeaways

Titan Rain exposed significant weaknesses in the cybersecurity defenses of the U.S. military and defense organizations. One of the critical lessons drawn from this case is the need for continuous monitoring and real-time detection capabilities. The attackers could operate undetected for extended periods, demonstrating that traditional security measures were insufficient for combating modern threats. Organizations must implement advanced threat detection mechanisms, including behavioral analysis and anomaly detection, to identify suspicious activities early.

Another key lesson is the importance of interagency collaboration. The lack of coordination between affected organizations and government agencies hindered the response efforts, allowing the attackers to maintain their network presence. Enhanced communication and cooperation between public and private sectors will be essential for improving national cybersecurity.

I assume that Titan Rain prompted significant changes in U.S. cybersecurity policy. In the years following the attack, there was an increased focus on creating comprehensive incident response plans and improving the overall cybersecurity posture of defense contractors. The introduction of frameworks like the National Institute of Standards and Technology Cybersecurity Framework can be seen as a direct response to incidents like Titan Rain, emphasizing the need for proactive risk management and the implementation of robust security controls.

Case Study Summary

The Titan Rain case illustrates the evolving nature of cyber threats and the importance of remaining vigilant in defending against nation-state actors. The key takeaways from this case include the need for continuous monitoring, improved detection capabilities, and enhanced collaboration between affected organizations and government entities. This attack serves as a reminder that even the most secure systems can be compromised, highlighting the importance of staying proactive in the face of evolving cyber threats.

OPERATION BUCKSHOT YANKEE (2008)

In 2008, the U.S. military experienced one of its most significant cybersecurity breaches, the defense of which was called Operation Buckshot Yankee. This incident highlighted vulnerabilities in military networks and set the stage for new approaches to cybersecurity in defense organizations. Operation Buckshot Yankee was the first known case where the U.S. Department of Defense (DoD) faced a cyberattack that threatened classified networks, forcing military leadership to take a more proactive stance on defending critical systems.

The attack targeted the Secret Internet Protocol Router Network (SIPRNet), the U.S. military's classified network for handling sensitive communications and operations. SIPRNet is also used heavily in tactical networks, and as an Armor officer, I was involved in the deployment and maintenance of SIPRNet in a tactical Army brigade in Iraq. This network was considered one of the most secure at the time, but the incident revealed weaknesses in its defense mechanisms. The technological landscape in 2008 was evolving, with increased reliance on digital systems across all military branches, but cybersecurity practices lagged. Antivirus programs and firewalls were standard, but there was insufficient focus on removable media security, which ultimately became the entry point for this attack.

Key stakeholders in Operation Buckshot Yankee included the DoD, military network administrators, the National Security Agency (NSA), and the newly established U.S. Cyber Command, which later took a leading role in managing the U.S. military's cybersecurity defenses. This breach catalyzed the formation of the U.S. Cyber Command, as it became clear that a centralized, coordinated response to cyber threats was necessary.

Unfolding the Attack

The attack that led to Operation Buckshot Yankee began when an infected Universal Serial Bus (USB) flash drive was inserted into a military laptop at a base in the Middle East. The USB drive contained malware known as Agent.btz, which quickly spread throughout the military's classified and unclassified networks. The malware was designed to automatically copy data and establish a backdoor, allowing external actors to steal sensitive information. The initial compromise came through what seemed like an innocuous action: the use of an infected removable device. This technique had not been considered a major threat up until that point.

Once the malware was introduced, it spread rapidly across military systems, exploiting vulnerabilities in how networks were segmented and monitored. The attackers used the malware to gather information silently, but their exact goals remain unclear. From the information I reviewed, I assume the malware was likely used for cyber espionage purposes, designed to gather intelligence on U.S. military operations and capabilities. The timeline of the attack suggests that the infection spread over a matter of days, with the military unaware of the full scope of the breach until much later.

The entry point—an infected USB drive—was a simple yet highly effective method of compromise. The attack exploited a significant vulnerability in the military's cybersecurity posture at the time: the lack of strict controls on the use of removable media. This vulnerability was particularly problematic given the classified nature of the networks involved. The attackers could use this weak point to bypass more robust perimeter defenses, effectively infiltrating even classified systems with relative ease.

Detection and Response Efforts

The discovery of the malware came months after the initial infection. It was first detected by military cybersecurity personnel during routine network monitoring. Once identified, the response effort quickly became one of the largest cybersecurity operations in U.S. military history. However, the timeline of the response was complicated by the malware's ability to evade detection for such a long period and by the uncertainty surrounding how far the infection had spread.

Initial response actions included isolating affected networks and systems to prevent the malware from spreading further. The DoD immediately initiated a full-scale investigation into the breach, with cybersecurity firms and government agencies like the NSA assisting in the containment and mitigation efforts. The military had to stop using removable media, conduct thorough scans of its networks, and manually remove the malware from infected systems.

It seems like there were delays in coordinating the response due to the lack of clear procedures for dealing with an attack of this scale and complexity. The involvement of external cybersecurity firms and government agencies helped accelerate the process, but the damage had already been done. The response ultimately included reevaluating the military's cybersecurity strategy and creating new policies and protocols to prevent future incidents.

Assessing the Impact

The immediate impact of the attack was the compromise of classified and unclassified military networks, though the full extent of the data stolen remains classified. The malware's presence in classified systems posed a significant risk to national security, leading to widespread concern within the DoD and among intelligence agencies. Although no operational disruptions were reported, the incident revealed critical weaknesses in the military's ability to protect its networks against sophisticated cyber threats.

Long-term consequences included damage to the U.S. military's reputation and a broader recognition that cyber warfare would become an integral part of national defense strategies. The breach increased scrutiny of the military's cybersecurity practices, focusing on using removable media and network segmentation. The formation of the U.S. Cyber Command in 2010 can be directly linked to the lessons learned from Operation Buckshot Yankee because it became clear that a centralized command structure was needed to coordinate and defend against cyber threats.

It can be assumed that the reputational damage extended beyond the U.S. military to the defense industry. The breach demonstrated that even the most secure networks could be compromised, highlighting the need for constant vigilance and proactive defense measures. The incident also likely accelerated the development of more advanced cybersecurity tools and technologies within the military and the defense contracting industry.

Lessons Learned and Takeaways

One critical lesson from Operation Buckshot Yankee is the importance of controlling and monitoring the use of removable media. Before this attack, the military did not have stringent policies for managing USB drives and other external devices. The attack showed how even a simple device could be used as a vector for a devastating cyber intrusion. Following the incident, the DoD banned using USB drives across its networks and implemented stricter policies for accessing and handling classified data.

Another key takeaway is the need for real-time monitoring and advanced threat detection capabilities. The malware used in the attack could evade detection for an extended period, largely because the military's cybersecurity infrastructure was not equipped to identify and respond to such sophisticated threats. In the years following the attack, there was a concerted effort to upgrade the military's cybersecurity capabilities, including using more advanced intrusion detection systems and network segmentation techniques.

From the information available, I assume that the breach also underscored the importance of interagency cooperation in responding to cyber threats. The involvement of multiple government agencies and external cybersecurity firms was critical to containing the malware and preventing further damage. In the aftermath of the attack, the military implemented new incident response procedures prioritizing collaboration and information sharing between different branches and agencies.

Case Study Summary

Operation Buckshot Yankee is a pivotal moment in the history of military cybersecurity. The key takeaways from this case include the need for strict control of removable media, real-time monitoring capabilities, and interagency collaboration in response efforts. The attack is a stark reminder that even the most secure networks are vulnerable to cyber threats, prompting the U.S. military to adopt a more proactive approach to cybersecurity.

Reflecting on the broader impact of Operation Buckshot Yankee, it is clear that the incident reshaped the military's approach to defending its digital infrastructure. The lessons learned from this attack helped shape the U.S. Cyber Command. They accelerated the development of more advanced cybersecurity tools and strategies, ultimately strengthening the defense against future cyber threats.

PENTAGON EMAIL BREACH (2015)

In July 2015, the Pentagon fell victim to a highly coordinated cyberattack that targeted its unclassified email system, affecting around 4,000 military and civilian personnel. The breach was significant not only because of its scale but also because it exposed the vulnerabilities within highly secure government networks. Although the email system was unclassified, the breach raised concerns about the security of more sensitive military and governmental communications.

The technological landscape of 2015 had evolved, with increased cybersecurity measures such as two-factor authentication and more advanced encryption methods becoming commonplace across government and military networks. However, the breach demonstrated that even these advanced measures could be bypassed when attackers leveraged sophisticated social engineering techniques and exploited human error. Cyber defense was still catching up with the rapidly evolving tactics of nation-state actors and cyber-criminal groups.

Key stakeholders in this case included the U.S. DoD, the Joint Chiefs of Staff, and external cybersecurity firms that were brought in to assist in the detection, analysis, and mitigation of the breach. The attack was widely attributed to Russian hackers, believed to be state-sponsored, although definitive attribution remains speculative. The incident heightened concerns over the ability of foreign adversaries to infiltrate critical U.S. defense systems.

Unfolding the Attack

The Pentagon email breach unfolded quickly, with attackers executing a spear-phishing campaign to trick users into providing access credentials. From the data made available, I assume that the attackers sent highly targeted emails that appeared to come from trusted sources, prompting recipients to click on malicious links or open infected attachments. Once inside the network, the attackers quickly escalated privileges and moved laterally, gaining access to a broad range of email accounts.

The attack was detected within hours of the initial compromise, but the damage had already been done. The timeline suggests that the hackers operated quite efficiently, stealing large amounts of data hours before the network was shut down to prevent further access. The entry point for the attack was likely a combination of social engineering techniques, which exploited the trust of military personnel in seemingly legitimate communications.

The attackers may have employed malware to maintain persistence in the network, allowing them to exfiltrate data without immediate detection. The vulnerability exploited here was not just technological but also human since the attackers were able to manipulate users into bypassing normal security protocols. This breach reflected a growing trend in cyberattacks at the time, where sophisticated social engineering tactics were used to gain initial access before launching more traditional malware attacks.

Detection and Response Efforts

The Pentagon's cybersecurity team quickly detected the breach, with signs of unusual activity appearing within hours of the attack. The response involved taking the entire unclassified email system offline to prevent further damage, immediately disrupting communications for thousands of personnel. While effectively stopping the attackers, this drastic measure highlighted the challenge of responding to cyber incidents without causing significant operational disruptions.

Once the breach was confirmed, the DoD brought in external cybersecurity firms to analyze the attack and mitigate its effects. Forensic analysis revealed that the attackers had stolen large amounts of data, though the exact nature of the information remains classified. The response timeline shows that the military acted swiftly to contain the breach, but the attack still exposed critical vulnerabilities in the Pentagon's cybersecurity infrastructure.

Based on the materials I analyzed, the involvement of external parties, including cybersecurity experts from the private sector, was crucial in understanding the scope of the breach and in implementing new measures to prevent similar incidents. While effective in stopping the immediate threat, the Pentagon's response highlighted the limitations of existing detection capabilities, particularly when dealing with advanced nation-state actors.

Assessing the Impact

The immediate impact of the Pentagon email breach was the disruption of the unclassified email system, which remained offline for nearly two weeks as cybersecurity teams worked to purge the network of any lingering threats. While the email system was unclassified, the breach raised alarms about the potential for more serious intrusions into classified networks. The attack also led to a status of heightened alert within the DoD and other government agencies, prompting a reassessment of cybersecurity protocols and policies.

Long-term consequences included a renewed focus on training personnel to recognize phishing and other social engineering attacks and an overhaul of the Pentagon's cybersecurity defenses. The breach also had diplomatic implications since the U.S. government accused Russia of being behind the attack. Although no official retaliation was confirmed, the incident increased tensions between the two nations, particularly in cyber warfare.

The reputational damage to the Pentagon was significant because the breach demonstrated that even the most secure government institutions were vulnerable to cyberattacks. The broader impact extended beyond the military, influencing how other federal agencies approached cybersecurity. It also likely accelerated the development of more advanced detection tools and strategies for responding to cyber incidents.

Lessons Learned and Takeaways

One key lesson from the Pentagon email breach, which simply cannot be stressed enough, is the critical importance of user awareness and training. The attack exploited human error, highlighting the need for ongoing education about phishing and other social engineering tactics. In the aftermath of the breach, the DoD implemented more rigorous cybersecurity training programs, emphasizing the role of individuals in defending against cyber threats.

Another significant takeaway is the need for real-time detection and rapid response capabilities. While the Pentagon detected and contained the breach relatively quickly, the attack demonstrated how quickly cyber adversaries can move once inside a network. To address this, the DoD invested in more advanced threat detection systems, including AI and machine learning tools designed to identify and respond to threats in real time.

The breach most likely prompted a reevaluation of interagency communication and cooperation in cybersecurity. The response to the attack involved multiple government agencies and private-sector experts, and the incident underscored the importance of collaboration in mitigating large-scale cyber threats. This experience likely contributed to broader efforts to strengthen cybersecurity coordination across all levels of government.

Case Study Summary

The Pentagon email breach in 2015 serves as a stark reminder of the vulnerabilities that exist even within highly secure government networks. The key takeaways from this case include the importance of user training, real-time threat detection, and interagency cooperation in responding to cyber incidents. The breach exposed critical weaknesses in the Pentagon's defenses, leading to significant changes in cybersecurity policies and practices across the U.S. government.

Reflecting on the broader impact of the attack, it is clear that the Pentagon email breach was a turning point in military cybersecurity. The lessons learned from this incident have helped shape how the U.S. government approaches cyber defense, emphasizing the need for constant vigilance, proactive threat detection, and a coordinated response to emerging cyber threats.

HACKING OF SOUTH KOREAN MILITARY SERVERS (2016)

In 2016, the South Korean military experienced a significant breach when its servers were compromised by North Korean hackers, highlighting the growing threat of cyber warfare on the Korean Peninsula. The attack targeted critical military infrastructure by stealing classified information and disrupting key systems. This incident underscored nation-states' increasing use of cyberattacks as a strategic tool, particularly in regions with long-standing geopolitical tensions.

Heightened cyber tensions between North and South Korea marked the technological landscape. South Korea had been investing in its cyber defense capabilities, but the attack exposed vulnerabilities in its military systems. Using outdated software and limited intrusion detection systems contributed to the successful breach. Key stakeholders included the South Korean Ministry of Defense, its military cybersecurity division, and various South Korean cybersecurity firms tasked with responding to the breach. Using state-sponsored hacking groups such as *Lazarus Group*, the North Korean government was widely suspected of orchestrating the attack.

Unfolding the Attack

The hacking of South Korean military servers unfolded over several months, with the attackers gaining access to highly sensitive systems through a spear-phishing campaign. South Korean military personnel were targeted with emails that contained malicious attachments or links, which, once opened, installed malware onto the military's network. From the information I have seen, I assume the attackers gained initial access by exploiting human vulnerabilities and manipulating personnel into downloading malicious software that opened backdoors for deeper infiltration.

The attack timeline indicates that the attackers moved quickly inside to escalate privileges and access key systems. The malware allowed the hackers to access military plans, operational details, and intelligence related to South Korea's defense posture. When the breach was detected, significant amounts of data had already been exfiltrated. The exact nature of the vulnerabilities exploited remains unclear, but the attack revealed weaknesses in South Korea's authentication protocols and patch management processes.

The attackers used advanced techniques to evade detection, moving laterally within the network and covering their tracks through encryption and obfuscation. The spear-phishing campaign's success and the malware's sophistication indicated that the attack was well-planned and likely supported by North Korean intelligence services.

Detection and Response Efforts

When cybersecurity personnel noticed unusual network activity, the South Korean military detected the breach several months after it began. By the time the attack was confirmed, and stop me if you have heard this before, the damage had already been done. The response involved isolating affected servers and conducting a comprehensive investigation into how the breach occurred. The response timeline shows that South Korean authorities acted quickly to contain the attack, but the initial detection delay allowed the attackers ample time to extract valuable data.

The South Korean government involved private cybersecurity firms to assist in the investigation and bolster the military's response capabilities. These firms helped to identify the malware and traced it back to North Korean hackers, reinforcing suspicions that the attack was state-sponsored. The involvement of external parties was crucial in helping the South Korean military understand the full scope of the breach and take steps to prevent further infiltration.

The information I studied leads me to believe the response likely included deploying more advanced cybersecurity tools and overhauling the military's network architecture to ensure future resilience. However, the fact that the attackers remained undetected for months points to a need for improved real-time monitoring and stronger defenses against social engineering attacks like spear-phishing.

Assessing the Impact

The immediate impact of the hacking of South Korean military servers was the loss of classified military information, which compromised South Korea's defense strategies and operational plans. Although the exact contents of the stolen data were not publicly disclosed, it is believed that North Korea gained access to sensitive intelligence regarding South Korea's military capabilities and defense posture in response to potential conflicts. This raised concerns about how this information could be used to undermine South Korea's national security.

The long-term consequences of the breach included a significant shake-up within the South Korean military's cybersecurity divisions, with increased funding and resources allocated to improve the country's cyber defenses. The incident also led to heightened tensions between North and South Korea, as it was seen as part of North Korea's ongoing strategy to destabilize its southern neighbor through cyber warfare. From the information available, I assume that the reputational damage to South Korea's military was considerable since the breach exposed weaknesses in its ability to protect critical systems.

The breach also had implications beyond South Korea, as it served as a wake-up call for other nations reliant on digital infrastructure to defend against increasingly sophisticated cyber threats. It demonstrated that even countries with advanced technological capabilities can fall victim to cyberattacks if proper defenses are not in place.

Lessons Learned and Takeaways

One of the key lessons learned from the hacking of South Korean military servers is the importance of securing networks against spear-phishing attacks. The attackers gained initial access by exploiting human vulnerabilities, underscoring the need for better training and awareness among military personnel regarding the dangers of social engineering. Following the attack, South Korea implemented more rigorous cybersecurity education and training programs for its armed forces.

Another takeaway is the necessity of real-time monitoring and advanced threat detection systems. The fact that the attackers remained undetected for several months highlights a critical weakness in the military's ability to identify and respond to sophisticated threats. South Korea has invested heavily in upgrading its detection capabilities, using AI and machine learning tools to identify abnormal behavior on its networks.

The breach also underscored the importance of collaboration between military and civilian cybersecurity experts. South Korea's reliance on private firms to help manage the response demonstrated the value of integrating external expertise into national defense strategies. Collaboration between the public and private sectors will be essential in defending against increasingly complex cyberattacks.

Case Study Summary

The 2016 hacking of South Korean military servers highlights the growing use of cyber warfare as a strategic tool by nation-states. The key takeaways from this case include the need for improved defenses against spear-phishing attacks, the importance of real-time threat detection, and the value of collaboration between military and civilian cybersecurity experts. The attack exposed critical weaknesses in South Korea's cybersecurity posture, prompting significant changes in how the country defends its military infrastructure.

Reflecting on the broader impact of the attack, it is clear that cyber warfare will continue to be a major component of geopolitical conflicts. The lessons learned from this incident have helped shape how South Korea and other nations approach cybersecurity, emphasizing the need for constant vigilance and proactive measures to defend against evolving cyber threats.

MICROSOFT EXCHANGE INTRUSION (2023)

In early 2023, the cybersecurity world was shaken by a massive intrusion targeting Microsoft Exchange servers. This incident followed a string of high-profile cyberattacks, underscoring the growing global threat organizations face. While the Microsoft Exchange platform has been a core part of many companies' communication infrastructures, it has also been an attractive target for cybercriminals and nation-state actors due to its widespread use and the valuable information it handles. The breach revealed significant vulnerabilities in the infrastructure, allowing attackers to compromise sensitive data and systems on a large scale.

The technological landscape at the time of the attack reflected a growing reliance on cloud services and hybrid environments, where companies were increasingly moving their operations to cloud platforms while maintaining on-premises systems. In particular, Microsoft Exchange was used in on-premises and cloud versions, giving attackers multiple vectors to exploit. Despite security improvements over the years, attackers exploited specific zero-day vulnerabilities that had yet to be patched, illustrating how even the most robust systems can be compromised when weaknesses remain unaddressed.

Key stakeholders in this incident included Microsoft and a wide range of organizations—private sector companies, government agencies, and military entities—that rely on Microsoft Exchange to manage their communications. The breach also drew attention from global cybersecurity firms, governments, and law enforcement agencies who collaborated to assess the damage and mitigate the risks posed by the attack.

Unfolding the Attack

The Microsoft Exchange Intrusion in 2023 unfolded as part of a coordinated effort by threat actors to exploit a series of vulnerabilities in Exchange servers. The attackers leveraged what appeared to be a zero-day vulnerability, gaining unauthorized access to Microsoft Exchange instances worldwide. The timeline of the attack suggests that once initial access was achieved, the attackers moved quickly to install web shells, creating backdoors that allowed them to maintain persistent access to compromised systems.

I assume that the initial compromise involved the attackers scanning for vulnerable Exchange servers and deploying exploits remotely, targeting weak points in the authentication and communication protocols of the servers. Once the entry point was secured, the attackers used advanced techniques to move laterally within networks, accessing critical data, including emails, sensitive files, and other business-critical information stored in Exchange databases.

The methods used were sophisticated, combining traditional hacking tools with new techniques designed to evade detection by security systems. The attackers' persistence in maintaining access and the ability to remain undetected for extended periods showcased the evolving nature of cyber threats. Exploited vulnerabilities in the authentication protocols of Exchange allowed them to impersonate legitimate users and escalate privileges, further deepening their access to critical systems.

Detection and Response Efforts

The detection of the Microsoft Exchange breach took time, with some organizations discovering the intrusion only after significant damage had been done. The breach was first reported by security researchers who identified unusual network activity and traced it back to compromised Exchange servers. Microsoft responded quickly by releasing emergency patches, but for many organizations, the response came too late to prevent data loss.

Once the attack was confirmed, a multipronged response was initiated. Microsoft worked closely with cybersecurity firms and law enforcement agencies to contain the breach and mitigate further damage. The company issued detailed guidance on how organizations could identify signs of compromise, remove malicious web shells, and patch their systems. The response timeline was critical, with Microsoft providing regular updates on the vulnerabilities and pushing emergency updates to affected systems.

It can be assumed many organizations faced challenges in applying the patches due to the complexity of their environments, particularly those running hybrid on-premises and cloud infrastructures. Involving external cybersecurity firms was key when supporting organizations without the *in-house* resources to respond quickly. Law enforcement agencies from several countries also played a role in investigating the attack, given its global reach and the involvement of state-sponsored actors suspected of being behind the intrusion.

Assessing the Impact

The immediate impact of the Microsoft Exchange intrusion was significant, affecting thousands of organizations worldwide, including government agencies, financial institutions, and private enterprises. Sensitive data, such as emails, internal documents, and personal information, was exposed, raising concerns about the potential misuse of this information. While the full extent of the damage is still unknown, the financial loss and operational disruptions caused by the breach were considerable.

Long-term consequences of the breach included heightened scrutiny of Microsoft's security practices and the security of cloud and on-premises hybrid environments. Many organizations were forced to reevaluate their cybersecurity strategies, particularly those related to email servers and communication platforms. The breach also prompted discussions around the need for faster patch management processes and greater transparency from technology providers regarding vulnerabilities.

After studying the existing information, I assume the reputational damage to Microsoft was substantial, although the company's swift response helped mitigate some of the fallout. The broader implications for the industry included a renewed focus on the security of critical business communication systems, especially in light of the rising number of sophisticated nation-state cyberattacks targeting such infrastructure. The incident highlighted the need for organizations to remain vigilant in updating their systems and adopting more robust monitoring and incident response protocols.

Lessons Learned and Takeaways

One of the critical lessons learned from the Microsoft Exchange intrusion is the importance of timely patching and vulnerability management. The attack exploited zero-day vulnerabilities, demonstrating how unpatched systems can become an entry point for attackers. Organizations must prioritize continuously monitoring their systems for known and emerging vulnerabilities and deploy patches as soon as they are available.

Another key lesson is the value of robust detection and response capabilities. The fact that attackers could maintain persistent access to compromised Exchange servers highlights the need for advanced detection tools, such as anomaly detection and threat hunting techniques, to identify malicious activity before significant damage occurs. The use of web shells as a persistent backdoor demonstrated that organizations must remain vigilant even after initial remediation efforts to ensure that attackers are fully eradicated from their networks.

The breach also underscored the importance of collaboration between private companies and government agencies in responding to large-scale cyber incidents. The coordinated effort between Microsoft, cybersecurity firms, and law enforcement was essential in containing the breach and preventing further damage. This incident serves as a reminder that responding to cyberattacks often requires a collective effort across industries and sectors.

Case Study Summary

The Microsoft Exchange intrusion in 2023 represents a critical moment in the evolution of cyber threats targeting communication infrastructure. The key takeaways from this case include the importance of timely patch management, the need for advanced detection capabilities, and the value of collaboration in responding to cyber incidents. The breach exposed significant vulnerabilities in Microsoft's email platform, forcing organizations to reassess their cybersecurity strategies.

Reflecting on the broader impact of the attack, it is clear that the Microsoft Exchange intrusion prompted widespread changes in how organizations approach email security and vulnerability management. The incident highlighted the need for constant vigilance and a proactive approach to cybersecurity, ensuring that even the most well-protected systems are defended against increasingly sophisticated threats.

CHAPTER CONCLUSION

The military hacks discussed in this chapter highlight the evolving nature of cyber warfare and its profound impact on global security. These incidents underscore the growing reliance on cyber capabilities to achieve strategic military objectives. Cyberattacks have increasingly become tools of geopolitical influence that are used by nation-states to undermine adversaries without resorting to direct physical conflict. The recurring theme of exploiting vulnerabilities in military communications, command-and-control systems, and operational infrastructure reveals the critical importance of securing digital assets in modern military operations. As militaries continue integrating technology into their operations, they must remain vigilant against evolving cyber threats that can disrupt operations and compromise national security.

For today's cybersecurity professionals, these historical cases offer valuable lessons on the importance of proactive defense and incident response strategies. Many of the attacks described in this chapter exploited human vulnerabilities—such as phishing and social engineering—highlighting the need for strong cybersecurity awareness training. Additionally, the ability of attackers to remain undetected for extended periods, as seen in the hacking of South Korean military servers, underscores the necessity of real-time monitoring and advanced threat detection tools. Cybersecurity professionals must prioritize continuous system monitoring, quick detection, and comprehensive response strategies to mitigate the damage caused by sophisticated adversaries.

These attacks demonstrate that a strong, multilayered defense is essential to protect critical military and civilian infrastructure.

Ultimately, the key takeaway for cybersecurity professionals is that the landscape of military and government cyber threats is complex, multifaceted, and continuously evolving. Cyber professionals must stay informed about the latest attack vectors and vulnerabilities and work to foster collaboration between government, military, and civilian sectors to strengthen defenses against cyberattacks. Investing in advanced tools, improving training programs, and ensuring rapid response capabilities are essential steps in addressing the challenges posed by state-sponsored cyberattacks. Cyber warfare continues to play a central role in geopolitical conflicts, therefore, cybersecurity professionals must be at the forefront, building defenses that can withstand the increasing sophistication of global cyber threats.

12

THE RISE AND IMPACT OF DISTRIBUTED DENIAL-OF-SERVICE ATTACKS

Ah, distributed denial-of-service (DDoS) attacks . . . those annoying digital tantrums that make your favorite websites go from hero to zero in seconds. Imagine if every time you tried to visit a website, a flood of unwanted visitors blocked the entrance, shouting nonsense and waving traffic signals in every direction. That is essentially what DDoS attacks do but with less personality and more bandwidth. If cyber threats were characters in a video game, DDoS would be the troll king, constantly reminding us that no matter how fast your server is, there is always someone with more firepower to slow it down.

Jokes aside, DDoS attacks have evolved into one of the most disruptive and dangerous weapons in the cyber arsenal. What began as a nuisance has grown into a powerful tool capable of crippling even the most resilient systems. These attacks, which flood networks and servers with overwhelming traffic, can easily bring down governments, financial institutions, and critical infrastructure. The scale and frequency of these incidents continue to rise, and understanding their evolution is key to defending against future threats. This chapter explores some of the most notorious DDoS attacks in recent history, analyzing how they unfolded, the methods attackers used, and the lasting impact they had on organizations and cybersecurity.

The purpose of this chapter is not just to recount these events but to extract valuable lessons for today's cybersecurity professionals. As these case studies demonstrate, DDoS attacks often exploit weak points in infrastructure, ranging from unsecured Internet of Things (IoT) devices to misconfigured Domain Name System (DNS) servers. The goal is to highlight the importance of securing these vulnerable systems and to emphasize the critical need for advanced DDoS mitigation strategies. However, in many cases, precise details about how organizations detected and responded to these attacks remain unclear. Where specific information does not exist, I have extrapolated from media reports and other available sources to provide insights into how the detection and response processes likely unfolded.

In exploring these historical DDoS attacks, this chapter aims to provide readers with a clearer understanding of the dynamic threat landscape and the defenses required to combat it. DDoS attacks are not going away; they are evolving in complexity and scale. Cybersecurity professionals can better prepare for the next wave of attacks by analyzing past incidents and identifying common vulnerabilities. Whether you are securing a global enterprise or a small business, the lessons learned here will help reinforce the importance of vigilance, adaptability, and collaboration in today's digital battleground.

WHAT IS A DISTRIBUTED DENIAL-OF-SERVICE ATTACK?

A DDoS attack is a type of cyberattack in which multiple systems flood the bandwidth or resources of a targeted server, website, or network, rendering it unavailable to legitimate users. In essence, the goal of a DDoS attack is to overwhelm the target with an enormous volume of traffic, so much so that the system can no longer handle the incoming requests. The result is a denial of service; legitimate users, whether customers, employees, or website visitors, cannot access the necessary resources.

In a typical DDoS attack, an attacker gains control of numerous computers or IoT devices, often forming a botnet network. These compromised devices, including personal computers, routers, and security cameras, are then used to bombard the target with traffic. Each device sends requests to the server, and the sheer volume of these requests makes it impossible for the system to differentiate between legitimate and malicious traffic. The server, unable to handle the load, becomes slow or crashes entirely, disrupting normal operations.

DDoS attacks can be carried out for various reasons, ranging from political motives and cyber warfare to simple financial extortion or personal vendettas. Some attackers aim to make a statement by taking down high-profile targets, while others may use the attack to gain leverage for a ransom. As these attacks have grown more sophisticated, so too have the tools to defend against them. However, DDoS attacks remain a major threat to businesses and organizations, particularly those that rely heavily on online services and continuous availability.

The following chart illustrates the timeline associated with the attacks that will be explored in this chapter (see Figure 12.1).

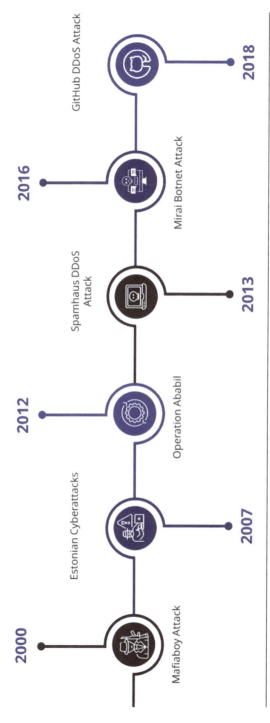

Figure 12.1   The timeline of DDoS attacks discussed in this chapter

MAFIABOY (2000)

The Mafiaboy attack in February of 2000 marked one of the first major DDoS attacks to target high-profile websites, sending shockwaves through the burgeoning internet landscape. Orchestrated by a Canadian teenager known online as *Mafiaboy*, this attack exploited the relatively weak security infrastructure of the time to take down major sites such as Yahoo!, Amazon, CNN, and eBay. The attack raised awareness of how vulnerable even well-known, seemingly secure websites could be to cyberattacks, especially as the internet economy was beginning to boom.

As the Internet was becoming a central hub for commerce, communication, and media, companies like Yahoo! and eBay were growing rapidly, and their availability was crucial to maintaining customer trust and operational efficiency. However, security practices were still evolving, and many organizations had yet to implement robust defenses to protect against DDoS attacks. The attack took advantage of this and highlighted the widespread lack of preparedness in defending against large-scale, coordinated attacks on network infrastructure.

Key stakeholders affected by the Mafiaboy attack included major e-commerce websites, news outlets, and their customers, who were disrupted by the outages. Additionally, cybersecurity firms and law enforcement agencies were tasked with investigating and responding to the attack. The high-profile nature of the attack brought the issue of cybersecurity into mainstream conversation and forced companies to reconsider their defense strategies to prevent similar incidents in the future.

Unfolding the Attack

The Mafiaboy attack unfolded over several days in early February 2000, with the attacker using a network of compromised computers, or botnets, to launch DDoS attacks on several major websites. From the information I was able to gather, I assume Mafiaboy's strategy was simple but effective; by overwhelming the targeted websites with traffic, he caused them to crash or become inaccessible to users. The first target was Yahoo!, which at the time was the most visited site on the Internet, and the attack quickly rendered it unusable for hours. Similar attacks on CNN, Amazon, and other high-profile sites followed.

The attack's entry point and initial compromise were based on Mafiaboy's ability to gain control over multiple unsecured computers, using them as a botnet to amplify the scale of the attack. He leveraged these compromised machines to send massive traffic to the targeted sites, effectively overwhelming their servers. While the technique itself was not particularly sophisticated, the scale and coordination of the attack were unprecedented at the time.

The timeline of the attack highlights its devastating impact. Over several days, Mafiaboy brought down some of the most heavily trafficked websites on the Internet. The attack clearly demonstrated how vulnerable even major websites were to large-scale DDoS attacks, forcing organizations to recognize the importance of securing their infrastructure against such threats.

Detection and Response Efforts

The Mafiaboy attack was detected relatively quickly due to the high-profile nature of the affected websites. Companies like Yahoo! and CNN immediately noticed the disruption, making their websites inaccessible to millions of users. From the available information, I assume the companies' initial response focused on restoring service while determining the cause of the outage. Since DDoS attacks were still relatively new, many organizations were unprepared to respond effectively to such a large-scale incident.

Cybersecurity firms and law enforcement agencies, including the Federal Bureau of Investigation (FBI), quickly became involved in investigating the attack. One of the challenges they faced was identifying the source of the attack, as it was carried out using a botnet of compromised computers. However, through coordinated efforts and network traffic analysis, investigators were eventually able to trace the attack back to the teenage hacker behind the Mafiaboy alias. He was arrested in April 2000 and later convicted for his role in the attacks.

The response efforts also led to a broader industry conversation about the need for stronger defenses against DDoS attacks. Many organizations began implementing more advanced traffic monitoring systems and improving their network infrastructure to prevent future incidents. While the immediate threat was contained, the attack underscored the growing importance of developing robust incident response plans to mitigate the damage caused by cyberattacks.

Assessing the Impact

The impact of the Mafiaboy attack was significant, with major websites like Yahoo!, CNN, Amazon, and eBay experiencing hours of downtime. This led to widespread disruption for businesses and users, as these websites were vital for e-commerce, news, and online transactions. The financial losses were substantial, as the downtime resulted in lost revenue and damaged customer trust. Yahoo!, for instance, was particularly hard hit, as the attack occurred when it was the leading search engine and internet portal.

In the long term, the Mafiaboy attack negatively affected how organizations approached cybersecurity. The attack exposed weaknesses in network infrastructure and forced companies to rethink their defense strategies. Many businesses realized they were unprepared for large-scale DDoS attacks, which led to increased investments in cybersecurity solutions designed to mitigate such threats. The attack also highlighted the importance of collaboration between companies and law enforcement agencies in investigating and responding to cyber incidents.

For Mafiaboy, the attack had personal consequences as well. The teenager was arrested and convicted for his involvement in the attacks, marking one of the first high-profile cybercrime cases. This case served as a deterrent for other would-be attackers, demonstrating that even young, unsophisticated hackers could face serious legal consequences for their actions.

Lessons Learned and Takeaways

The Mafiaboy attack offered several critical lessons for the cybersecurity community. First, it demonstrated the effectiveness of DDoS attacks in disrupting major websites and services. The attack highlighted the need for businesses to invest in DDoS mitigation strategies, including traffic filtering, load balancing, and real-time network traffic monitoring. Many companies implemented these measures after the attack to prevent future incidents.

Another key takeaway was the importance of securing vulnerable systems. Mafiaboy executed the attack by exploiting a network of compromised computers called a botnet. This emphasized the need for stronger security practices, such as regular software updates, stronger passwords, and better user education to prevent machines from being hijacked and used in cyberattacks. The attack also underscored the need for businesses to collaborate with law enforcement and cybersecurity firms to address large-scale threats.

Finally, the Mafiaboy attack showed that the Internet's growing role in commerce and communication made it a prime target for cybercriminals. As a result, organizations began to adopt more comprehensive cybersecurity policies and develop more sophisticated incident response plans. This attack catalyzed improving defenses against DDoS attacks and other large-scale cyber threats.

Case Study Summary

The Mafiaboy attack of 2000 was a pivotal moment in the history of cyber-security, illustrating how vulnerable major websites were to DDoS attacks. The attack caused significant operational disruption and financial loss for companies like Yahoo! and Amazon, raising awareness of the importance of securing network infrastructure. Key takeaways include the need for DDoS mitigation strategies, stronger security practices to prevent botnet exploitation, and more robust incident response plans.

Reflecting on the broader impact of the attack, Mafiaboy's actions forced organizations to take cybersecurity more seriously as the Internet grew in importance. The attack prompted significant improvements in network se-curity practices and set the stage for future advancements in protecting against large-scale cyberattacks. The lessons learned from the Mafiaboy incident continue to shape modern cybersecurity defenses, particularly in DDoS prevention and incident response.

ESTONIAN CYBERATTACKS (2007)

The Estonian cyberattacks in 2007 marked one of the earliest instances where a nation-state experienced large-scale, coordinated cyber assaults. These attacks came in response to Estonia's decision to relocate a Soviet-era monument, a move that sparked political tensions with Russia. Estonia, a Baltic nation known for its digital society and extensive internet infrastructure, became the target of what many believe was politically motivated DDoS attacks. The Estonian government, financial institutions, media outlets, and other critical infrastructure were affected, showcasing the vulnerabilities of even the most tech-savvy nations.

At the time, Estonia was considered one of the most digitally advanced countries in the world, having developed an extensive e-government system that allowed its citizens to access services online. This reliance on digital in-frastructure made the country particularly vulnerable to cyberattacks. Key stakeholders involved in this incident included the Estonian government, various private sector entities, and their international allies, including NATO, which had to step in to support Estonia during the crisis.

The technological landscape in 2007 was still evolving, with cybersecu-rity still in its infancy compared to today's standards. The understanding of DDoS attacks was limited, and the event served as a wake-up call to many nations and industries about the potential for cyberattacks to disrupt national security. Estonia's position as a small yet highly digitalized nation became both a strength and a vulnerability, making this case a pivotal moment in cybersecurity history.

Unfolding the Attack

The cyberattacks against Estonia began on April 27, 2007, shortly after the Estonian government decided to move the Bronze Soldier monument. What initially seemed like isolated incidents of website defacement quickly escalated into a full-blown cyber assault. Attackers utilized DDoS techniques, flooding Estonian websites with traffic from botnets worldwide, rendering key governmental, financial, and media websites inaccessible.

The timeline of events unfolded over several weeks, with different sectors of Estonia's infrastructure being targeted in waves. The first wave primarily focused on government and media websites, followed by a second wave that expanded to banks and other financial institutions. The attackers overwhelmed these systems by sending massive data requests, causing the servers to crash or become so overloaded that they could no longer respond to legitimate users.

The entry point for these attacks was the public-facing websites of critical organizations, and the attackers exploited vulnerabilities in the websites' server infrastructures. At the time, Estonia's preparedness for large-scale attacks was minimal, and the attackers capitalized on these weaknesses. The methods involved massive botnets, many believed to have been operated from outside Estonia. From the information available, it can be assumed that the attack was coordinated across various groups, potentially with state backing. However, direct involvement from the Russian government has never been officially confirmed.

Detection and Response Efforts

Estonia quickly realized that the cyberattacks were not isolated incidents but a coordinated effort to disrupt the country's infrastructure. The attacks were detected almost immediately due to the massive surge in traffic, but the response was slow as the nation had never dealt with such an event. Estonian officials, private cybersecurity firms, and international partners scrambled to put up defenses.

Initial response actions involved blocking foreign Internet Protocol (IP) addresses from accessing the country's web services and rerouting traffic to servers in other countries that could help absorb the influx of data. The involvement of external parties, such as NATO's Cooperative Cyber Defence

Centre of Excellence, played a crucial role in helping Estonia mitigate the effects of the attacks. Law enforcement agencies and cybersecurity professionals worked together to trace the attack's origins, but the decentralized nature of botnets made it difficult to pinpoint the exact perpetrators.

The response timeline stretched several weeks, with Estonian officials gradually restoring access to essential services. By implementing temporary technical fixes, such as filtering traffic and relying on international assistance, Estonia was able to regain some control. However, the attacks demonstrated the vulnerabilities of interconnected systems and the difficulty of responding to large-scale DDoS attacks in real time.

Assessing the Impact

The impact of the Estonian cyberattacks was profound, both in terms of immediate disruptions and long-term consequences. In the short term, the attacks brought down critical websites, including those of the government, banks, and media outlets, crippling communications and financial transactions for several days. While no direct financial loss was attributed to stolen data, the operational disruption caused significant economic damage as businesses could not function normally.

In the long term, Estonia's reputation as a digital leader was challenged. The event raised concerns over the vulnerabilities inherent in relying heavily on digital infrastructure, especially for critical national functions. The attack also set a precedent for how cyberattacks could be used as a political tool, bringing attention to cyber warfare as a legitimate threat to national security.

Stakeholders, including the Estonian government, private sector organizations, and international allies, had to reconsider their approach to cybersecurity. The attacks highlighted the need for improved defenses and policies to protect against similar future events. While the immediate effects were disruptive, the broader implications of the attacks resonated far beyond Estonia's borders, affecting global cybersecurity strategies.

Lessons Learned and Takeaways

The Estonian cyberattacks provided critical lessons for the country and the international community. One of the key lessons was the importance of having a robust cybersecurity infrastructure in place, particularly for nations heavily reliant on digital services. Estonia's preexisting technological advancement proved to be both a strength and a vulnerability, and the attacks exposed weaknesses in their ability to respond to cyber threats.

A major security weakness was the lack of coordinated defenses against DDoS attacks. At the time, Estonia did not have the resources or technical capability to withstand such a sustained cyber assault, leading to a reevaluation of the country's cybersecurity posture. Following the attack, Estonia implemented a series of changes, including bolstering its cyber defenses, collaborating with NATO, and advocating for a more coordinated international response to cyber warfare.

The broader implications for the industry were also significant. The attacks underscored that no country or organization is immune to cyberattacks, regardless of their technological sophistication. The incident demonstrated that cyber warfare was not a futuristic concept but a present-day threat, one that required nations to reconsider how they protect their critical infrastructure from malicious actors.

Case Study Summary

The 2007 cyberattacks on Estonia served as a watershed moment in the evolution of cybersecurity threats. The attacks highlighted the vulnerabilities of digital infrastructure, especially in countries that rely heavily on online services for governance, commerce, and communication. While the attackers remain officially unidentified, the impact of their actions was felt across the globe.

This case emphasizes the need for vigilance, proactive defense strategies, and international collaboration in cybersecurity. It provides valuable lessons in preparing for, detecting, and responding to large-scale DDoS attacks, underscoring the necessity for continuous improvement in cyber defenses. The events in Estonia marked the beginning of a new era in cyber warfare, where the Internet became a tool for communication and a battlefield in its own right.

OPERATION ABABIL (2012)

Operation Ababil, one of the most significant cyberattacks in the financial sector, was launched in 2012 against major U.S. banks. It was carried out by a group calling itself the *Izz ad-Din al-Qassam Cyber Fighters*. The attackers claimed the operation was in response to a controversial video that insulted the Prophet Muhammad, which led to unrest across the Middle East. However, many cybersecurity experts believe that the operation was likely state-sponsored, given the sophistication of the attack and its scale, although direct evidence linking a government to the attack remains circumstantial.

The primary targets of this attack were large American financial institutions, including Bank of America, JPMorgan Chase, and Wells Fargo. As integral parts of the global financial system, these organizations rely heavily on digital infrastructure for transactions and customer services, making them vulnerable to large-scale DDoS attacks. At the time of the attack, the global financial sector had already transitioned to more digitally interconnected systems, increasing the risk of cyber disruptions.

The technological landscape in 2012 was in flux, with financial institutions adopting more complex online banking systems that, while offering greater convenience to customers, also expanded the potential attack surface. Key stakeholders involved included the banks and their customers and U.S. regulatory bodies such as the Department of the Treasury and the Federal Financial Institutions Examination Council, which played pivotal roles in coordinating responses.

Unfolding the Attack

Operation Ababil unfolded in waves for several months, beginning in September 2012. The attackers employed a series of high-volume DDoS attacks against the websites of the targeted banks, overwhelming their servers and rendering them unable to process legitimate traffic. This resulted in significant disruptions to online banking services for both individual and corporate clients, leading to widespread frustration and concern about the security of the financial system.

The timeline of events suggests a highly coordinated effort. Each wave of attacks lasted several days, with the first phase occurring in the fall of 2012 and subsequent waves hitting into early 2013. The entry point for these attacks was the banks' publicly accessible web interfaces, specifically targeting their customer-facing systems. From the information available, it can be assumed that the attackers used botnets of compromised computers to flood the banks' systems with traffic. These botnets were spread across various regions, making it difficult to mitigate the attacks.

The methods and techniques used in this operation were relatively straightforward from a technical standpoint but devastating in their impact. The attackers relied on sheer volume, leveraging botnets to overwhelm the banks' defenses. Unlike more sophisticated attacks that infiltrate internal systems, the focus was on creating a denial of service. The vulnerabilities exploited were not inherent flaws in the banks' security systems but rather the inability of their systems to handle the massive influx of traffic.

Detection and Response Efforts

The banks quickly detected DDoS attacks due to the sudden surge in traffic that caused their websites to slow down or crash entirely. The immediate response involved attempts to mitigate the attack by filtering out malicious traffic and routing legitimate traffic through alternative systems. However, due to the scale and persistence of the attacks, many banks struggled to maintain full functionality throughout the waves of assaults.

In response, the banks worked with external cybersecurity firms and law enforcement agencies, including the FBI and the Department of Homeland Security, to strengthen their defenses and identify the attackers. One of the primary initial actions was deploying traffic-scrubbing technologies designed to filter out malicious traffic. Despite these efforts, due to the scale of the botnet-driven attacks, the response took considerable time to become effective, causing some services to remain disrupted for days.

The timeline of the response efforts varied from bank to bank, with some institutions better prepared than others to handle the sustained onslaught. Cybersecurity firms were brought in throughout the operation to help develop more robust defenses, and information sharing between banks and regulatory agencies became critical. The involvement of external parties, particularly U.S. law enforcement and cybersecurity experts, was essential in mitigating the attacks and investigating their origins.

Assessing the Impact

The immediate effects of Operation Ababil were felt across the U.S. financial sector. Customers of the affected banks faced significant disruptions to online services, with many unable to access their accounts or complete transactions during critical periods. While no sensitive data was stolen, and there were no reports of financial loss due to unauthorized access, the operational disruption caused by the DDoS attacks led to a loss of customer confidence in the security of online banking systems.

Long-term consequences included a heightened awareness of the vulnerability of financial institutions to cyberattacks, particularly DDoS attacks. The reputational damage was not insignificant, as customers questioned the ability of these major financial institutions to protect their digital assets. In addition to customer dissatisfaction, the attacks highlighted the regulatory gaps in cybersecurity preparedness within the financial sector, prompting calls for more stringent security measures.

The impact on stakeholders was significant, including the banks, their customers, and the broader financial system. While the attacks did not result in the theft of funds or data breaches, the operational disruption underscored the fragility of digital infrastructures. Regulatory bodies were forced to reconsider their cybersecurity frameworks, and banks were compelled to invest heavily in upgrading their DDoS mitigation strategies and overall cybersecurity postures.

Lessons Learned and Takeaways

Operation Ababil offered critical lessons for financial institutions and the broader cybersecurity community. One of the primary takeaways was the importance of having comprehensive DDoS mitigation strategies in place. The attack exposed the limitations of existing defenses, particularly in the face of sustained, high-volume assaults. The financial sector, in particular, learned that even without direct access to sensitive data, attackers could cause significant disruption simply by overwhelming public-facing systems.

A key security weakness identified was the reliance on reactive defenses rather than proactive measures. Many banks did not have sufficient DDoS mitigation tools at the time of the attacks, leading to prolonged service outages. From this, the financial sector learned the necessity of investing in advanced DDoS protection technologies and ensuring they are integrated into broader cybersecurity strategies.

In response to the attacks, many banks implemented more robust defenses, including using traffic-scrubbing services, enhanced monitoring capabilities, and improved incident response protocols. Additionally, the attacks led to increased collaboration between financial institutions and regulatory bodies to ensure the industry was better prepared for future cyber threats. For the industry, Operation Ababil was a reminder of the evolving nature of cyber threats and the importance of continuous investment in cybersecurity.

Case Study Summary

Operation Ababil is a pivotal moment in the evolution of DDoS attacks, particularly in the financial sector. The attacks demonstrated the power of large-scale botnet-driven assaults and the vulnerability of even the most well-resourced institutions. Although no data was stolen or funds lost, the operational disruption caused significant reputational and regulatory consequences for the affected banks.

The case underscores the importance of proactive cybersecurity measures, particularly in sectors where digital infrastructure is critical to daily operations. It also highlighted the need for collaboration between private companies, cybersecurity firms, and regulatory bodies in responding to cyber threats. Operation Ababil remains a case study of how DDoS attacks can be a disruption tool and a wake-up call for organizations to strengthen their defenses against increasingly sophisticated cyber threats.

SPAMHAUS DDOS ATTACK (2013)

The 2013 DDoS attack on Spamhaus, a nonprofit organization that maintains lists of servers involved in spamming, is often cited as one of the largest DDoS attacks in history at the time. The attack highlighted the growing use of DDoS as a weapon for cybercriminals to disrupt services, harm reputations, and target organizations fighting against malicious online activities. Spamhaus was particularly targeted because of its role in blacklisting domains and IP addresses involved in spamming, making it a natural adversary for entities operating in the dark corners of the Internet.

Founded in 1998, Spamhaus has been a global cornerstone of email security and anti-spam efforts. Its service allows Internet service providers (ISPs) and other organizations to filter and block email traffic from known spammers. By 2013, Spamhaus had grown into a critical infrastructure for the global email system, playing a pivotal role in preventing unsolicited emails from flooding inboxes. The attack against Spamhaus sought to disrupt this anti-spam service and discredit its efforts to regulate online space.

DDoS attacks were becoming more sophisticated and prevalent at the time of the attack. The technological landscape was defined by the rise of large botnets, which could be employed to launch mass attacks of unprecedented scale. Key stakeholders in this incident included Spamhaus, its ISPs, third-party DDoS mitigation firms, and global law enforcement agencies tasked with investigating the attack.

Unfolding the Attack

The Spamhaus DDoS attack began in March 2013 and quickly escalated into one of the most significant cyber incidents of the year. Initially, the attack targeted Spamhaus's DNS servers, overwhelming them with massive traffic volumes. The attackers employed a technique known as DNS amplification, which leveraged vulnerable DNS servers to amplify traffic toward Spamhaus's infrastructure. The attack reached a staggering peak of over 300 Gbps, setting a new record for DDoS attacks.

The timeline of events suggests that the attackers, who were reportedly linked to a Dutch hosting provider known for questionable practices, initiated the attack in retaliation for Spamhaus's efforts to blacklist their servers. The botnets used for the attack included tens of thousands of compromised devices, contributing to the vast scale of the DDoS assault. I assume the attackers likely coordinated with multiple groups to sustain the prolonged attack since it lasted for several days and included various increasing intensities.

The entry point for the attack was Spamhaus's publicly available DNS servers. The attackers could amplify small requests into large responses by exploiting the lack of secure configurations in open DNS resolvers, thereby overwhelming Spamhaus's network infrastructure. The vulnerabilities exploited were not specific to Spamhaus itself. Still, they were a systemic issue within the broader Internet infrastructure, where DNS servers were not properly secured against this amplification attack.

Detection and Response Efforts

Spamhaus detected the attack almost immediately as its services became overwhelmed by the sudden surge in traffic. However, due to the sheer scale of the DDoS assault, the organization struggled to mitigate the impact on its own. As the attack progressed, Spamhaus turned to Cloudflare, a leading DDoS mitigation firm, for assistance in mitigating the flood of traffic. Cloudflare's global infrastructure helped absorb much of the attack, but even their systems were strained due to the unprecedented traffic volume.

The immediate response involved rerouting traffic and deploying additional DDoS mitigation strategies, such as filtering out malicious requests and using anycast routing to distribute traffic across multiple servers. The attackers responded by escalating the attack, shifting their focus to Cloudflare's infrastructure, and targeting key internet exchanges, which affected broader internet traffic across Europe.

The timeline of response efforts demonstrated the challenges of defending against such a large-scale DDoS attack. Over several days, multiple cybersecurity firms, ISPs, and law enforcement agencies became involved in controlling the attack. The collaboration between Spamhaus, Cloudflare, and other parties was critical in eventually mitigating the attack's impact, although some services remained disrupted for an extended period.

Assessing the Impact

The immediate impact of the Spamhaus DDoS attack was the disruption of Spamhaus's services, which affected its ability to provide real-time updates to its blacklists, causing a ripple effect on organizations and ISPs relying on Spamhaus to filter out spam emails. For a brief period, email security across the globe was compromised, leading to increased spam and phishing attacks during the downtime. However, the attack did not result in direct financial loss or data breaches because the goal was purely to disrupt services.

Long-term consequences included heightened awareness of the vulnerabilities inherent in DNS infrastructure and the need for more secure configurations to prevent DNS amplification attacks. The incident also demonstrated the growing power of botnets and the need for more advanced DDoS mitigation techniques. Reputationally, Spamhaus emerged relatively unscathed, as the attack was widely seen as an effort by malicious actors to silence an organization dedicated to combating spam and cybercrime.

The broader impact of the attack extended beyond Spamhaus since it exposed weaknesses in the Internet's core infrastructure. The attack reached a scale that affected not only Spamhaus and Cloudflare but also major Internet exchanges and service providers. Stakeholders across the internet ecosystem were forced to reconsider their defenses against large-scale DDoS attacks, leading to increased investment in mitigation technologies and more collaborative approaches to defending against cyber threats.

Lessons Learned and Takeaways

The Spamhaus DDoS attack provided critical lessons for the cybersecurity industry and internet infrastructure providers. One of the key lessons was the importance of securing DNS infrastructure against amplification attacks. The attack highlighted how vulnerable open DNS resolvers could be exploited to launch large-scale DDoS attacks, leading to widespread disruption.

A major security weakness identified was the lack of global coordination in securing critical internet infrastructure. After studying the existing information, I assume that many DNS resolvers used in the attack were not properly configured, allowing them to be leveraged for amplification. This attack prompted many organizations to adopt best practices for securing DNS servers, such as implementing rate-limiting and restricting access to DNS queries.

Several organizations, including Spamhaus and Cloudflare, strengthened their DDoS defenses in response to the attack. Additionally, the attack led to broader industry efforts to secure DNS infrastructure and improve collaboration between cybersecurity firms and ISPs in responding to large-scale cyber threats. The incident also raised awareness of the evolving threat landscape, where attackers could leverage botnets and poorly configured infrastructure to cause massive disruptions.

Case Study Summary

The 2013 Spamhaus DDoS attack marked a turning point in the evolution of DDoS attacks. It showcased the immense power of DNS amplification and botnets and the vulnerability of global internet infrastructure to such

continued

attacks. While Spamhaus ultimately recovered, the attack underscored the need for more secure configurations of DNS servers and the importance of collaboration in mitigating large-scale cyber threats.

This case study illustrates how attackers can exploit systemic weaknesses in internet architecture to launch highly disruptive attacks. The broader implications of the attack for the cybersecurity industry include the need for continuous innovation in DDoS mitigation strategies and the importance of securing critical internet services against emerging threats. The Spamhaus incident remains a critical example of how cyberattacks can evolve in scale and sophistication, challenging defenders to stay vigilant and proactive.

MIRAI BOTNET ATTACK (2016)

The Mirai botnet attack of 2016 is one of the most notorious DDoS attacks, primarily due to its unprecedented scale and the widespread disruption it caused. The attack leveraged an army of compromised IoT devices, including cameras, routers, and DVRs, to launch massive DDoS attacks on prominent websites and critical infrastructure. The primary target of the attack was Dyn, a major DNS provider, which resulted in significant downtime for major websites, including Twitter, Netflix, and Reddit. The Mirai botnet attack demonstrated the vulnerabilities of IoT devices and the growing risk they posed as attackers began to exploit them in new ways.

At the time, IoT devices were rapidly increasing across the consumer and business markets, but security for these devices was often weak or nonexistent. Many compromised devices used in the Mirai botnet were found to have default factory credentials, making them easy targets for attackers. This attack highlighted the failure of IoT manufacturers to prioritize security and how this negligence could have catastrophic consequences. Key stakeholders in this incident included Dyn, the companies affected by the downtime, IoT device manufacturers, and law enforcement agencies working to investigate and respond to the attack.

The technological landscape of 2016 was heavily shaped by the increasing reliance on cloud services and web-based applications, which meant that any disruption to DNS services could have far-reaching consequences. The Mirai botnet attack exploited this centralization of services, using DDoS to cripple a fundamental aspect of the internet's infrastructure, resulting in global service outages.

Unfolding the Attack

The Mirai botnet attack occurred in several stages, with the most significant event happening on October 21, 2016, when the botnet launched a massive DDoS attack against Dyn, a DNS provider responsible for routing much of the internet's traffic. Prior to this, smaller attacks were observed, allowing attackers to test their capabilities. The botnet used hundreds of thousands of compromised IoT devices to generate vast amounts of traffic, overwhelming Dyn's servers and causing disruptions to websites dependent on their DNS services.

The timeline of events suggests that the attackers had been systematically scanning the Internet for vulnerable IoT devices to infect with the Mirai malware that could brute-force default login credentials. Most likely, the attack was orchestrated by several individuals who had significant technical expertise in botnet operations. The Mirai botnet first appeared in September 2016, when the malware's source code was publicly released on hacker forums, allowing others to deploy similar attacks.

The entry point for the attack was unsecured IoT devices scattered across the globe. The attackers exploited weak or default passwords left unchanged by device owners, allowing them to take control of these devices. Once compromised, these IoT devices became part of the Mirai botnet, which sent overwhelming amounts of traffic to targeted servers. The vulnerabilities exploited were largely related to IoT devices' lack of security standards such as shipping with hardcoded or weak credentials.

Detection and Response Efforts

Dyn and other cybersecurity firms quickly detected the attack due to the sudden surge in DNS queries overwhelming their servers. Dyn's immediate response involved attempts to mitigate the attack by rerouting traffic and employing traffic-scrubbing techniques to filter out malicious requests. However, the scale of the botnet's attack overwhelmed these defenses, leading to significant service outages for several hours. The attack affected Dyn's services and the broader internet ecosystem, with users across North America and Europe reporting access issues.

Initial response actions included shutting down compromised endpoints and working with ISPs to block traffic originating from infected devices. Despite these efforts, the botnet's distributed nature made it difficult to contain. Dyn collaborated with external parties, including cybersecurity firms and government agencies, to analyze the attack and mitigate its effects. Law enforcement agencies, such as the FBI, became involved in investigating the attack's origins, though it took several months before arrests were made.

The timeline of the response effort was extended, as the sheer number of infected IoT devices meant that mitigating the attack and preventing further occurrences required long-term collaboration between ISPs, manufacturers, and cybersecurity experts. Over the following weeks and months, law enforcement tracked down the creators of Mirai, resulting in the arrest of several individuals involved in the development and deployment of the malware.

Assessing the Impact

The Mirai botnet attack had far-reaching consequences, both in the immediate disruption it caused and the longer-term implications for cybersecurity. The attack on Dyn led to widespread outages for several major websites, frustrating millions of users and causing financial losses for businesses that relied on these online services. While no sensitive data was stolen, and there was no direct financial theft, the operational disruption was significant. The attack underscored the fragility of internet infrastructure and how reliance on centralized DNS services made the web vulnerable to large-scale attacks.

The attack led to greater scrutiny of IoT device security in the long term. The fact that such a massive attack was made possible by exploiting poorly secured consumer devices revealed a serious problem in the industry. Manufacturers faced increased pressure to improve the security of their products, and new regulatory efforts began to take shape to address these vulnerabilities. Additionally, organizations began to rethink their DDoS defense strategies, recognizing the need for more sophisticated mitigation techniques to handle future attacks of this scale.

The impact on stakeholders, including Dyn, IoT manufacturers, and users affected by the downtime was considerable. IoT manufacturers, in particular, faced reputational damage since the attack brought attention to their failure to secure devices adequately. Meanwhile, the broader internet ecosystem had to confront the reality that DDoS attacks were evolving and that new defensive strategies were required to protect critical infrastructure from future threats.

Lessons Learned and Takeaways

The Mirai botnet attack offered several critical lessons for the cybersecurity community and IoT industry. One of the primary takeaways was the importance of securing IoT devices, particularly concerning default credentials. The attack demonstrated that even simple security measures, such as changing default passwords, could have mitigated much of the damage. From the information available, I assume many device owners were unaware of the risks posed by leaving these default settings in place, highlighting the need for better consumer education around IoT security.

A major security weakness identified was the lack of oversight in the IoT industry, where devices were mass-produced with little regard for security. This lack of accountability contributed to the scale of the attack, as hundreds of thousands of insecure devices were easily hijacked and used as part of the botnet. The attack also underscored the need for better industry standards and regulations to ensure that IoT devices are secure out of the box.

In response to the attack, the cybersecurity industry began advocating for more robust defenses against DDoS attacks, including adopting automated threat detection systems and more aggressive traffic-filtering techniques. Additionally, the attack prompted calls for manufacturers to adopt better security practices such as eliminating hardcoded credentials and enabling automatic software updates to patch vulnerabilities. The broader implications for the industry included a renewed focus on securing IoT ecosystems and ensuring that future devices would not be as easily exploited.

Case Study Summary

The 2016 Mirai botnet attack highlighted the vulnerabilities of IoT devices and the catastrophic consequences of failing to secure them. The attack disrupted major internet services and demonstrated the power of large-scale DDoS attacks and the evolving threat landscape. While the attack did not result in financial theft or data breaches, its impact on internet infrastructure was profound, revealing significant weaknesses in the security of IoT ecosystems.

This case emphasizes the need for vigilance in securing critical infrastructure and consumer-grade devices that can be exploited on a massive scale. The lessons learned from the Mirai attack have had lasting effects on the cybersecurity industry, driving efforts to improve IoT security and prompting organizations to develop more advanced DDoS defense strategies. The Mirai incident remains a critical example of how cyberattacks continue to evolve, and it serves as a reminder of the importance of proactive cybersecurity measures in an increasingly connected world.

GITHUB DDOS ATTACK (2018)

In February 2018, GitHub, the world's leading platform for software development collaboration, experienced one of the largest DDoS attacks ever recorded. The attack peaked at 1.35 terabits per second (Tbps), making it an unprecedented event in terms of scale and complexity. GitHub, a vital service for millions of developers, was targeted because of its open-source nature and critical role in supporting global software development.

GitHub had grown significantly by 2018, becoming the go-to platform for developers worldwide to host, manage, and collaborate on software projects. At the time of the attack, GitHub handled massive volumes of data, with millions of repositories hosting crucial software infrastructure. The technological landscape was evolving rapidly, with cloud-based services, content delivery networks (CDNs), and DDoS mitigation strategies becoming integral parts of web infrastructure. Key stakeholders in this case included GitHub's platform administrators, the developers who rely on it, and Akamai, the CDN service that played a critical role in mitigating the attack.

Unfolding the Attack

The GitHub DDoS attack occurred on February 28, 2018, and unfolded within minutes. The attackers used a technique called Memcached amplification, which dramatically increased the amount of traffic directed at GitHub's servers. Memcached, a popular open-source tool used to cache data and reduce server loads, was exploited to amplify the attack by a factor of 50,000. Attackers sent small requests to vulnerable Memcached servers, which then responded with massive volumes of data, overwhelming GitHub's infrastructure.

The timeline of events suggests that GitHub's monitoring systems quickly detected the incoming traffic spike, but the sheer scale of the attack initially overwhelmed the platform's defenses. After studying the existing information, I assume the attackers likely knew of GitHub's infrastructure and targeted the platform specifically due to its global visibility and reliance on constant uptime. The attack peaked at 1.35 Tbps and lasted for several minutes before GitHub's systems started to mitigate it effectively.

The entry point for the attack was the vulnerable Memcached servers, which had been left exposed to the public Internet without proper configuration. The attackers exploited this weakness to launch an immense DDoS attack, using only a small amount of their bandwidth while leveraging the amplification effect of Memcached servers. The primary vulnerability in this attack lay not with GitHub but with the misconfigured Memcached servers across the Internet, which allowed the attackers to generate such large volumes of traffic.

Detection and Response Efforts

GitHub's internal monitoring tools immediately detected the unusual spike in traffic. Within minutes of the attack, GitHub activated its DDoS response plan, rerouting traffic through Akamai's DDoS mitigation service, Prolexic. Akamai's infrastructure absorbed and filtered the attack traffic, preventing most of it from reaching GitHub's servers. Within approximately 10 minutes, the attack had been mitigated, and GitHub's services were fully restored.

GitHub's team's initial response actions involved throttling incoming traffic and rerouting it through Akamai's scrubbing centers, where malicious traffic was filtered out. Akamai's response was critical in preventing more extensive service disruption. Despite the scale of the attack, GitHub experienced only brief downtime.

The involvement of external parties, particularly Akamai, was vital in mitigating the attack. Akamai's distributed network of scrubbing centers helped handle the massive influx of traffic. GitHub also collaborated with cybersecurity firms to analyze the attack, understand the Memcached amplification method, and prevent further exploits in the future.

Assessing the Impact

The immediate effects of the GitHub DDoS attack were limited to a brief service disruption that affected developers worldwide. GitHub's swift response and reliance on Akamai's DDoS mitigation services prevented more significant financial loss or prolonged downtime. Despite the size of the attack, GitHub's quick recovery ensured minimal disruption to its user base, and no sensitive data was compromised.

In the long term, the attack prompted greater awareness of the vulnerabilities associated with Memcached servers. It also underscored the importance of robust DDoS defenses, particularly for platforms like GitHub, which is critical to the global software development community. GitHub's reputation remained intact due to the speed and effectiveness of its response, but the attack highlighted the potential for massive disruption in future DDoS incidents.

For stakeholders, including GitHub's developers and the broader internet community, the attack served as a reminder of the fragility of the internet's infrastructure in the face of increasingly sophisticated cyber threats. The incident also highlighted the need for better security configurations for services like Memcached, which had not been designed with DDoS amplification in mind.

Lessons Learned and Takeaways

The GitHub DDoS attack taught the cybersecurity community and web-based service providers valuable lessons. One of the key takeaways was the importance of securing infrastructure that could be exploited for amplification attacks, such as Memcached servers. Following the attack, many organizations took steps to configure their Memcached services properly, ensuring they were not publicly accessible or vulnerable to misuse.

In response to the attack, GitHub and Akamai further bolstered their DDoS defenses, recognizing that the scale of future attacks could grow even larger. Additionally, the attack led to an industry-wide push for better DDoS mitigation technologies and improvements in the security of internet-facing services that could be leveraged in such attacks. The broader implications for the industry included a renewed focus on securing the infrastructure that underpins the Internet and ensuring that services critical to the global digital economy were better protected against future DDoS threats.

Case Study Summary

The GitHub DDoS attack of 2018 marked a significant moment in the evolution of cyber threats, particularly due to the use of Memcached amplification to generate massive volumes of traffic. Despite the attack's unprecedented scale, GitHub's response was swift, limiting the impact to a brief service outage. This case highlights the vulnerabilities in internet infrastructure, particularly in the context of amplification attacks, and underscores the importance of robust DDoS mitigation strategies.

The attack also catalyzed change, leading to better security practices across the industry and prompting organizations to reconsider the security of their online services. The GitHub incident remains a critical example of the dynamic nature of DDoS threats and the need for continued vigilance and proactive defense measures in an increasingly connected world.

CHAPTER CONCLUSION

The details of the DDoS attacks explored in this chapter—from the Estonian cyberattacks in 2007 to the GitHub incident in 2018—highlight how these attacks have evolved in scale, sophistication, and impact. A common theme across all these incidents is the exploitation of system vulnerabilities—whether in public-facing websites, IoT devices, or misconfigured servers—to disrupt critical infrastructure. These attacks have shown that no organization, no matter how well-prepared, is immune to the risks of determined attackers. What began as relatively simple yet massive attacks in the early 2000s has grown into a sophisticated tool capable of crippling global infrastructure, as measured by the increasing number of attacks of 50 Gbps or more per year (see Figure 12.2).

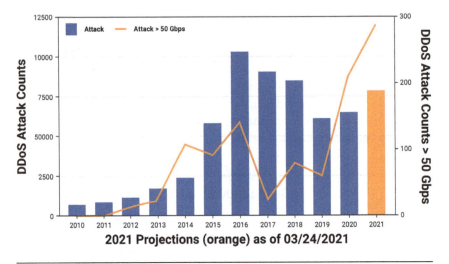

Figure 12.2   The changing impact of DDoS attacks (*source*: Statista Search Department)

For today's cybersecurity professionals, these cases emphasize the importance of maintaining robust defense mechanisms and staying ahead of evolving threats. Each attack demonstrates the necessity of constant vigilance and the importance of updating security protocols regularly. Organizations must proactively secure public-facing systems, properly configure critical infrastructure, and implement advanced DDoS mitigation strategies to respond to these threats in real time. Moreover, collaboration between private organizations, cybersecurity firms, and governmental agencies has repeatedly proven essential to managing and mitigating large-scale attacks, as seen in cases like Operation Ababil and the GitHub DDoS attack.

It is important to note that in many of these cases, the specific details of detection and response efforts were extrapolated from available media reports and information. The lack of complete transparency from targeted organizations often leaves gaps in our understanding of the exact steps to mitigate these attacks. As an author, I have relied on my analysis of the available information to conclude how certain organizations may have responded. This underscores a broader issue within cybersecurity: the need for clearer communication and documentation of lessons learned from significant incidents because this information can be invaluable to professionals facing similar challenges.

The key takeaway from these case studies is that preparation is critical for cybersecurity professionals. Investing in the right technologies, including DDoS mitigation tools and traffic-scrubbing services, is essential. However, building a security culture that prioritizes proactive measures, collaboration, and adaptability is just as important. The dynamic nature of DDoS threats demands continuous learning to keep up with evolving strategies as attackers continue to refine their methods. By drawing on the lessons learned from these historical incidents and committing to best practices, today's cybersecurity professionals can better protect their organizations from the ever-growing threat of DDoS attacks.

REFERENCES

Administrator. (2024, March 25). *The MafiaBoy DDoS attack—101 Computing*. 101 Computing—Boost Your Programming Skills! https://www.101 computing.net/the-mafiaboy-ddos-attack/.

Alijo, H. (2001, February 16). *Purported 'Anna' virus toolkit author yanks files from site*. ZDNET. https://www.zdnet.com/article/purported-anna-virus -toolkit-author-yanks-files-from-site/.

Anderson, N. (2012, June 1). *Confirmed: US and Israel created Stuxnet, lost control of it*. ars TECHNICA. https://arstechnica.com/tech-policy/2012 /06/confirmed-us-israel-created-stuxnet-lost-control-of-it/.

B., D. (2020, August 5). *History of Hacking: John "Captain Crunch" Draper's Perspective*. Privacy PC. https://privacy-pc.com/articles/history-of-hacki ng-john-captain-crunch-drapers-perspective.html.

Batty, D. (2017, July 15). *Timeline: Gary McKinnon's fight against extradition to the US*. The Guardian. https://www.theguardian.com/world/2009/nov /26/gary-mckinnon-extradition-timeline.

BBC. (2001, February 13) | *SCI/TECH | Kournikova computer virus hits hard*. BBC News. http://news.bbc.co.uk/2/hi/science/nature/1167453.stm.

Belot, H. and Borys, S. (2017, May 16). *Ransomware attack still looms in Australia as Government warns WannaCry threat not over*. ABC News. http:// www.abc.net.au/news/2017-05-15/ransomware-attack-to-hit-victims-in -australia-government-says/8526346.

BetaFred. (2023, March 1). *Microsoft Security Bulletin MS03-026—Critical*. Microsoft Learn. https://learn.microsoft.com/en-us/security-updates/se curitybulletins/2003/ms03-026.

Bradshaw, P. (2016, April 8). *In the wake of Ashley Madison, towards a journalism ethics of using hacked documents*. Online Journalism Blog. https://on linejournalismblog.com/2015/07/20/ashley-madison-ethics-journalism -hacked-documents/.

CAIDA Analysis of Code-Red. (2020, July 30). CAIDA. https://www.caida.org /archive/code-red/.

Caña, P. J. (1970, January 1). *Filipino Creator of the 'I Love You' Virus Just Did It So He Could Get Free Internet.* Esquiremag.ph. https://web.archive.org/ web/20200607094321/https://www.esquiremag.ph/culture/tech/filipino -creator-of-the-i-love-you-virus-free-internet-a00289-20200504.

Captain Crunch on Apple—An interview with John Draper. Stories of Apple. (2008, December 4). https://www.storiesofapple.net/captain-crunch-on -apple-an-interview-with-john-draper.html.

Case Study: What We've Learned from the Target Data Breach 2013. (2023, May 19). CardConnect. https://www.cardconnect.com/launchpointe/payment -trends/target-data-breach/.

Chen, T. M. and J. Robert. (2004). *The evolution of viruses and worms* (pp. 289–310). CRC Press. doi.org/10.1201/9781420030884-19.

Chin, M. (2017, October 11). *Equifax hackers got 10 million driver's licenses.* Mashable. https://mashable.com/article/equifax-hackers-got-drivers-licenses.

Cloud computing data breaches: A review of U.S. regulation and data breach notification literature. (2021, October 28). IEEE Conference Publication | IEEE Xplore. https://ieeexplore.ieee.org/document/9629173.

Cohen, G. (2022, August 15). *Throwback Attack: Three teens stoke fears of a cyber war with the Solar Sunrise attack.* Industrial Cybersecurity Pulse. https://www.industrialcybersecuritypulse.com/threats-vulnerabilities/ throwback-attack-three-teens-stoke-fears-of-a-cyber-war-with-the-sol ar-sunrise-attack/.

Cyber Safety Review Board, Silvers, R., Sr. and Alperovitch, D., Jr. (2024). *Review of the Summer 2023 Microsoft Exchange Online Intrusion.* https:// www.cisa.gov/sites/default/files/2024-04/CSRB_Review_of_the_Summ er_2023_MEO_Intrusion_Final_508c.pdf.

Discoveries—Video—The Spread of the Code Red Worm | NSF—National Science Foundation. (n.d.). https://www.nsf.gov/discoveries/disc_videos.jsp ?org=NSF&cntn_id=100075&media_id=51501.

Draper, J. T., C. W. Fraser, S. Wozniak, T. Barbalet, and R. Draper. (2018). *Beyond the Little Blue Box: The biographical adventure of John T. Draper (aka Captain Crunch). Notorious 'Phone Phreak,' legendary internet pioneer and ardent privacy advocate. Amazon.com: Books.* https://www.ama zon.com/Beyond-Little-Blue-Box-Biographical/dp/1525505696.

Duncan, F. (2009, January 23). Escenic. *The Telegraph.* https://www.telegra ph.co.uk/news/worldnews/northamerica/usa/4320901/Gary-McKinnon -profile-Autistic-hacker-who-started-writing-computer-programs-at-14 .html.

EP 23: *Vladimir Levin*. Darknet Diaries. (n.d.). https://darknetdiaries.com/tr anscript/23/.

Equifax to Pay $575 Million as Part of Settlement with FTC, CFPB, and States Related to 2017 Data Breach. (2023, June 2). Federal Trade Commission. https://www.ftc.gov/news-events/news/press-releases/2019/07/equifax -pay-575-million-part-settlement-ftc-cfpb-states-related-2017-data-br each.

Extortionists Target Ashley Madison Users. (2015, August 31). https://krebson security.com/2015/08/extortionists-target-ashley-madison-users/.

FBI arrests 'stupid' Blaster.B suspect. vnunet.com. (2003, September 1). https:// web.archive.org/web/20081101140521/http://www.vnunet.com/vnunet /news/2123165/fbi-arrests-stupid-blaster-b-suspect.

From snitch to cyberthief of the century. (2009, August 23). Newspapers.com. https://www.newspapers.com/article/the-miami-herald-from-snitch-to -cyberthi/148309063/.

Gallagher, S. (2015, June 24). *Encryption "would not have helped" at OPM, says DHS official*. ars TECHNICA. https://arstechnica.com/information -technology/2015/06/encryption-would-not-have-helped-at-opm-says -dhs-official/.

Giles, M. (2024, August 22). *Triton is the world's most murderous malware, and it's spreading*. MIT Technology Review. https://www.technologyrevi ew.com/2019/03/05/103328/cybersecurity-critical-infrastructure-triton -malware/.

Gillis, A. S. (2021, December 7). *Melissa virus*. Search Security. https://www.te chtarget.com/searchsecurity/definition/Melissa-virus.

Goodin, D. (2015, September 10). *Once seen as bulletproof, 11 million+ Ashley Madison passwords already cracked*. ars TECHNICA. https://arstechnica .com/information-technology/2015/09/once-seen-as-bulletproof-11-mi llion-ashley-madison-passwords-already-cracked/.

Goodin, D. (2016, September 22). *Yahoo says half a billion accounts breached by nation-sponsored hackers*. ars TECHNICA. https://arstechnica.com/ information-technology/2016/09/yahoo-says-half-a-billion-accounts-br eached-by-nation-sponsored-hackers/.

Gorelik, M. (2022, February 25). *Inside the ASUS Supply Chain Attack*. Mor phisec Breach Prevention Blog. https://blog.morphisec.com/asus-supply -chain-attack.

Greenberg, A. (2021, February 8). *A Hacker Tried to Poison a Florida City's Water Supply, Officials Say*. WIRED. https://www.wired.com/story/olds mar-florida-water-utility-hack/.

Greenberg, A. (2021, May 20). *The Full Story of the Stunning RSA Hack Can Finally Be Told*. WIRED. https://www.wired.com/story/the-full-story-of-the-stunning-rsa-hack-can-finally-be-told/.

Guerrero-Saade, J. A. (2021, September 2). *MeteorExpress | Mysterious Wiper Paralyzes Iranian Trains with Epic Troll—SentinelLabs*. SentinelOne. https://www.sentinelone.com/labs/meteorexpress-mysterious-wiper-pa ralyzes-iranian-trains-with-epic-troll/#:~:text=On%20July%209th%2C %202021%20a,of%20Supreme%20Leader%20Ali%20Khamenei.

Haselton, T. (2017, September 8). *Credit reporting firm Equifax says data breach could potentially affect 143 million US consumers*. CNBC. https://www.cnbc.com/2017/09/07/credit-reporting-firm-equifax-says-cyber security-incident-could-potentially-affect-143-million-us-consumers .html.

Heightened DDoS Threat Posed by Mirai and Other Botnets | CISA. (2016, October 14). Cybersecurity and Infrastructure Security Agency CISA. https://www.cisa.gov/news-events/alerts/2016/10/14/heightened-ddos -threat-posed-mirai-and-other-botnets.

Hern, A. (2017, September 8). *Equifax told to inform Britons whether they are at risk after data breach*. The Guardian. https://www.theguardian.com /technology/2017/sep/08/equifax-told-to-inform-britons-whether-they -are-at-risk-after-data-breach.

Hersher, R. (2015, February 7). *Meet Mafiaboy, The 'Bratty Kid' Who Took Down The Internet*. NPR. https://www.npr.org/sections/alltechconsider ed/2015/02/07/384567322/meet-mafiaboy-the-bratty-kid-who-took-do wn-the-internet.

http://www.gsdesign.com. (n.d.). *NEOHAPSIS—Peace of Mind Through Integrity and Insight*. Copyright (©) 2007 Neohapsis. https://web.archive .org/web/20090219072809/http://archives.neohapsis.com/archives/ntb ugtraq/2003-q1/0010.html.

Jazeera, A. (2023, December 18). *Iran points at Israeli-linked group as cyberattack disrupts fuel network*. Al Jazeera. https://www.aljazeera.com/news /2023/12/18/iran-says-cyberattack-disrupts-petrol-stations-across-coun try#:~:text=Tehran%20says%20Israel%2Dlinked%20Predatory%20Spar row%20group%20is%20behind%20the%20disruption.&text=A%20cyb erattack%20has%20disrupted%20services,of%20being%20behind%20th ose%20attacks.

Jones, C. (2022, May 3). *Warnings (& Lessons) of the 2013 Target Data Breach*. Red River | Technology Decisions Aren't Black and White. Think Red. https://redriver.com/security/target-data-breach.

Keizer, G. (2009, April 9). *Conficker cashes in, installs spam bots and scareware.* Copyright (©) 2009 Computerworld Inc. All Rights Reserved. https://web.archive.org/web/20090417165448/http://www.computerworld.com/action/article.do?command=viewArticleBasic&taxonomyName=Security&articleId=9131380.

Kelly, S. CNN Business. (2021, May 16). *The bizarre story of the inventor of ransomware.* CNN. https://web.archive.org/web/20210516125654/https://edition.cnn.com/2021/05/16/tech/ransomware-joseph-popp/index.html.

Khan, S., I. Kabanov, Y. Hua, and S. Madnick. (2022). *A Systematic Analysis of the Capital One Data Breach: Critical Lessons Learned.* ACM Transactions on Privacy and Security, *26*(1), 1–29. https://doi.org/10.1145/3546068.

Leader of Hacking Ring Sentenced for Massive Identity Thefts from Payment Processor and U.S. Retail Networks. Office of Public Affairs | United States Department of Justice (2014, September 16). https://www.justice.gov/opa/pr/leader-hacking-ring-sentenced-massive-identity-thefts-payment-processor-and-us-retail.

Leyden, J. (2011, September 16). *Ten years on from Nimda: Worm author still at large.* The Register. https://www.theregister.com/2011/09/17/nimda_anniversary/.

Little, A. (2021, June 9). The World's Food Supply Has Never Been More Vulnerable. *Bloomberg.* https://www.bloomberg.com/opinion/articles/2021-06-09/jbs-cyberattack-shows-vulnerability-of-world-food-supplies?srf=CIpmV6x8.

McKinney, C. and D. Mulvin. (2019). *Bugs: Rethinking the History of Computing.* Communication Culture and Critique, *12*(4), 476–498. https://doi.org/10.1093/ccc/tcz039.

Millions of internet users hit by massive Sony PlayStation data theft—Telegraph. (n.d.). https://web.archive.org/web/20110428161228/http://www.telegraph.co.uk/technology/news/8475728/Millions-of-internet-users-hit-by-massive-Sony-PlayStation-data-theft.html.

Minnesota Man Sentenced to 18 Months in Prison for Creating and Unleashing a Variant of the MS Blaster Computer Worm (January 28, 2005). (n.d.). https://www.justice.gov/archive/criminal/cybercrime/press-releases/2005/parsonSent.htm.

Mitnick, K. D. and W. L. Simon. (2001). *The Art of Deception: Controlling the Human Element of Security.* In John Wiley & Sons, Inc. eBooks. http://mario.elinos.org.mx/docencia/seginfo/the_art_of_deception.pdf.

Mungo, P. and B. Clough. (1993). *Approaching zero: the extraordinary underworld of hackers, phreakers, virus writers, and keyboard criminals.* Choice Reviews Online, *31*(03), 31–1561. https://doi.org/10.5860/choice.31-1561.

Naked Security—Sophos News. (n.d.). Sophos News. https://news.sophos.com/en-us/category/serious-security/.

NASA-hacker McKinnon kan VS toch vermijden. (n.d.). Security.NL. https://www.security.nl/posting/34253/NASA-hacker+McKinnon+kan+VS+toch+vermijden.

Newman, L. H. (2018, March 1). *A 1.3-Tbs DDoS Hit GitHub, the Largest Yet Recorded*. WIRED. https://www.wired.com/story/github-ddos-memcached/.

Newman, L. H. (2018, April 17). *Inside the Unnerving CCleaner Supply Chain Attack*. WIRED. https://www.wired.com/story/inside-the-unnerving-supply-chain-attack-that-corrupted-ccleaner/.

PBS News Hour. (2016, July 30). *Clinton's campaign and the DCCC are cyber hacked—was it the Russians?* PBS News. https://www.pbs.org/newshour/show/clintons-campaign-dccc-cyber-hacked-russians.

Petcu, A. G. (2022, June 8). *The Curious Case of the Baltimore Ransomware Attack: What You Need to Know*. Heimdal Security Blog. https://heimdalsecurity.com/blog/baltimore-ransomware/.

Pinsent Masons. (2019, May 20). *Confession by author of Anna Kournikova virus*. Pinsent Masons. https://www.pinsentmasons.com/out-law/news/confession-by-author-of-anna-kournikova-virus.

Podcast, M. L. (n.d.). *Malicious Life Podcast: The Real Story of Citibank's $10M Hack*. https://www.cybereason.com/blog/malicious-life-podcast-the-real-story-of-citibanks-10m-hack.

Poulsen, K. (2001, August 1). *Justice mysteriously delayed for 'Melissa' author*. The Register. https://www.theregister.com/2001/08/01/justice_mysteriously_delayed_for_melissa/.

Poulsen, K. (2010, May 4). May 4, 2000: *Tainted 'Love' Infects Computers*. WIRED. https://www.wired.com/2010/05/0504i-love-you-virus/.

PSN reactivation delayed for "further testing," likely not coming back this week. (2011, May 6). Joystiq. https://web.archive.org/web/20110508234950/http://www.joystiq.com/2011/05/06/psn-reactivation-delayed-for-further-testing-not-coming-back/.

PurpleSec. (2024, May 10). *Saudi Aramco $50 Million Data Breach Explained*. https://purplesec.us/breach-report/saudi-aramco-data-breach-explained/.

Radware. (n.d.). *The Story of the Mirai Botnet | Radware*. https://www.radware.com/security/ddos-knowledge-center/ddospedia/mirai/.

Reporter, G. S. (2021, July 12). *'Cyber-attack' hits Iran's transport ministry and railways*. The Guardian. https://www.theguardian.com/world/2021/jul /11/cyber-attack-hits-irans-transport-ministry-and-railways#:~:text= On%20Friday%2C%20Iran's%20railways%20also,trains%20acro ss%20Iran%20reportedly%20failed.&text=The%20Fars%20news%20ag ency%20reported,possible%20cyber%2Dattacks%20though%20ransom ware.

Reporters Sans Frontières. *Russian and Georgian websites fall victim to a war being fought online as well as in the field*. (2008, August 13). https://web.ar chive.org/web/20101206114656/http://en.rsf.org/georgia-russian-and -georgian-websites-fall-13-08-2008,28167.html.

Rhoads, C. (2013, January 17). *The Twilight Years of Cap'n Crunch*. Wall Street Journal.

Roberts, P. (2003, August 12). *Blaster worm spreading, experts warn of attack*. InfoWorld. https://www.infoworld.com/article/2224815/blaster-worm -spreading-experts-warn-of-attack-2.html.

Sanabria, A. (2024, April 16). *A Meta-Review of the Summer 2023 Microsoft Exchange Online Intrusion*. The Cyber Why. https://www.thecyberwhy .com/p/a-meta-review-of-the-summer-2023.

Sanders, S. (2015, June 4). *Massive Data Breach Puts 4 Million Federal Employ-ees' Records At Risk*. NPR. https://www.npr.org/sections/thetwo-way/20 15/06/04/412086068/massive-data-breach-puts-4-million-federal-empl oyees-records-at-risk.

Seals, T. (2020, December 18). *The SolarWinds Perfect Storm: Default Pass-word, Access Sales and More*. Threatpost. https://threatpost.com/solarwi nds-default-password-access-sales/162327/.

SOLAR SUNRISE After 25 Years: Are We 25 Years Wiser? (2023, February 28). National Security Archive. https://nsarchive.gwu.edu/briefing-book/ cyber-vault/2023-02-28/solar-sunrise-after-25-years-are-we-25-years -wiser.

Speed, R. (2020, May 5). *It has been 20 years since cybercrime woke up to social engineering with an intriguing little email titled 'ILOVEYOU.'* The Regis-ter. https://www.theregister.com/2020/05/05/iloveyou_20_years/.

Staff, A. (2024, October 23). *Five Most Famous DDoS Attacks and Then Some*. A10 Networks. https://www.a10networks.com/blog/5-most-famous-dd os-attacks/.

Staff, D. R. (2023, December 8). *Pro-Iranian Attackers Claim to Target Israeli Railroad Network*. https://www.darkreading.com/ics-ot-security/pro-ira nian-attackers-target-israeli-railroad-network.

Standard. (2012, October 16). *Gary McKinnon: Profile*. The Standard. https://www.standard.co.uk/news/uk/gary-mckinnon-profile-8212771.html.

Steinberg, S., Neary K. Adam, and Picker Center Digital Education Group. (2021). *Target Cyber Attack: A Columbia University Case Study*. In G. Rattray and J. Healey (Eds.), SIPA [Case study]. https://www.sipa.columbia.edu/sites/default/files/2022-11/Target%20Final.pdf.

Stoll, C. (2024). *The Cuckoo's Egg: Tracking a Spy Through the Maze of Computer Espionage*. Simon and Schuster.

Stutz, M. (1997, December 9). *Yahoo Hack: Heck of a Hoax*. WIRED. https://www.wired.com/1997/12/yahoo-hack-heck-of-a-hoax/.

Stuxnet attackers used 4 Windows zero-day exploits. (n.d.). ZDNet. https://web.archive.org/web/20141125225130/http://www.zdnet.com/blog/security/stuxnet-attackers-used-4-windows-zero-day-exploits/7347.

Suddath, C. (2009, August 19). *Master Hacker Albert Gonzalez*. TIME. https://time.com/archive/6906352/master-hacker-albert-gonzalez/.

Target Settles 2013 Hacked Customer Data Breach for $18.5 Million. (2017, May 24). NBC News. https://www.nbcnews.com/business/business-news/target-settles-2013-hacked-customer-data-breach-18-5-million-n764031.

Taylor, C. (2023, February 16). *SQL Slammer Virus (Harbinger of things to come)*. CyberHoot. https://cyberhoot.com/cybrary/sql-slammer-virus/.

The DDoS That Almost Broke the Internet. (2024, October 10). The Cloudflare Blog. https://blog.cloudflare.com/the-ddos-that-almost-broke-the-internet.

The DDoS That Knocked Spamhaus Offline (And How We Mitigated It). (2013, March 20). The Cloudflare Blog. https://blog.cloudflare.com/the-ddos-that-knocked-spamhaus-offline-and-ho.

Thomsen, S. (2015, July 20). *Extramarital affair website Ashley Madison has been hacked and attackers are threatening to leak data online*. Business Insider. https://www.businessinsider.com/cheating-affair-website-ashley-madison-hacked-user-data-leaked-2015-7.

Thomson, I. (2015, August 20). *The Ashley Madison files—are people really this stupid?* The Register. https://www.theregister.com/2015/08/20/the_ashley_madison_files_are_people_really_this_stupid/.

Turton, W., Riley, M., and Jacobs, J. (2021a, May 13). *Colonial Pipeline Paid Hackers Nearly $5 Million in Ransom*. Bloomberg. https://www.bloomberg.com/news/articles/2021-05-13/colonial-pipeline-paid-hackers-nearly-5-million-in-ransom.

United States Department of State. *Reward Offers for Information to Bring DarkSide Ransomware Variant Co-Conspirators to Justice.* (2021, November 5). United States Department of State. https://www.state.gov/reward -offers-for-information-to-bring-darkside-ransomware-variant-co-cons pirators-to-justice/.

UPI Archives. *John Draper, dubbed 'Capt. Crunch' for using toy whistles....* (1987, February 25). UPI. https://www.upi.com/Archives/1987/02/25/John-Dr aper-dubbed-Capt-Crunch-for-using-toy-whistles/3750541227600.

Vanden Brook, T. and Winter, W. (2015, August 7). *Hackers penetrated Pentagon email.* USA TODAY. https://www.usatoday.com/story/news/nati on/2015/08/06/russia-reportedly-hacks-pentagon-email-system/31228 625/.

Vasquez, C. (2023, April 11). *Did someone really hack into the Oldsmar, Florida, water treatment plant? New details suggest maybe not.* CyberScoop. https://cyberscoop.com/water-oldsmar-incident-cyberattack/.

W32.Sircam.Worm@mm | Technical Details | Symantec. (n.d.). https://web.ar chive.org/web/20101205222127/http://www.symantec.com/security_re sponse/writeup.jsp?docid=2001-071720-1640-99&tabid=2.

Waddell, K. (2016, May 10). *The Computer Virus That Haunted Early AIDS Researchers.* The Atlantic. https://www.theatlantic.com/technology/arc hive/2016/05/the-computer-virus-that-haunted-early-aids-researchers /481965/.

Whittaker, Z. (2019, May 13). *Two years after WannaCry, a million computers remain at risk.* TechCrunch. https://techcrunch.com/2019/05/12/wannacry -two-years-on/.

Who Are Hackers - Notable Hacks | *Hackers.* FRONTLINE | PBS. (2015, November 18). https://www.pbs.org/wgbh/pages/frontline/shows/hackers/ whoare/notable.html.

Wikipedia contributors. (2023, June 18). *Democratic Congressional Campaign Committee cyber attacks.* Wikipedia. https://en.wikipedia.org/wiki/Dem ocratic_Congressional_Campaign_Committee_cyber_attacks#:~:text= On%20Friday%20July%2029%2C%202016,National%20Committee&ap os;s%20computer%20systems.

Wikipedia contributors. (2023, November 2). *Titan Rain.* Wikipedia. https:// en.wikipedia.org/wiki/Titan_Rain.

Wikipedia contributors. (2024, April 29). *Sircam.* Wikipedia. https://en.wikip edia.org/wiki/Sircam.

Wikipedia contributors. (2024, May 1). *Havex.* Wikipedia. https://en.wikiped ia.org/wiki/Havex.

Wikipedia contributors. (2024, May 16). *Russo-Ukrainian cyberwarfare*. Wikipedia. https://en.wikipedia.org/wiki/Russo-Ukrainian_cyberwarfare.

Wikipedia contributors. (2024, July 18). *Health Service Executive ransomware attack*. Wikipedia. https://en.wikipedia.org/wiki/Health_Service_Executive_ransomware_attack.

Wikipedia contributors. (2024, August 22). *Operation Aurora*. Wikipedia. https://en.wikipedia.org/wiki/Operation_Aurora.

Wikipedia contributors. (2024, September 4). *2021 Microsoft Exchange Server data breach*. Wikipedia. https://en.wikipedia.org/wiki/2021_Microsoft_Exchange_Server_data_breach#:~:text=A%20global%20wave%20of%20cyberattacks,connected%20devices%20on%20the%20same.

Wikipedia contributors. (2024, September 4). *The Shadow Brokers*. Wikipedia. https://en.wikipedia.org/wiki/The_Shadow_Brokers.

Wikipedia contributors. (2024, September 9). *2017 Equifax data breach*. Wikipedia. https://en.wikipedia.org/wiki/2017_Equifax_data_breach.

Wikipedia contributors. (2024, September 11). *History of Target Corporation*. Wikipedia. https://en.wikipedia.org/wiki/History_of_Target_Corporation#2013_security_breach.

Wikipedia contributors. (2024, September 11). *Triton (malware)*. Wikipedia. https://en.wikipedia.org/wiki/Triton_(malware).

Wikipedia contributors. (2024, September 12). *2020 United States federal government data breach*. Wikipedia. https://en.wikipedia.org/wiki/2020_United_States_federal_government_data_breach.

Wikipedia contributors. (2024, September 14). *Colonial Pipeline ransomware attack*. Wikipedia. https://en.wikipedia.org/wiki/Colonial_Pipeline_ransomware_attack.

Wikipedia contributors. (2024, September 16). *DarkHotel*. Wikipedia. https://en.wikipedia.org/wiki/DarkHotel.

Wikipedia contributors. (2024, September 16). *Red October (malware)*. Wikipedia. https://en.wikipedia.org/wiki/Red_October_(malware).

Wikipedia contributors. (2024, September 22). *2013 South Korea cyberattack*. Wikipedia. https://en.wikipedia.org/wiki/2013_South_Korea_cyberattack.

Wikipedia contributors. (2024, September 26). *John Draper*. Wikipedia. https://en.wikipedia.org/wiki/John_Draper.

Wikipedia contributors. (2024, September 26). *Nimda*. Wikipedia. https://en.wikipedia.org/wiki/Nimda.

Wikipedia contributors. (2024, September 27). *Code Red (computer worm)*. Wikipedia. https://en.wikipedia.org/wiki/Code_Red_(computer_worm).

Wikipedia contributors. (2024, September 29). *Blaster (computer worm)*. Wikipedia. https://en.wikipedia.org/wiki/Blaster_(computer_worm).

Wikipedia contributors. (2024, October 1). *2011 PlayStation Network outage.* Wikipedia. https://en.wikipedia.org/wiki/2011_PlayStation_Network_ou tage.

Wikipedia contributors. (2024, October 8). *2007 cyberattacks on Estonia.* Wikipedia. https://en.wikipedia.org/wiki/2007_cyberattacks_on_Estonia.

Wikipedia contributors. (2024, October 12). *Kaseya VSA ransomware attack.* Wikipedia. https://en.wikipedia.org/wiki/Kaseya_VSA_ransomware_at tack.

Wikipedia contributors. (2024, October 12). *Morris worm.* Wikipedia. https:// en.wikipedia.org/wiki/Morris_worm.

Wikipedia contributors. (2024, October 14). *Yahoo data breaches.* Wikipedia. https://en.wikipedia.org/wiki/Yahoo_data_breaches.

Wikipedia contributors. (2024, October 19). *SQL Slammer.* Wikipedia. https:// en.wikipedia.org/wiki/SQL_Slammer.

Wikipedia contributors. (2024, October 22). *2014 Sony Pictures hack.* Wikipedia. https://en.wikipedia.org/wiki/2014_Sony_Pictures_hack.

Wikipedia contributors. (2024, October 23). *Michael Calce.* Wikipedia. https:// en.wikipedia.org/wiki/Michael_Calce.

Wikipedia contributors. (2024, October 24). *2008 malware infection of the United States Department of Defense.* Wikipedia. https://en.wikipedia .org/wiki/2008_malware_infection_of_the_United_States_Department _of_Defense.

Wikipedia contributors. (2024, October 24). *2019 Baltimore ransomware attack.* Wikipedia. https://en.wikipedia.org/wiki/2019_Baltimore_ransom ware_attack.

Wikipedia contributors. (2024, October 24). *Cyberattacks during the Russo-Georgian War.* Wikipedia. https://en.wikipedia.org/wiki/Cyberattacks_du ring_the_Russo-Georgian_War.

Wikipedia contributors. (2024, October 24). *JBS S.A. ransomware attack.* Wikipedia. https://en.wikipedia.org/wiki/JBS_S.A._ransomware_attack.

Wikipedia contributors. (2024, October 24). *Operation Ababil.* Wikipedia. https://en.wikipedia.org/wiki/Operation_Ababil.

Wikipedia contributors. (2024, October 25). *2015 Ukraine power grid hack.* Wikipedia. https://en.wikipedia.org/wiki/2015_Ukraine_power_grid_hack.

Wikipedia contributors. (2024, October 25). *Ehud Tenenbaum.* Wikipedia. https://en.wikipedia.org/wiki/Ehud_Tenenbaum.

Wikipedia contributors. (2024, October 25). *WannaCry ransomware attack.* Wikipedia. https://en.wikipedia.org/wiki/WannaCry_ransomware_attack.

Wikipedia contributors. (2024, October 28). *Blue box.* Wikipedia. https:// en.wikipedia.org/wiki/Blue_box.

Wikipedia contributors. (2024, October 29). *Shamoon*. Wikipedia. https://en.wikipedia.org/wiki/Shamoon.

Wikipedia contributors. (2024, October 31). *Ashley Madison data breach*. Wikipedia. https://en.wikipedia.org/wiki/Ashley_Madison_data_breach.

Wikipedia contributors. (2024, November 4). *Conficker*. Wikipedia. https://en.wikipedia.org/wiki/Conficker.

Wikipedia contributors. (2024, November 4). *Vladimir Levin (hacker)*. Wikipedia. https://en.wikipedia.org/wiki/Vladimir_Levin_(hacker).

Wikipedia contributors. (2024, November 6). *2016 Democratic National Committee email leak*. Wikipedia. https://en.wikipedia.org/wiki/2016_Democratic_National_Committee_email_leak.

Wikipedia contributors. (2024, November 6). *Bangladesh Bank robbery*. Wikipedia. https://en.wikipedia.org/wiki/Bangladesh_Bank_robbery.

Wikipedia contributors. (2024, November 6). *ILOVEYOU*. Wikipedia. https://en.wikipedia.org/wiki/ILOVEYOU.

Wikipedia contributors. (2024, November 7). *Albert Gonzalez*. Wikipedia. https://en.wikipedia.org/wiki/Albert_Gonzalez.

Wikipedia contributors. (2024, November 9). *2014 Ukrainian presidential election*. Wikipedia. https://en.wikipedia.org/wiki/2014_Ukrainian_presidential_election.

Wikipedia contributors. (2024, November 9). *2017 Macron e-mail leaks*. Wikipedia. https://en.wikipedia.org/wiki/2017_Macron_e-mail_leaks.

Wikipedia contributors. (2024, November 10). *Anna Kournikova (computer virus)*. Wikipedia. https://en.wikipedia.org/wiki/Anna_Kournikova_(computer_virus).

Wikipedia contributors. (2024, November 10). *Fancy Bear*. Wikipedia. https://en.wikipedia.org/wiki/Fancy_Bear.

Wikipedia contributors. (2024, November 10). *Lazarus Group*. Wikipedia. https://en.wikipedia.org/wiki/Lazarus_Group.

Wikipedia contributors. (2024, November 10). *Office of Personnel Management data breach*. Wikipedia. https://en.wikipedia.org/wiki/Office_of_Personnel_Management_data_breach.

Wikipedia contributors. (2024, November 10). *Petya (malware family)*. Wikipedia. https://en.wikipedia.org/wiki/Petya_(malware_family).

Wikipedia contributors. (2024, November 10). *Stuxnet*. Wikipedia. https://en.wikipedia.org/wiki/Stuxnet.

Wikipedia contributors. (2024, November 11). *Capital One*. Wikipedia. https://en.wikipedia.org/wiki/Capital_One.

Winder, D. (2021, June 30). *This 20-Year-Old Virus Infected 50 Million Windows Computers In 10 Days: Why The ILOVEYOU Pandemic Matters In 2020*. Forbes. https://www.forbes.com/sites/daveywinder/2020/05/04/this-20-year-old-virus-infected-50-million-windows-computers-in-10-days-why-the-iloveyou-pandemic-matters-in-2020/?sh=3c9c24683c7c.

Zetter, K. (2014, December 3). *Sony Got Hacked Hard: What We Know and Don't Know So Far*. WIRED. https://www.wired.com/2014/12/sony-hack-what-we-know/.

Zetter, K. (2016, February 24). *The Sony Hackers Were Causing Mayhem Years Before They Hit the Company*. WIRED. https://www.wired.com/2016/02/sony-hackers-causing-mayhem-years-hit-company/.

INDEX

Note: Page numbers followed by *f* refer to figures.